'Architectural Design' 1991 £10-
Magazine.

9781854900593

A DECADE
OF ARCHITECTURAL DESIGN

ABOVE: IM Pei, Extension to the Louvre, Paris, France.
OVERLEAF: Bernard Tschumi, Parc de la Villette, *Folies*, First Phase, Paris, France.

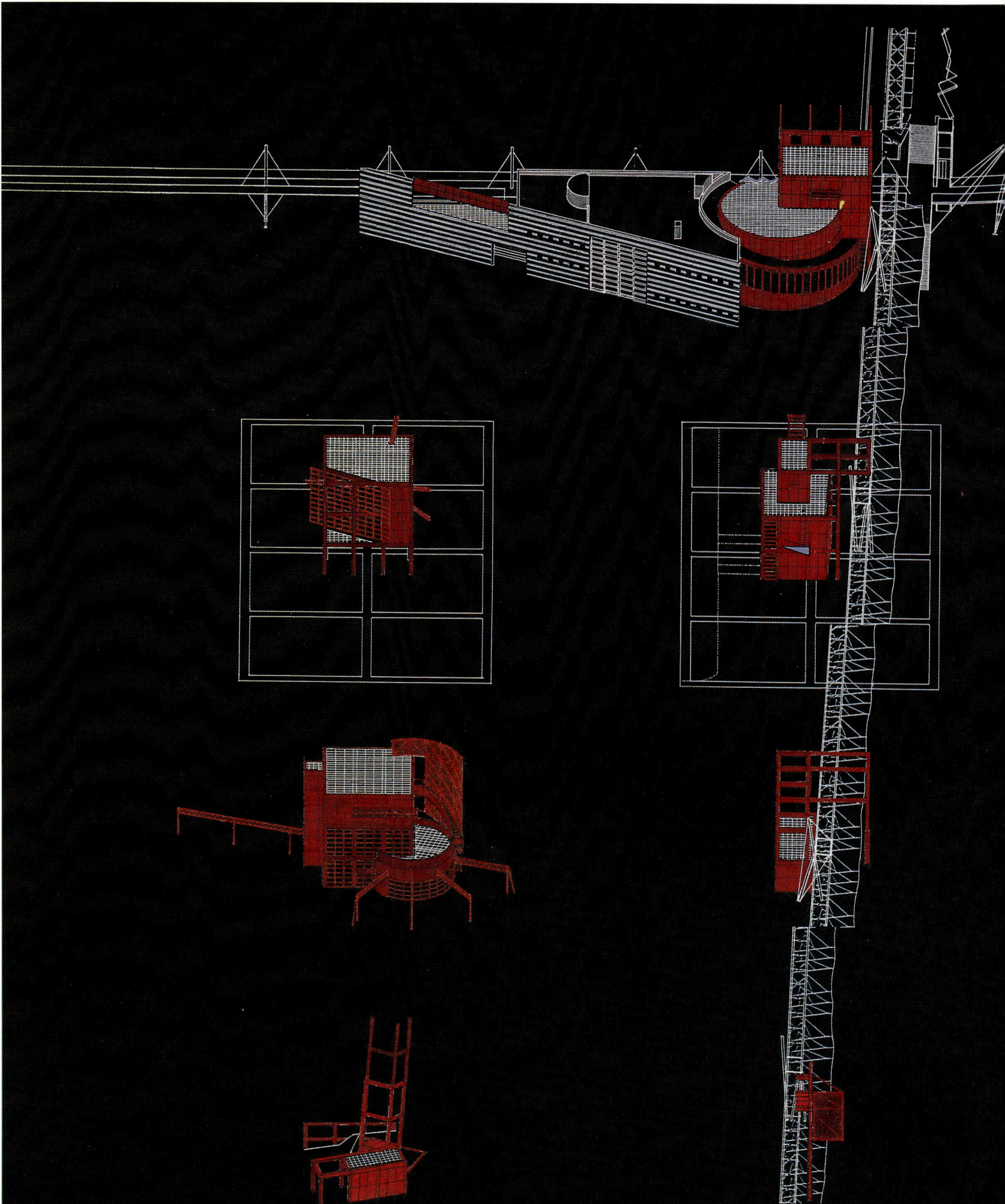

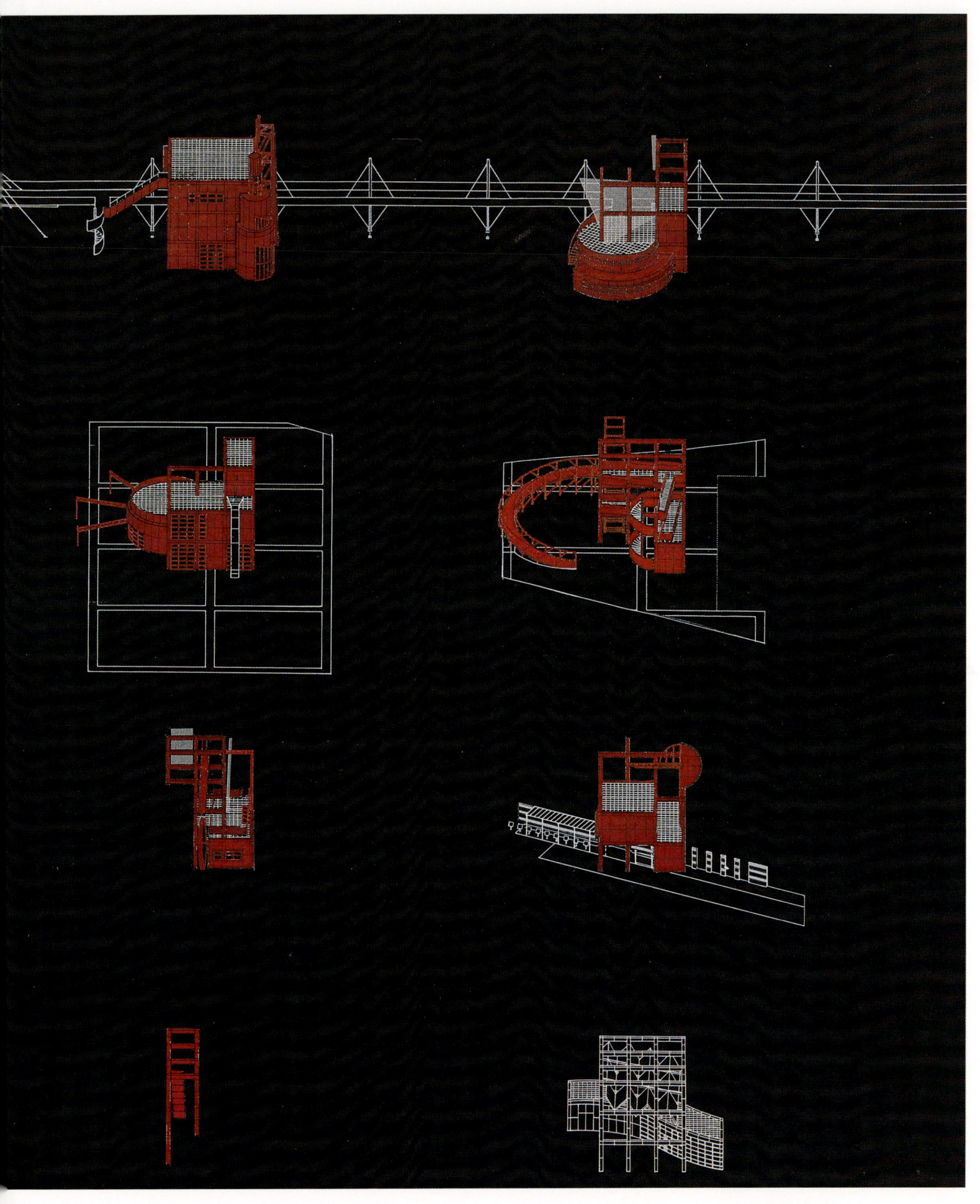

Andreas Papadakis
in collaboration with James Steele
and editorial staff of Architectural Design

A DECADE
OF ARCHITECTURAL DESIGN

OPPOSITE: Aldo Rossi, Il Palazzo, Fukuoka, Japan.
ABOVE: Odile Decq, The Model is the Message.

Editorial Note

This anthology owes its existence almost entirely to *Architectural Design* Magazine. As Editor, I have had the opportunity to follow consistently the work of international architects, particularly over the last ten years. This volume has been produced as a collaboration between James Steele and myself, together with the editorial and production team at Academy Editions. The publication owes a debt to the numerous authors and architects who have worked with *Architectural Design* in the past years and more recently with this project. I am especially indebted to Robert Adam, Ada Louise Huxtable, Charles Jencks, Richard Meier, Demetri Porphyrios and Robert Stern for allowing us to reproduce written contributions. Most of the material used in this volume has appeared, over the past decade, in issues of *Architectural Design* Magazine and related publications. Many thanks are extended to the architects who have been so generous in providing illustrative material.

I wish to express my gratitude in particular to James Steele who has contributed the texts on individual architects and annotations to the illustrations. The volume is produced very much as a team effort and thanks are therefore due to the staff at Academy Editions who have worked with great enthusiasm: Andrea Bettella, Maggie Toy, Sharon Anthony, Helen Castle, Nicola Hodges, Vivian Constantinopoulos, Mario Bettella and Ian Huebner.

Andreas Papadakis

First published in Great Britain in 1991 by
ACADEMY EDITIONS
an imprint of the Academy Group Ltd, 7 Holland Street, London W8 4NA

Copyright © 1991 Academy Group Ltd
All rights reserved
No part of this publication may be reproduced or transmitted in any form or by any means, whether by photocopying, recording or facsimile machine or otherwise howsoever without permission in writing from the Publishers.

ISBN 1 85490 059 5

Contents

Introduction
Andreas Papadakis 8

Tradition & Classicism
Demetri Porphyrios: The Relevance of Classical Architecture 10
Leon Krier 12. Robert A M Stern 18. Rob Krier 24. Andres Duany & Elizabeth Plater-Zyberk 28. Allan Greenberg 30. Robert Adam 34. Quinlan Terry 36. Demetri Porphyrios 40. Aldo Rossi 44.
Robert Adam: Tin Gods 50.

Modernism & High-Tech
Ada Louise Huxtable: On Modern Architecture 66
Richard Meier 68. Tadao Ando 74. Helmut Jahn 80. Fumihiko Maki 82. Itsuko Hasegawa 84. Henri Ciriani 86. I M Pei 88. Mario Botta 90. Norman Foster 92. Richard Rogers 100. Cesar Pelli 106. Michael Hopkins 112. Jean Nouvel 116.
Richard Meier: The Subject of Architecture 118.

Post-Modernism
Robert A M Stern: The Doubles of Post-Modernism 120
Michael Graves 122. Robert Venturi & Denise Scott Brown 128. O M Ungers 134. James Stirling 136. Hans Hollein 142. Ricardo Bofill 146. Terry Farrell 148. Charles Vandenhove 152. Nigel Coates 154. Japanese Post-Modernism 162.
Charles Jencks: Post-Modernism and Discontinuity 156.

The New Moderns
Andreas Papadakis: Deconstruction and Architecture 166
Peter Eisenman 168. Zaha Hadid 174. Bernard Tschumi 180. Coop Himmelblau 186. Frank Gehry 190. Daniel Libeskind 196. Günter Behnisch 202. Morphosis 204. OMA 208. Emilio Ambasz 210. Site 212. Philippe Starck 214.

Acknowledgements
218

Index
219

A DECADE OF ARCHITECTURAL DESIGN

Introduction

Architecture today has changed to an extent that would have been inconceivable a decade ago, and it would be no exaggeration to say that those changes have been unparalleled, in recent years, in both rapidity and scope. The alienation created by old style Modernism, as represented by the Post-War building boom, has finally culminated in a pluralist ideology that now runs the gamut from the machine aesthetic of high-tech at one end, through to traditional design, covering a number of gradations in between. This pluralist climate has encouraged a variety of architectural attitudes and ideologies to co-exist in a way that has reinvigorated the entire profession right across the spectrum and has allowed it to appeal to many different beliefs and tastes. In retrospect, it may be argued that the polemical reactions against Modernism did not destroy it, but have instead made architects reconsider several of its most important ideas, making them more relevant to the new social conditions that exist today. Changes have not happened easily, and influences have come from both within and outside architecture, evidenced by the theoretical influence of polemical Post-Modernism on the one hand, and the humanistic approach of Prince Charles on the other, which have all acted to bring about the freedom of expression that is present today.

Perhaps this freedom is best reflected by the new images of Deconstruction, an ideology that has appealed to students, architects and clients of the avant-garde alike. While confined to the drawing board for some time, those images are now becoming a reality all over the world. It is in Paris, especially, where this new direction has been most widely realised. The *folies* in the Parc de la Villette have dramatically shown the tectonic possibilities of this new direction, as well as demonstrating its civic potential, by transforming what had been alacklustre urban space into a totally unique park for our time.

While an equally valid selection of work could have included many other architects, there is no doubt that those shown have made important contributions to the contemporary architectural debate. The one thing the architects presented in this volume have in common, whatever their style or ideology, is a freshness of imagery and high quality of design that have enriched the built environment, and the city in particular. Above all, the choice is biased towards architects whose work has had an influence on students and the younger architects who will ultimately decide the future direction of architecture for the generation to come.

Nocturne (painting by Rita Wolff)

Tradition & Classicism

Demetri Porphyrios: The Relevance of Classical Architecture

As regards the aesthetics of architecture, the classicists adopt the theory of imitation. Art, it is argued, imitates the real world by turning selected significant aspects of it into mythical representations. Consider the following comparison. A documentary record of the atrocities of civil war can be contrasted with Goya's or Ruben's *Atrocities of War* that depict Saturn devouring his children. The documentary can only provoke disgust. Goya's imitative representation of the real world, however, does afford us aesthetic pleasure. This is so exactly because it establishes a distance from reality which allows us to contemplate our universal human predicament.

Similarly, a classicist would argue, architecture is the imitative celebration of construction and shelter qualified by the myths and ideas of a given culture. Such myths might have to do with life, nature or the mode of production of a given society. Ultimately, architecture speaks of these myths and ideas but always through the language of construction and shelter, celebrating construction and shelter by means of tectonic order.

Surely, many modernists have spoken about 'honest construction'. But, I want to stress here that classical imitation has nothing in common with the structural functionalism of modern architecture. Modernism makes no distinction between building and architecture. Modernism does *not* imitate construction and shelter; it simply uses raw building material without any imitative mediation. In that sense, Modernism has produced buildings but, as yet, no architecture. The result has been a century of mute realism in the name of industrial production. On the contrary what makes classical architecture possible is the dialogic relationship it establishes between the craft of building and the art of architecture. Our imagination traverses this dialogic space between, say, a pergola and a colonnade, and establishes hierarchies, levels of propriety and communicable systems of evaluation.

Classical architecture needs also another dialogic relationship: this time the relationship between one building and another. This point is very important. Today the market ethic of the original and authentic is based on the pretence that every work of art is an invention singular enough to be patented . . .

Let me finish by saying that architecture has nothing to do with 'novelty-mania' and intellectual sophistries. Architecture has nothing to do with transgression, boredom or parody. It has nothing to do with parasitic life, excremental culture or the cynical fascination with the bad luck of others. Architecture has to do with decisions that concern the good, the decent, the proper. Decisions about what Aristotle called the *EU ZEIN*, the good and proper life. Surely, what constitutes proper life varies from one historical period to another. But it is our responsibility to define it anew all the time. If we choose to embrace the tradition of the classical we will find no recipes but we will encounter again and again a kind of genius for practical life, a kind of genius that is actually less of a gift than a constant task of adjustment to present contingencies. In that sense we can speak of the classical as that which endures; but this defiance of time is always experienced as a historical present.

Demetri Porphyrios, House in Chelsea Square (painting by Rita Wolff).

A DECADE OF ARCHITECTURAL DESIGN

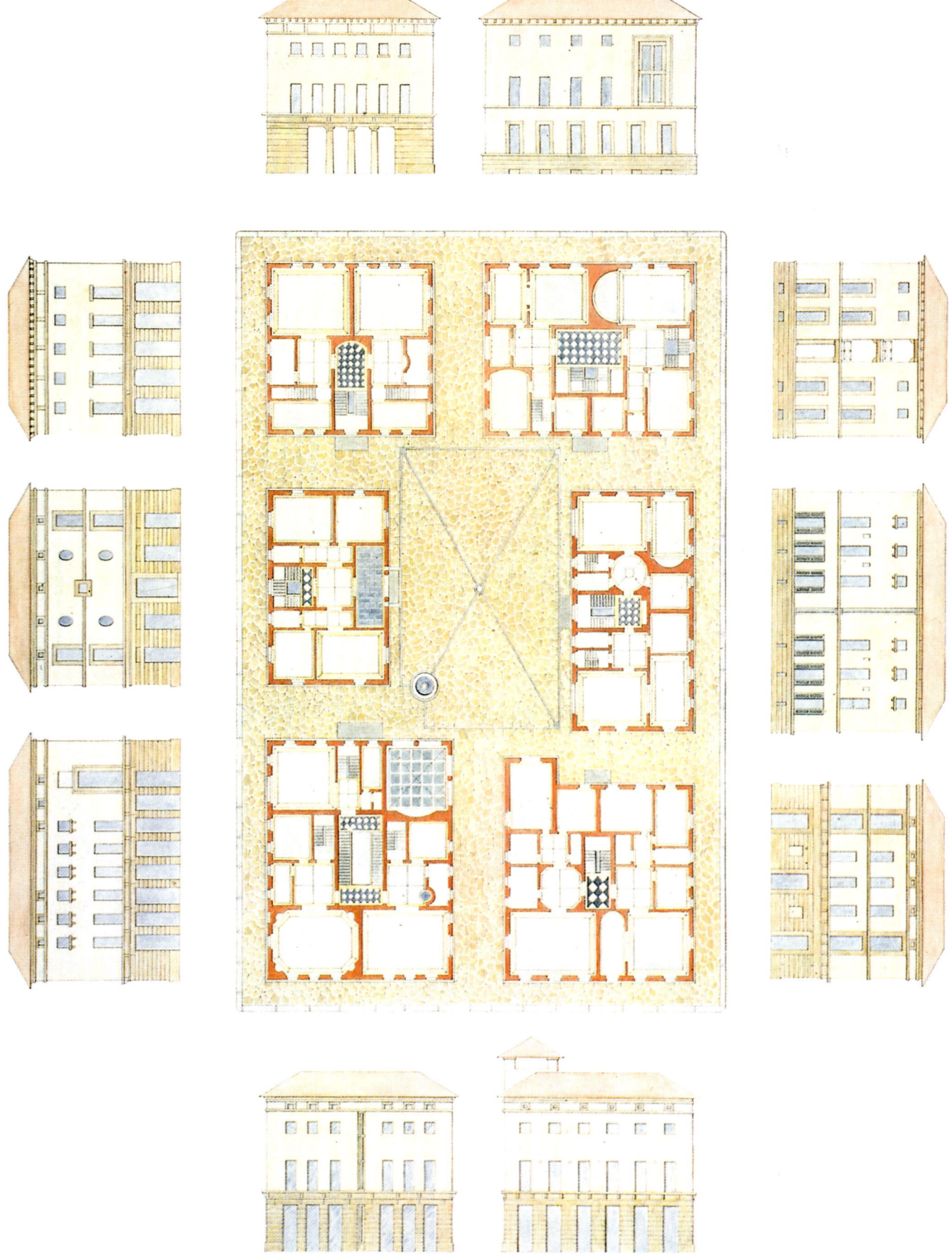

12

Leon Krier

Rather than rejecting the title of polemicist, Leon Krier enthusiastically accepts it, along with all of its martial implications. Like his older brother Robert, and others who have expressed grave concern about the destruction of the city as a basic human institution, he has had to do intellectual battle against the deeply ingrained establishment prejudices that have now come to hinder the perpetuation of the urban patterns of the past. He realistically sees prejudice to be an inevitable product of the political and economic conglomerations that have developed in the 20th century, and the more and more grandiose 'urban renewal' programmes that have resulted from them. His goal, then, as he describes it in an *Architectural Design* article entitled 'Urban Components', is:

' . . . not just to describe an irreversible historical fatality, but to establish a hypothesis: the social and cultural complexity of a city has necessarily to do with its physical and structural complexity and density . . . My main affirmation as regards urban design will be: *urban blocks should be as small in length and width as is typologically viable; they should form as many well defined streets and squares as possible in the form of a multi-directional horizontal pattern of urban spaces.*'

Through his relentless defence of this hypothesis, over the last decade, he has managed not only to bring many city planners and architects around to his way of thinking, but has also won influential patronage that will insure his ideas now have a much wider hearing. While he has placed great emphasis, in the past, on the need for an architect to remain somewhat aloof from the commercial forces that corrupt art, he has now found it necessary to wrestle with them, and to do so in a way that doesn't compromise his ideals. As his drawings show, those ideals are very clear.

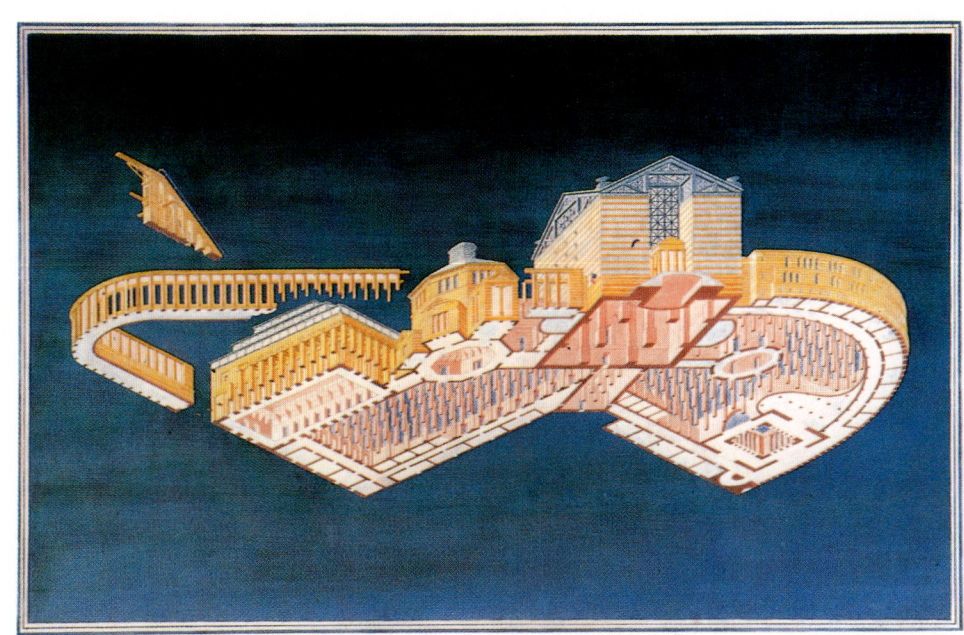

While Leon Krier has said that he prefers to draw rather than build, the evocative quality of his recently completed house at Seaside, Florida, makes it easier to imagine the architectural and spatial quality that proposals, such as Atlantis, would have.

OPPOSITE & LEFT: Proposal for redevelopment, Tegel, Berlin, Germany. (Painting by Rita Wolff)
OVERLEAF, LEFT: Turris Bubonis; RIGHT: School, St Quentin-en-Yvelines, France.

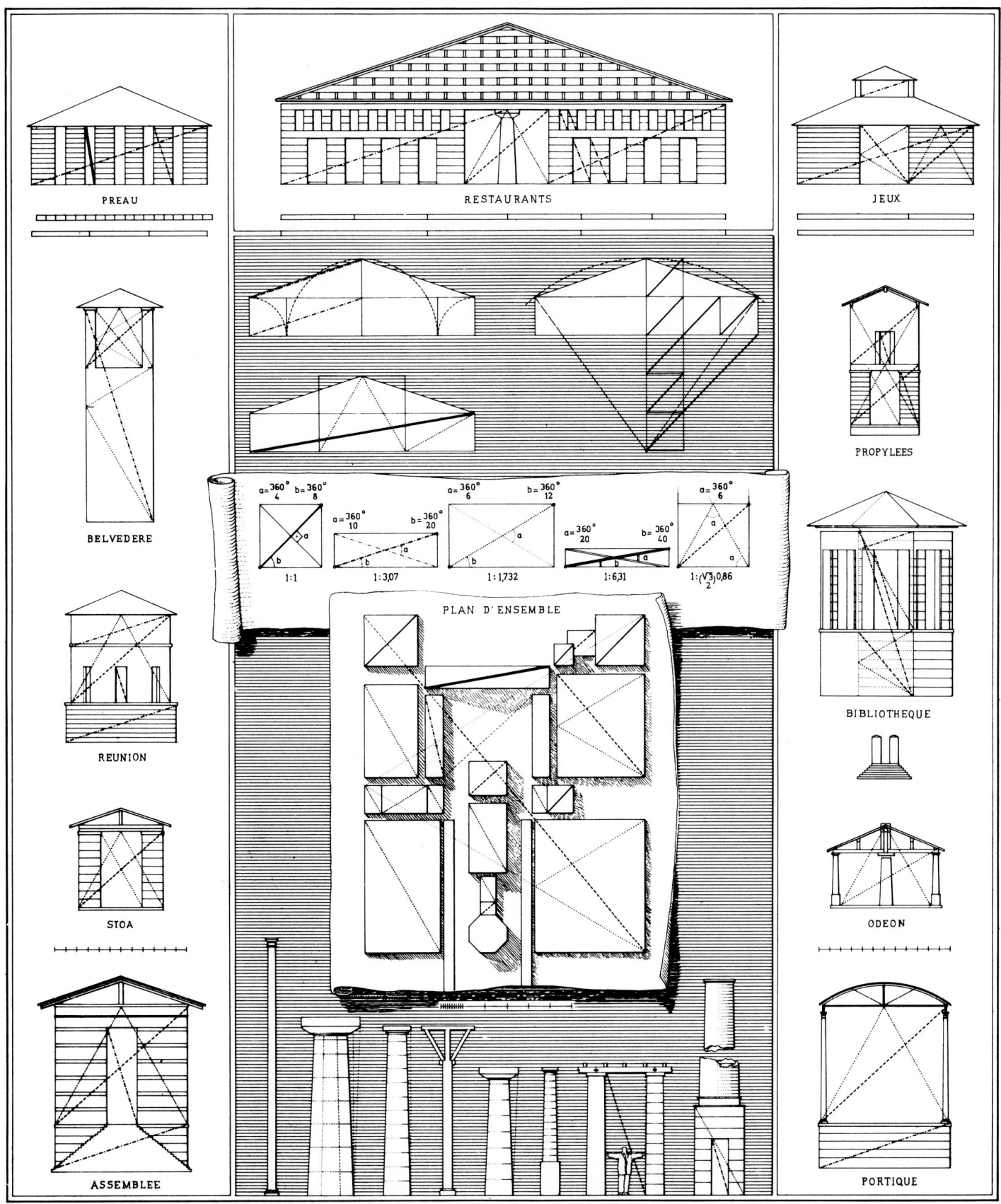

THE ELEMENTS OF THIS ENSEMBLE OF BUILDINGS ARE REGULATED IN PLAN, ELEVATION AND VOLUME BY A SYSTEM OF PROPORTIONS AND GEOMETRICAL REGULATING LINES.
THE REPETITION OF A LIMITED NUMBER OF FIXED HARMONIC RELATIONS CONFERS BEAUTY BOTH ON THE ENSEMBLE AND ON THE DETAILS. THIS IS UNDOUBTEDLY THE MAIN JOB OF THE GOOD ARCHITECT, A CONSIDERABLE AND FASCINATING JOB WHICH REQUIRES PRECISION. ATTENTION TO MINUTE DETAIL AND FANATICISM. THE REWARD TO BE GAINED FROM THIS JOB IS NEITHER MORE MYSTERIOUS NOR LESS ENIGMATIC THAN THE BEAUTY WE ADMIRE IN THE MOST BEAUTIFUL WORKS OF NATURE.

A DECADE OF ARCHITECTURAL DESIGN

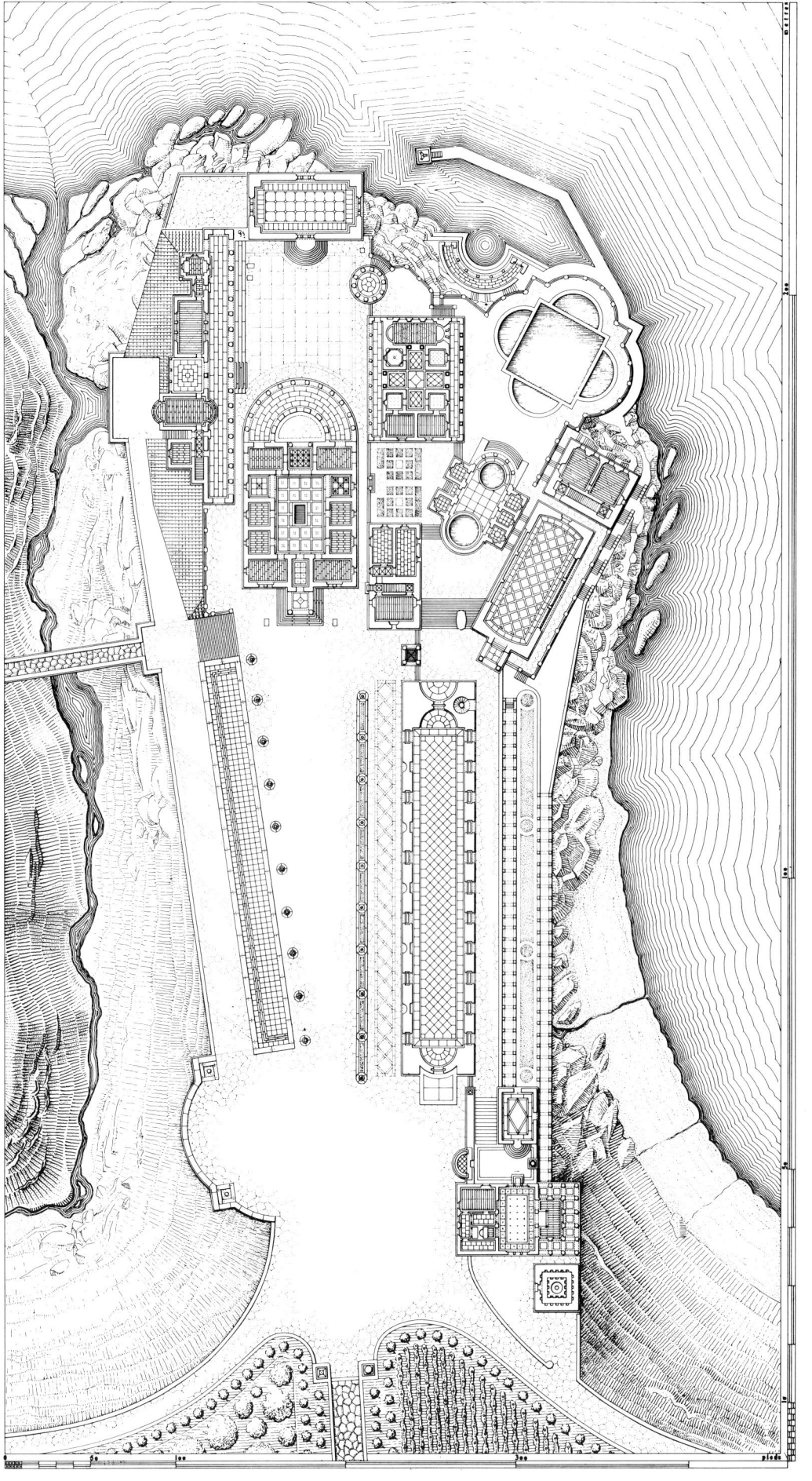

LEON KRIER

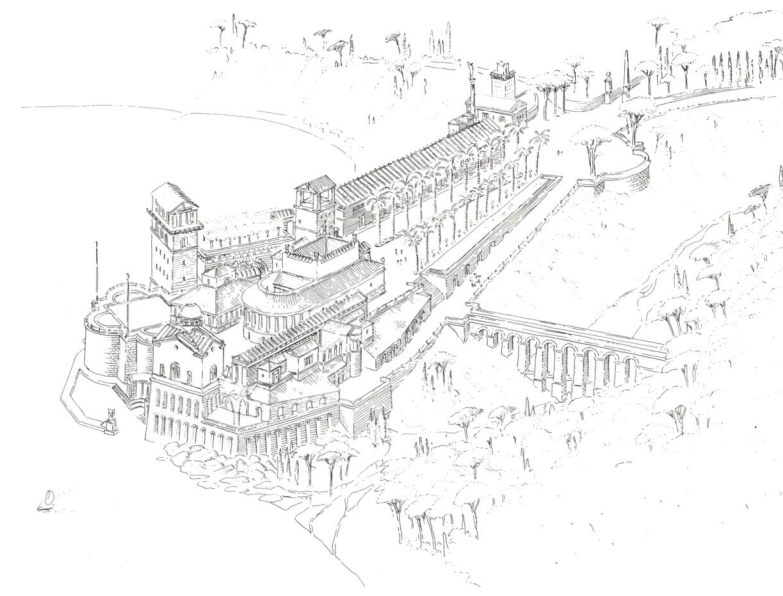

Regulating lines, proportion, order and harmony, all play an important role in Leon Krier's work.

OPPOSITE, LEFT & ABOVE: Pliny's villa, Laurentum, Italy. (Painting by Rita Wolff)

Robert A M Stern

While Robert Stern has most recently been consistent in his rejection of Modern doctrine, the architectural expression of that rejection has shifted noticeably since his own declaration of the basic principles of Post-Modernism more than a decade ago. In that declaration, which subsequently appeared in Paolo Portoghesi's *After Modern Architecture* in 1982, Stern said that he believed in an associative, contextual, ornamental, historically referential and communicative architecture, based on cultural responsiveness, not rejection. In doing so, he helped to give focus to many who sympathised with these ideas, but were unable to combine them into a cohesive philosophy. In an article for *Architectural Design* that followed soon afterwards, called 'The Doubles of Post-Modernism', he further clarified his theoretical stance by defining Modernism in a way that is still of particular value today, as he said:

'What can be called the *Modern Period* begins in the 15th century with the birth of Humanism. The International Style of *circa* 1920-60 is also a modern style, often thought to be *the* Modern Style in which the meaning of the word *Modern* is transformed and limited so as to represent only those values more properly described as *modernist*. Modernism, in the most oversimplified terms, represents a moralistic application of a superior value to that which is not only new but also independent of all previous production.' In contrast to others who were then categorising the trend away from Modernism, Stern tended to ascribe an American, and particularly an academic, rather than an international basis to it, revealing the same cultural chauvinism that makes his vernacular renditions so convincing today. Since issuing his declaration, his clearly stated commitment to historicism has seemed to increase in character, providing dramatic evidence that the actual results of a given set of criteria can be interpreted quite differently. As is the case with several other Traditionalists and Classicists today, Stern continues to didactically support his individual point of view quite effectively, backing it up with thorough research. So that his deep love of history has now begun to reveal itself in a far more authentic way.

In comparison to his work of 15 years ago, such as the widely publicised Bourke Poolhouse which was done when Post-Modernism was in full swing, these current projects are far more traditional.

OPPOSITE & OVERLEAF: Observatory Hill Dining Hall, University of Virginia.
LEFT & ABOVE: House at Marblehead, Massachusetts.

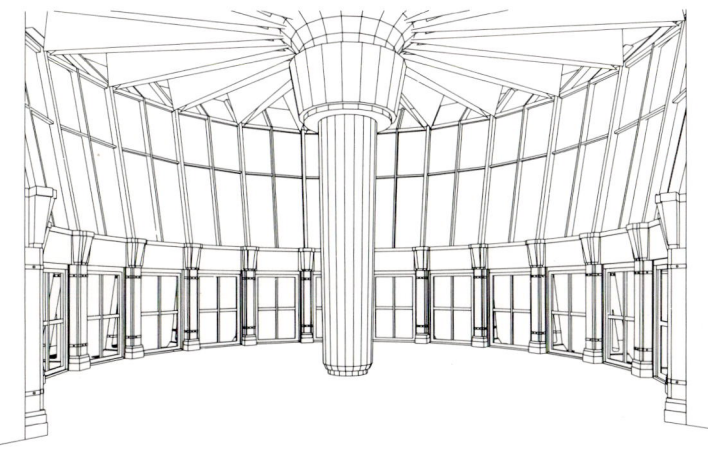

Utilising high contrast between materials and styles, as well as reflection, Stern has provided a surprising interplay of form.

OPPOSITE, LEFT & ABOVE: Mexx International Headquarters, The Netherlands.

A DECADE OF ARCHITECTURAL DESIGN

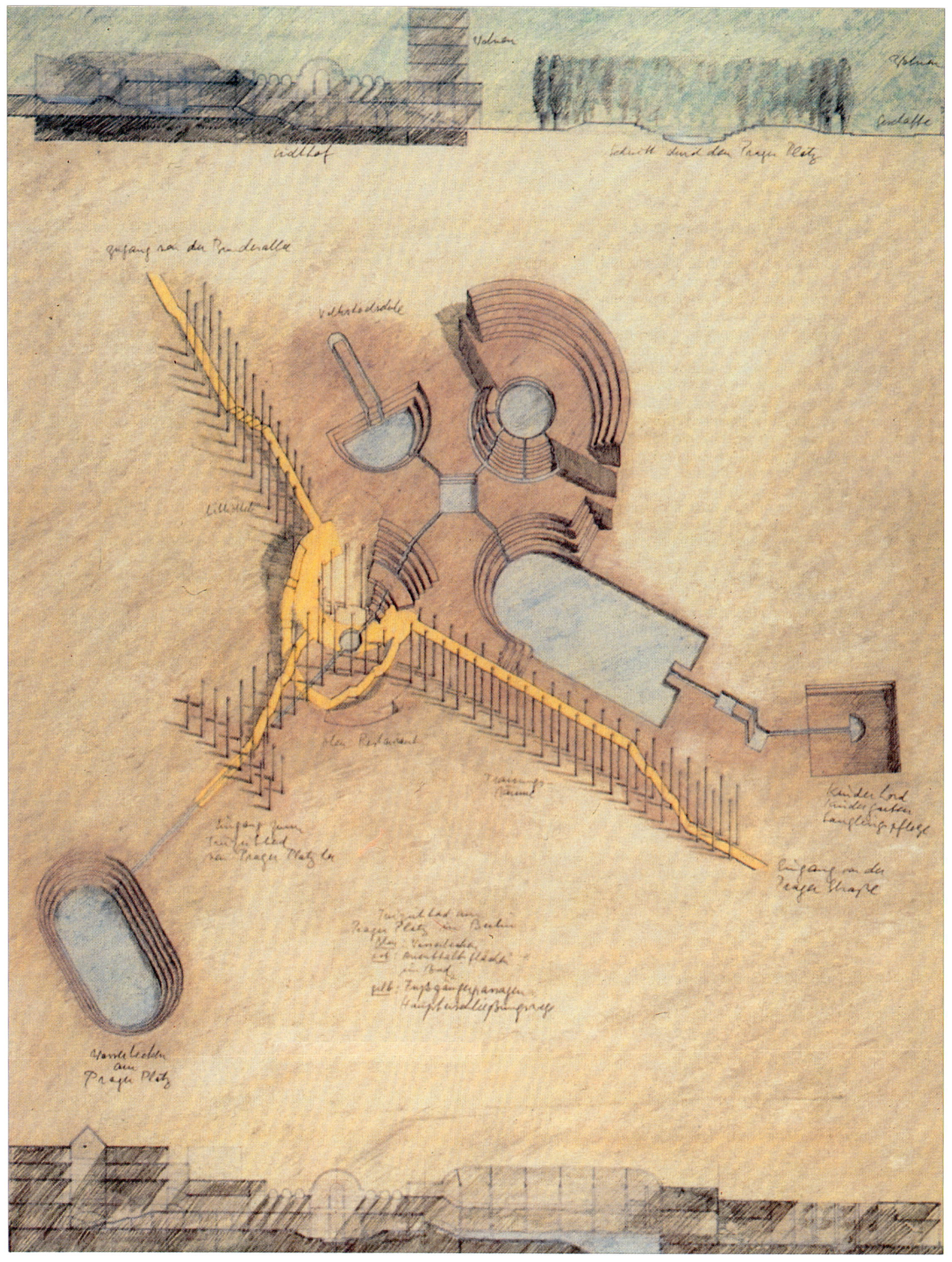

Rob Krier

Rob Krier has a perspective that encompasses entire cities rather than their individual parts. In his belief that architects have entirely lost the ability to design buildings that link with others to form a larger entity, he has focused on typologies as the way to create urban fabric that has been lost.

After World War II many European cities obviously needed reconstructing. Unfortunately the chance that this offered architects to reinterpret the traditional urban environment also coincided with the emergence of the Modern Movement, which as Marshall Berman has so succinctly put it 'hated cities'. The results of this unhappy historical coincidence, has given Krier's work an added sense of urgency. His studies have mainly focused around the perception that the city is made up of what he calls 'building blocks' and he notes that the analysis of such blocks is not included in the curriculum of architectural schools, where individuality reigns supreme. By bringing attention to this neglected subject he has made one of the most significant contributions to his field since Camillo Sitte, and by seeking to recreate the urban complexity of the past, he has proposed a viable alternative to the sterile legacy of the International Style that is considerably more likely to stand the test of time.

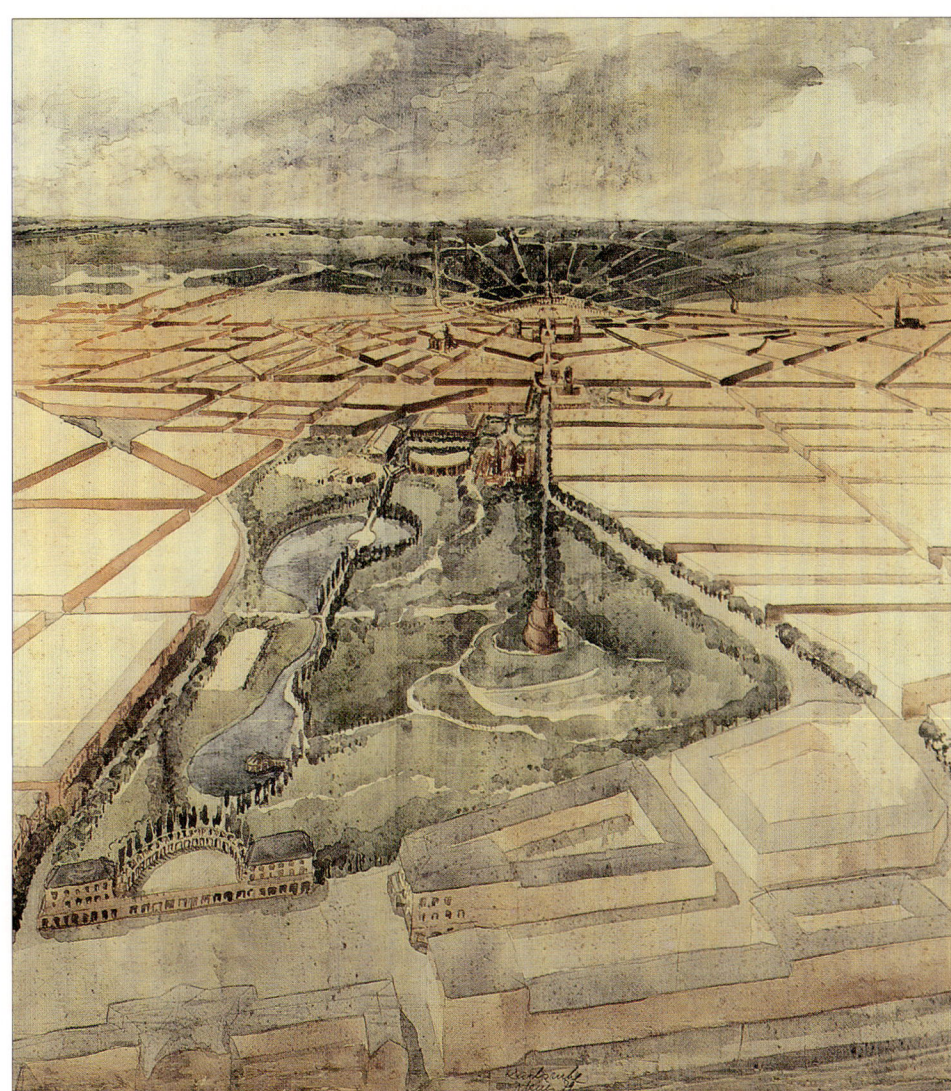

The intellectual appeal of Rob Krier's arguments has been considerably broadened by the seductive aesthetic of the way that they are rendered.

OPPOSITE: Prager Platz, Berlin, Germany.
LEFT: Re-design of the 'Via Triumphalis', Karlsruhe.

A DECADE OF ARCHITECTURAL DESIGN

Aerial perspectives are a favourite device of this architect, because they are more effective in presenting the city as an entity, rather than the sum of individual parts.

OPPOSITE: General Plan for City of 25,000 inhabitants, Marne la Vallée, Paris.
ABOVE: Breitenfurterstrasse, Vienna.
LEFT: The Column, Ink and Pastel on Linen.

A DECADE OF ARCHITECTURAL DESIGN

28

Andres Duany & Elizabeth Plater-Zyberk

It is no exaggeration to say that Andres Duany and Elizabeth Plater-Zyberk have revolutionised urban planning concepts, particularly regarding the function of zoning in both controlling and guiding suburban growth. By drawing clear comparisons between what exists in the American suburbs today, and what those suburbs have replaced, Duany and Plater-Zyberk have effectively raised the question of why the traditional town, which has been such a central part of the national psyche, had to be replaced at all. In the process each practical detail of current planning practice has been put under cross-examination, and when found to be at odds with the common-sensical patterns of the past, has been isolated for criticism. Much of this examination has, by necessity, focused on the automobile, which has obviously been a major cause of the roadside architecture that is now so endemic to their country. Unlike other advocates of this clutter, who have found it to be 'almost all right' Duany and Plater-Zyberk have questioned its inevitability, and have proposed a realistic alternative. In the place of single use roadside strips, which cater to what they consider to a basically anti-social machine, these architects have proposed the mixed-usages that were characteristic of the most memorable communities of the past and which typically resulted in buildings and streets of different sizes. Rather than being outdated, as planners claim, such a hierarchy of streets has been shown by them to actually regulate traffic flow, and to be very flexible. As a bonus, such a network also promotes the pedestrian use of sidewalks, encouraging more social interaction, and reverses the American reliance on the car. This change of an institutionally sanctioned habit and countless smaller victories have now been implemented in new towns such as Seaside, Florida. Positive public response has shown that these architects have struck a deep chord with their arguments.

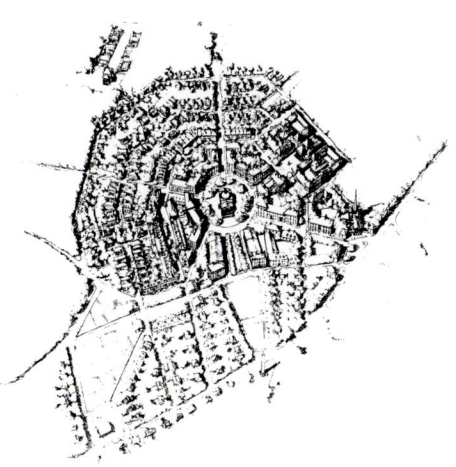

The sources quoted in private, residential designs, as well as in planning projects such as Crab Creek and Seaside, have been varied, but have always been sympathetic to their use.

OPPOSITE: Seaside, Florida.
LEFT: Kentlands, Maryland.
ABOVE: Crab Creek, Maryland.

Allan Greenberg

While working within the realm of what might be called historical representation, Allan Greenberg differs from others in this category in his precise attention to detail, and the level of his ability to adapt the canons of the past to the predilections of the present. Such representation has been especially popular in the Washington DC area, where a Federalist style predominates, and has come to symbolise continuity of government as well as an architectural fashion of choice. In doing so Greenberg has helped to satisfy the needs of a large group of public and private clients that had not previously been recognised by the architectural establishment. With a client list that reads like a *Who's Who* of government officials, and corporations his work has certainly been an accurate barometer of that omission, and in correcting it he has shown the wide divergence of architectural tastes that exist today.

A notable feature of his work is that the level of finish achieved regardless of the scale of each project is consistently high. This achievement is all the more remarkable considering the difficulty involved in finding the craftsmen necessary to execute details that have now passed out of regular use, as well as the care required in re-introducing those details in new ways, and in new proportions, as Greenberg does.

'The history of classical architecture over the past three millennia may be likened to a great river which flows into the future and from the past. Each of its many tributaries represents various natures and cultures. These, in turn, are fed by a multiplicity of smaller rivers and streams representing the architecture of different regions and cities within each nation. The smallest brooks and rills are works by individual architects. The fine degree of difference between the architecture of different nations, or individuals, is easily read because the formal language of classical architecture is so highly developed that it is possible to tell the hand of a great architect even in small details like mouldings.'

Neglected techniques of craftsmanship are now being reintroduced in details like this pendant moulding in the George G Marshall Reception Room in Washington DC.

OPPOSITE, LEFT & ABOVE: Department of State Building, Washington DC.
OVERLEAF: Farmhouse in Connecticut.

ALLAN GREENBERG

DOGMERSFIELD
PARK
TRIVMPHAL ARCH
END PAVILION
FOR NEW BVILDING
ROBERT ADAM·ARCHITECT
MCMLXXXV·ONE METRE·SCALE

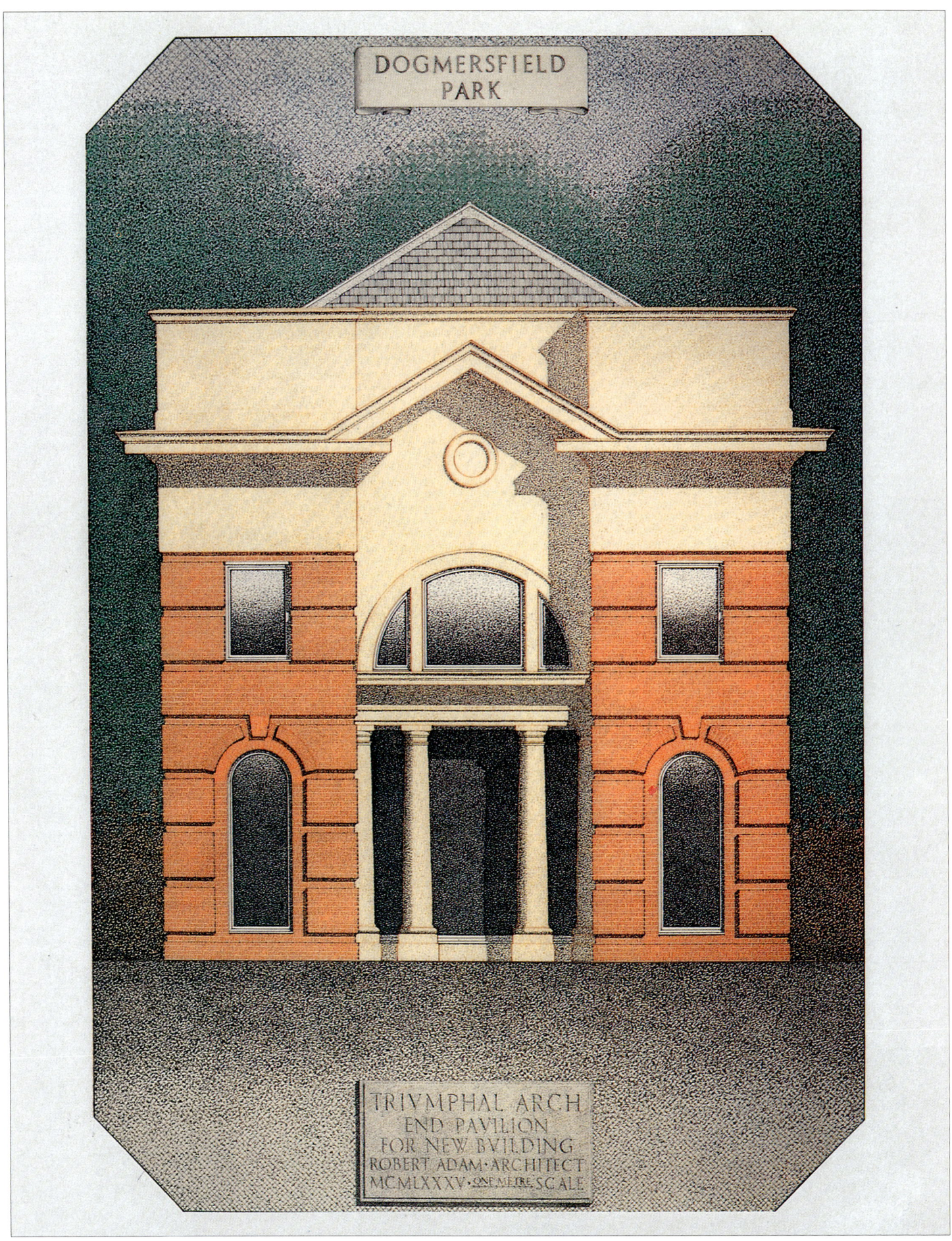

Robert Adam

The recent labelling of Robert Adam as a 'maverick Classicist' by the British press not only shows to what extent the public has come to accept Classicism as a viable alternative in today's pluralist climate, but also gives a good indication of Adam's philosophical position within that group. Where others may claim to offer a pure translation of the Classical vocabulary and system of orders, Adam doubts that any such translation is technically possible, given the difficulties inherent in finding an absolute model to work from. Instead, he notes that each of the three periods of Classical Revival in the past, while attempting to imitate what were believed to be reliable models, were actually interpretive, and were based on the subjective vision that each successive age has had of history. In addition, he strongly believes that what he has called the 'constructional fundamentalism' of other Classicists has not only been a pointless reaction to the sterility of the Modern Movement, but he has also tended to limit the future possibilities of the direction in which he is working. As an alternative, Adam iconoclastically suggests that the positive benefits of technology be reconsidered, since, the true meaning of 'techne' is craftsmanship in Greek, and Classicism has originally incorporated the latest construction methods in its detailing.

In his essay called *Tin Gods*, for example, he says ' Now, where *does* technology stand in society? Technology is not a *thing*, it is an *activity* and has no physical existence except by way of artefacts or products – technology *produces* things. When we talk of the level of technological development of a society, we are talking about the sum total of the technological processes involved in the use, operation, or manufacture of the products generate by that society.'

Modernism, on the other hand, had ironically limited the technological growth it had originally sought to express by its elitist, exclusive attitude, ultimately preventing such integration. Instead of being limiting, Adam sees Classicism as being open to originality and invention, as well as technology, making it just as reflective of the values of this age as other revivals have been of theirs.

While appearing at first to be bonafide member of the Classicist fraternity, Adam's renditions soon reveal variations when considered in detail.

OPPOSITE: Dogmersfield Park, Hampshire.
LEFT: Crooked Pightle House, Hampshire.
ABOVE: Bordon Library, Hampshire, (with Evans, Roberts & Partners).

A DECADE OF ARCHITECTURAL DESIGN

Quinlan Terry

While other classical architects may support their belief in this tradition through elaborate arguments based on Aristotle, Vitruvius and Petrarch, Quinlan Terry goes for the jugular, basing his defence on what he perceives to be unanimous, popular dissatisfaction with both the appearance and durability of modern buildings. Getting down to details quickly, he rhetorically asks, for example, why is it that 'old materials last for hundreds of years, whereas modern materials do not,' or why 'old buildings are so easy on the eye, whereas modern buildings are not.' In his opinion, the answers are obvious and the choice is between what he has categorised as 'the short-lived lusts of a throw-away society with their glossy, space-age structures, which suck out the earth's resources and leave behind a scrap heap of unrecyclable rubbish' on the one hand, and traditional techniques of building on the other. In order to clarify the issue further, he frequently points out that traditional building techniques are not only more environmentally friendly, because they involve natural, rather than man-made materials, but also that such materials are more compatible to human sensibilities. When his buildings are compared with this *apologia*, the physical results are far more convincing. While not to everyone's taste, his architecture reveals an impressive understanding of his craft in all its aspects, including an ability to create surprise and enclosure, as well as to choreograph movement through space.

Richmond Riverside is the most ambitious project undertaken by the architect to date, demonstrating all of the complexities of combining individual buildings together *de nuovo*.

OPPOSITE: Howard Building, Downing Collage, Cambridge, England.
LEFT: Dower House, Roydon, England.
OVERLEAF: Richmond Riverside Development, Richmond, England.

A DECADE OF ARCHITECTURAL DESIGN

QUINLAN TERRY

A DECADE OF ARCHITECTURAL DESIGN

Demetri Porphyrios

Several themes emerge when Demetri Porphyrios discusses his work. One of these, guaranteed to get a reaction from both professionals and a general public who have become increasingly accustomed to thinking of architecture in the same way that one regards Haute Couture or the *Times* Best Seller list, is that Classicism is not a Style. Pointing to such identifiable elements as gable roofs and columns, this architect convincingly draws from a number of literary and historical sources to show that they are all conventions that represent a symbolic recognition of culturally based empirical knowledge. Classical forms go back to the origins of building that are the basis of architecture itself. A second theme, closely related to that of convention, is mimesis, which has been poorly translated as imitation. Mimesis does not imply a replica of the natural world, but an interpretation and transformation of it. Incomplete understanding of Aristotlean texts and Classical monuments led many scholars to misdirect inadvertently this idea of transformation. While his own reading led him to say 'It is the same in architecture as with all of the arts, its principles are founded on nature itself and in the processes of nature are to be found clearly indicated, all of the rules of architecture,' a public that was increasingly enthusiastic for Classicalism, reduced this to the aphorism 'art must imitate nature.' In stressing that such imitation not only implies a translation of the natural world, but other buildings in the same tradition as well, Porphyrios lends authority to the argument that each generation must discover the validity of Classical conventions for itself, and not slavishly copy them. The last, and most paramount of all, is the controversial question of the connection between architecture and art. When considered in relation to these ideas of convention and transformation, there is no conflict between them because selection is necessary in each case, based upon socially determined criteria of relevance.

Because Classicism transcends fashion, it is not tied to questions of taste and provides a timelessly elegant setting for a serene lifestyle.

OPPOSITE, LEFT & ABOVE: House in Chepstow Villas, London, England.

A DECADE OF ARCHITECTURAL DESIGN

DEMETRI PORPHYRIOS

In working within a tradition that he sees as being based on the architect's transformation of the natural world, Demetri Porphyrios perceptively interprets that world, using time-tested conventions.

OPPOSITE & LEFT: House in Kensington, London, England.

A DECADE OF ARCHITECTURAL DESIGN

Aldo Rossi

Few architects have been as definitive in their opinions about what should be done to reverse the destruction of the traditional context of the European city as Aldo Rossi. In his *L'Architettura della Cittá*, published in 1966, he presents a thorough assessment of all aspects of this problem, such as the continuing part to be played by typology in restructuring the urban fabric. After defining the concept of type as 'something that is permanent and complex, a logical principle that is prior to form and that constitutes it,' Rossi goes on to systematically refine that definition. Referring to Quatremère de Quincy, he notes a type is not a model to be exactly copied or endlessly repeated; but is a rule, that is 'the structuring principle of architecture,'. 'Thus', he concludes, 'typology presents itself as the study of types of elements that cannot be further reduced, elements of a city as well as an architecture.' In his study, he also examines the role that monuments have had in the continuous growth of a city, building upon the theory of 'permanence' or 'persistences' put forward by both Poète and Lavedan to arrive at the critical distinction between what he calls 'propelling' and 'pathological' elements in urban form. While the Roman Temple of Jupiter in Damascus, which was later converted into a Mosque by the Ummayads and has since served as a key monument for Islam, may readily be seen to be a propelling presence in that city, rigorous application of the principles he put forward sheds quite a different light on such beloved monuments as the Alhambra in Granada, which is pathological or non-generative, in nature.

Since the English translation of his book in 1982, Rossi has acknowledged that inexorable forces of change have brought totally new pressures upon the post-industrial city. In his recognition of the regenerating powers of propelling elements, he has encouraged those who are concerned about the contextual casualties in traditional cities today to focus instead on saving surviving monuments, in the firm belief that they will recreate urbanity in totally new, and unexpected, ways. The alternative, in his view, is to abandon these cities altogether, and to make them museums of a way of life that has now disappeared forever.

Like the painter Giorgio De Chirico, Aldo Rossi tries to create a silent empty world in which his architecture stands as a permanent, regenerating force.

OPPOSITE & LEFT: Administration Centre, Perugia, Italy.

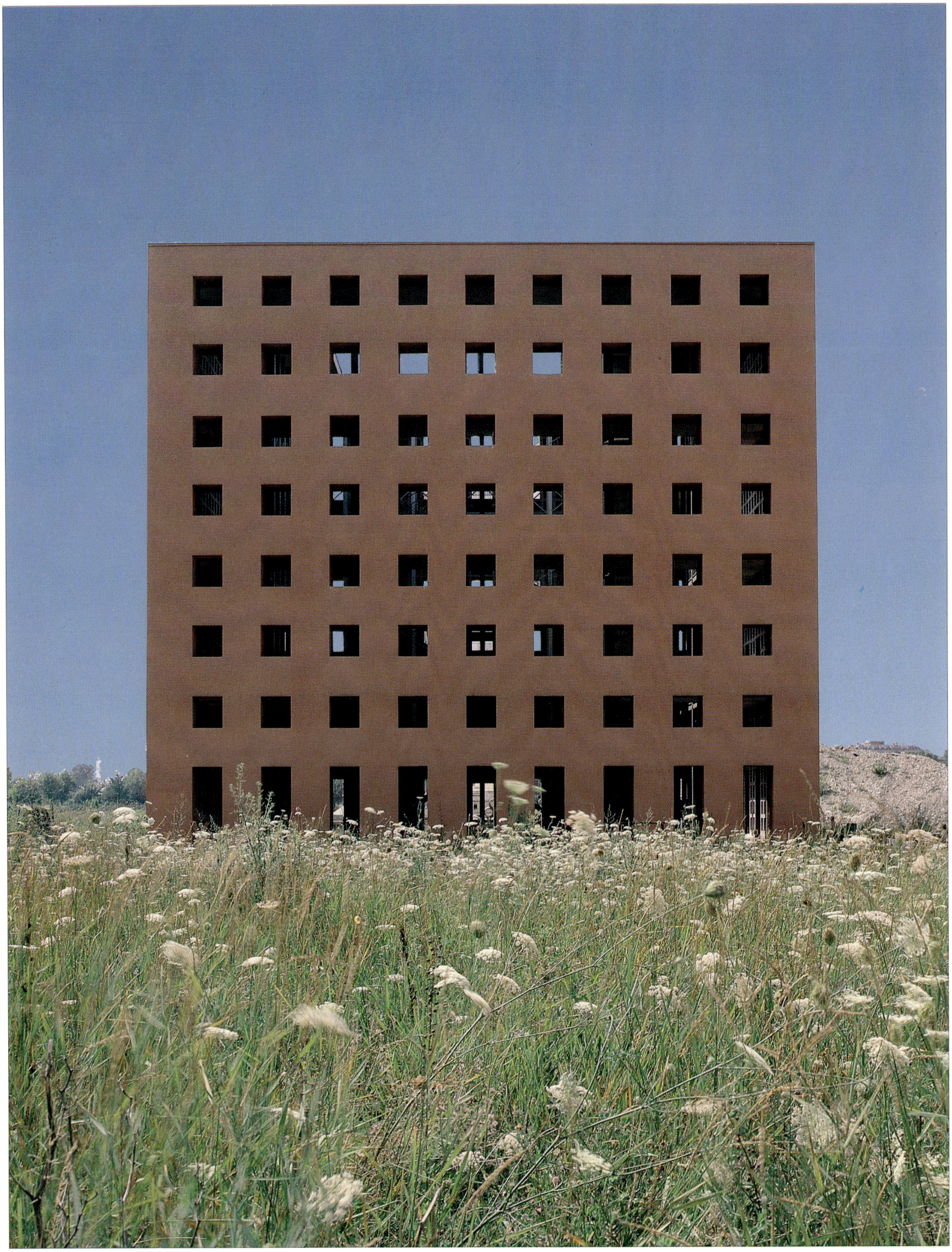

ALDO ROSSI

Platonic solids are favoured as being the most easily comprehensible and visually powerful of all forms, as well as the most susceptible to mathematical proof.

OPPOSITE: Cemetery, Modena, Italy.
LEFT & ABOVE: Friedrichstadt housing, Berlin, Germany.

A DECADE OF ARCHITECTURAL DESIGN

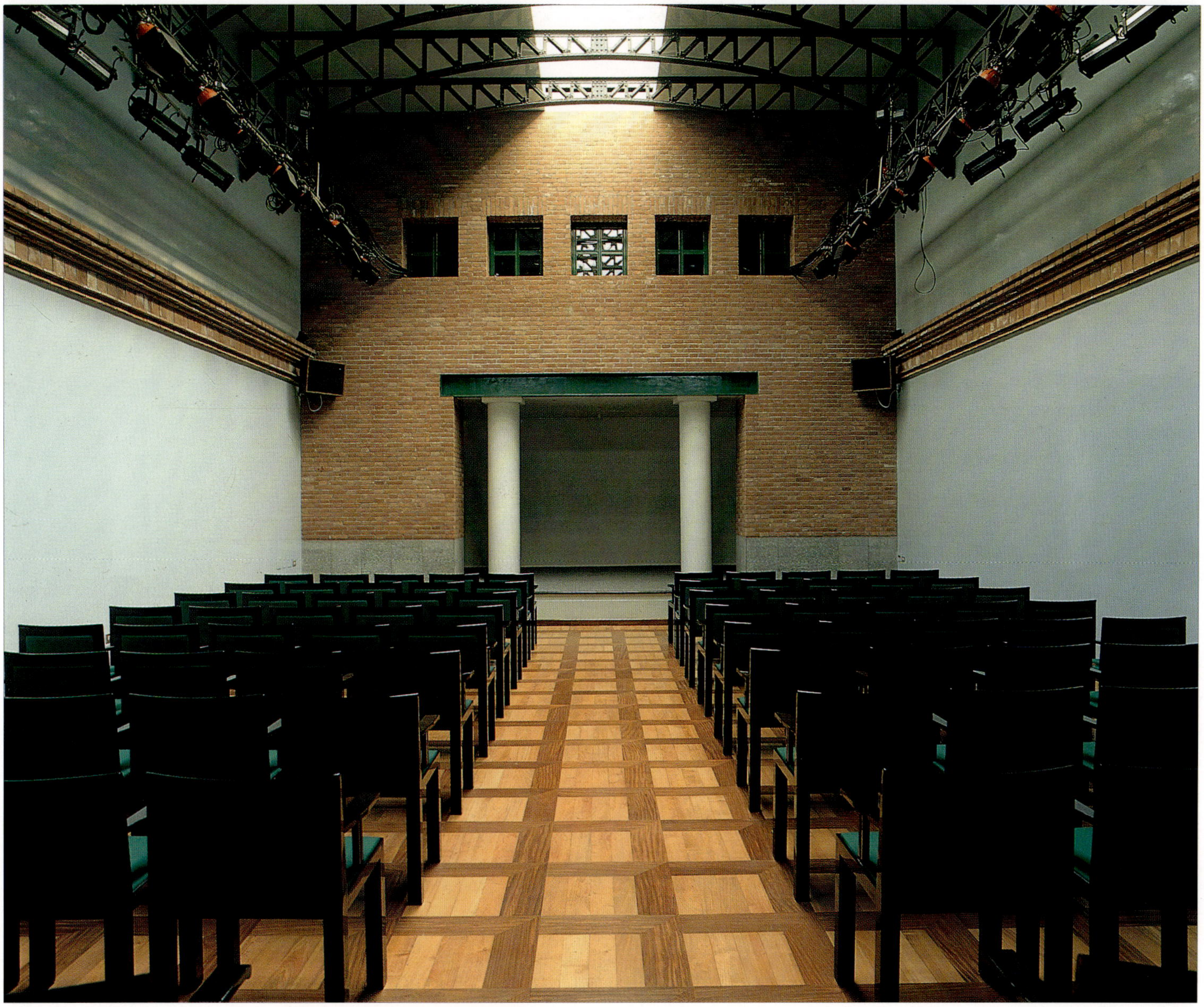

ALDO ROSSI

Typologies of street, arcade and entrance re-occur in buildings of diverse function, in order that the type itself may be studied and refined.

OPPOSITE, LEFT & ABOVE: Casa Aurora, Turin, Italy.

A DECADE OF ARCHITECTURAL DESIGN

Robert Adam
Tin Gods

The Modern Movement is alive and well and living in Lime Street. In spite of ambitious promises from Post-Modernists, Classicists and others, in spite of the almost total dominance of the Neo-Vernacular in everyday architecture, the spirit of the machine age keeps coming back to re-inspire a profession which has clung to its Modernist dreams for 50 years. Inside every monster cottage office block there is a Lloyds Building begging to be let out.

At the heart of every debate about new, and generally historicist, directions in architecture, lies the issue of technology. To those educated in the Modern Movement, and this is nearly the whole profession, the adoption of any architectural forms that evoke a pre-industrial revolution aesthetic is not true to the Modern age. When the 20th century is defined by its motor cars and computers what possible relevance can columns or decorated gables have to an architecture which has a duty to reflect its age? To most of the design professions, this technological view of contemporary life removes any hope of giving any credibility to Classicism, Post-Modernism or other historically-biased movements. Alastair Best summed it up in his discussion of the Hong Kong Shanghai Bank in *Architectural Review*:

> Norman Foster and Richard Rogers are the only architects of international status who are now practising with their Modern Movement ideals more or less intact. Both still cling tenaciously to an architecture which is anti-suburban in form, committed to social integration, and wholly, even ostentatiously, dedicated to technology at its leading edge. These are values worth fighting for, but they are out of fashion. Those who have abandoned the struggle – through fecklessness or expediency, or both – must now watch from the ten-guinea seats while Foster and Rogers carry on the heroic struggle alone.

Strong stuff, but the Modern Movement has always been convinced of its absolute rightness. The most extreme counter to this comes from Quinlan Terry. His belief in the Divine origins of the Orders via Moses and Solomon's Temple runs parallel with his belief in the rightness of ignoring 19th- and 20th-century technological advance in building techniques. This view is so extreme it barely contributes to the debate but merely lets Terry settle back into an impregnable position always guarded against argument by Divine approval. I would go further and say that both views, the High-Technology argument and the case for technological retrogression are the reverse sides of the same very distinctly modern coin. Both relate to a 19th- and 20th-century obsession with technology. This obsession can express itself by turning that technology into a god or by turning it into a devil.

Similar attitudes can be found in other walks of life. On the one hand we have the quite common view that technological advance has a will of its own and moves forward like a vast juggernaut incapable of being stopped. On the other hand we have the conservationist or the anti-fluoride campaigner. Both sides are obsessed with technology, one positively and the other negatively. This obsession has been created by the rapid changes society has experienced since the early 19th century. But an obsession with technology and its visual counterpart, the machine aesthetic, is

The Doric Order.

not an inevitable consequence of significant technological change. There have been other periods when collective advances in technology have changed society.

In 15th-century Europe the invention of printing transformed written communication. The development of efficient artillery revolutionised the vital political and physical art of warfare. The invention of the sea-quadrant and the development of the modern sailing ship opened up the world to European explorers. Scientific cartography and major advances in canal locks opened new possibilities in land transport. And yet the commercial and technological centre was in the Mediterranean where that revival of Classical Antiquity in design, the Renaissance, was growing alongside these new developments.

Equally, the late 18th and early 19th centuries saw some of the most important technological advances before the introduction of electrical power. Watts steam pumping engines came into use in 1776, the first commercial paddlesteamer was commissioned in New York in 1807, and the Stockton and Darlington railway line, the first in the world, opened in 1825. Add this to the extensive use of factory production, the invention of the Spinning Jenny, the use of wrought iron, the introduction of the rifle and many more revolutionary advances and we have an age which was, indeed, dominated by its technological progress.

But this precise period saw the dominance of Neo-Classical architecture throughout Europe. Neo-Classical buildings, employing wrought iron beams and cast iron decoration, were used for the first railway stations and, indeed, came to symbolise the political revolutions of America and France which paralleled the technological and social revolutions of the same period.

It would be possible to cite northern Europe in the late 17th century or the Classical world in the first century BC, but I think the point is made. It is not made to say that technological advance *must* or *should* be accompanied by revivals in architecture and design. It is made to point out that such advance does not of *necessity* bring about a corresponding aesthetic based on the products or processes associated with that advance.

So, what underlies the idea that it would be untruthful, even immoral, to use an historically-inspired architecture in an age noted for technical change? It cannot, as we have seen, be the technical change itself that forces the aesthetic on the designer, so it must be a particular attitude of mind exclusive to the 20th century. In order to understand this we must examine the origins and history of this attitude of mind.

The 20th-century love affair with machines has its roots in the middle of the 19th century, when familiarity with machines and confidence in technology led some to a mechanistic and aesthetic view of the world.

In Germany philosophers like Buchner saw existence itself obeying 'mechanical laws' and Darwin's theory of natural selection dismissed the concept of any supernatural benign force in creation, substituting a chilling scientific concept of an unceasing struggle for resources.

Above all it was Karl Marx who drew together these strands into a single philosophical system that laid the foundations both of Communism and Modernism. He combined a wholly technological view of society with a belief that history was rolling relentlessly towards a predestined end, and considered that only a revolutionary destruction of the old order could create a truly modern world unencumbered with its past.

Early printing technology.

The ordained end of this historical process was the rule of the proletariat. The proletariat *had* to transcend the other classes because they were 'the special and essential product' of modern industry. The Marxist analysis of history was overwhelmingly technological. *Technology* makes society, not society technology. So, 'the hand-mill gives you the society with the feudal lord; the steam-mill the society with the industrial capitalist'.

This old world had to be destroyed because 'the tradition of all the dead generations weighs like a nightmare on the brain of the living . . . the social revolution of the 19th century cannot draw its poetry from the past, but only from the future. It cannot begin with itself before it has stripped off all superstition in regard to the past'.

The strong resemblance between this view of progress and technology and the writings of Sant'Elia, Le Corbusier and other Modernist theorists may be coincidental. It is not, however, coincidental that Marx, who brought together Determinist, Materialist and Revolutionary ideas current in the 19th century, should have found similarity with the Modernists. His writings were in general currency at the turn of the century and serve to locate the common roots they share with the Modern Movement in a mechanistic 19th-century view of inevitable technology-driven progress towards a better society and the revolution required to create it.

The new century seemed to many to be the dawn of a new machine age. A few artists sought a new aesthetic which would overturn the 'use of materials that are massive, bulky, durable, and expensive all opposed to the complexity of modern culture' (Ugo Nebbia on Sant'Elia 1914) and 'rule out "architecture" in the Classical and traditional sense' (Sant'Elia and Marinetti: *Futurist Architecture*).

The new direction could not, therefore, be drawn from architecture and art itself – this would be retrogressive, not a revolution. The Modernists had to look elsewhere and it was to an analogous relationship with the most up-to-date products of the new century that they turned for the revolutionary new aesthetic.

Much of this is very familiar, but it is worth reiterating the essential views of the Modern Movement towards technology in order that we can be reminded of how this vision of a technological future lies at the centre of the Modern Movement. It is eloquently expressed by the comparatively recent development of so called High-Tech architecture which has given new hope to embittered purists like Peter Cook who said in 1983 that they had 'remained committed throughout to the belief that architecture owed its honour to the forward movement of civilisation' and can once again feel that 'after the great wars, great speeds, great ships, great feats of technology, there can be buildings that are of a similar order'.

Modern Movement ideas about technology can be reduced to two fundamental beliefs. The first is that modern history is technology-led and has a momentum that is so powerful that it is largely outside the control of individuals and even of society, and has such a dynamic character that it will compel society to accommodate itself to the introduction of new technologies which will bring about a better society. The second is that contemporary design should cast aside the historical aesthetic as irrelevant to a society that is defined by its rapidly advancing technology and that a new aesthetic should be found by an analogous relationship with the most up-to-date and significant products of that advanced technology.

In order to progress the debate, we must go to the very heart of these beliefs and examine the role of technology in society. And first we must try and define what we

Sant'Elia, drawing.

mean by technology. Technics, or technological activities, are that class of activities that humans engage in that involve a skill and can be called useful, the useful arts. Generally it involves the manipulation of tools but not of necessity. Basket making is a primitive technology but need not employ any tools. In common usage, however, technology generally implies something at least faintly connected with manufacture or industry. It is, nonetheless, important to remember that the practise of some form of technology is one of the most basic of human activities.

Now, where *does* technology stand in society? Technology is not a *thing*, it is an *activity* and has no physical existence except by way of artefacts or products – technology *produces* things. When we talk of the level of technological development of a society, we are talking about the sum total of the technological processes involved in the use, operation, or manufacture of the products generated by that society. So in the 18th-century list there would be the steam engine, the inland canal and Wedgwood pottery; and in the 20th-century list the motor car, the computer and something simple like the brick industry.

These technological processes are all joined together to form an operating technological system specific to a society. In other words one product can be part of the technological process involved in the manufacture of another product. At the same time, each product is brought into existence or is operated by an industry specific to that product. So there is the electrical tool industry, the motor manufacturing industry, the micro-computer industry, the ceramics industry, or the building industry. Although each industry is related to many other industries, it is also independent. It is generally financed and managed independently, and if it consists of several firms each firm competes with other firms within that industry.

In examining the operation of technology in society it is not only practical but realistic to examine how technological change affects an industry, and therefore the industrial system in general.

I have here a model of the active forces in the creation of a product. This is a general model and applies to almost any industry. It will require some explanation.

The primary factor is the population for whom the product is brought into existence. As this may not represent the whole population, it is referred to in the square box on the right as the 'market', as any product, be it a house or a hairdryer, is produced for a sector of the population which is commercially, although not architecturally, referred to as a market. This market is never static and it is important for the survival of a firm or an industry to understand how this market is moving and so the general buying or commissioning public is referred to as 'market change'. The types of change that can take place are noted in the circular box on the right: Social, Political, Demographic, Economic and Cultural. There may be others.

The next thing is the product itself and the principal forces which bring it into being. A product exists to satisfy a demand and, in the commercial as in the architectural world, if it does not satisfy that demand, be it of the purchaser, the client, or some secondary end user, the product will fail and either be destroyed, modified, or not repeated. This aspect of the product is labelled in the square box at the top 'Demand Satisfaction'. It is very important to note, for reasons that I will explain later, that this demand can be of a very simple nature – such as to get around easily, or to do sums more easily and accurately, or to provide shelter. It can be quite complex such as wanting a car that will get me to my aunt's house in Scotland in six hours, for a relatively small sum of money, allow me to enjoy the drive and impress her no end when she sees my car.

The types of demand will, therefore, vary a great deal from industry to industry, and from product to product. I believe, nonetheless, that they will generally include one or more of the categories noted in the circular box at the top: Functional, Economic, Performance, and Aesthetic. So, the desire to get about easily is purely functional whereas my car for my trip to Scotland has all four ingredients. A building will, generally, have a demand for a high aesthetic satisfaction but not inevitably. A military fortification, for example would have high functional and performance demands to satisfy, if necessary, at the expense of economy and appearance.

To bring a product into being which satisfies the demands of the market it has to be produced, and this is labelled in the square box at the bottom, rather obviously, the 'Production Process'. This involves the factors set out in the bottom circular box: Product Design, Supply of Capital, Supply of Materials, Supply of Labour, Manufacturing or Assembly Processes, and – if appropriate – Marketing and Distribution.

Before moving on to the burning question in the square box on the left I would like to discuss the arrowed links between the boxes mentioned so far.

The link between 'Demand Satisfaction' and the 'Production Process' is obvious. The production process creates the product to satisfy a demand and the desire for satisfaction of that demand is the force of the production process.

The link between the 'Production Process' and 'Market Change' is not so obvious. A change in the economy or demography of the market may have a direct effect on production, independent of that production processes' function of creating a product. For example, a change in the economy and a rise in wage demands could create a need for automation. Equally, the production process could influence changes in the market. Limitations in available distribution systems for agricultural products, for example, could lead to a population shift to agricultural areas.

Most important, however, is the two-way link between 'Demand Satisfaction' and 'Market Change'. The fact that a change in the market will produce new or varied demands to be satisfied almost goes without saying. For example, if the immigrant population of Bradford increases, the demand for food stuffs will change. What is significant is that the satisfaction of a demand often has an effect on the market itself. This market change could then change the demand on the original product. Once people have tried something new, they want it to perform better, function better, look nicer or cost less.

This effect is particularly marked when an industry operates in a competitive situation. So, for example, an improved weapon will satisfy a demand in one country for military superiority. This will then create a new demand in another country that previously had superiority but had now lost it. This see-saw effect between demand satisfaction and market change can operate very slowly or extremely rapidly according to the nature or strength of demand and the ability of competitors within an industry to modify their products in the most appropriate way to satisfy the demand. So, the demand for the movement of people and produce has always been with us. The development of light-wheeled animal-drawn vehicles satisfied that demand for that market or society. It also had a demographic effect on the population permitting greater distances between producing centres. This more dispersed market then created a demand for yet more efficient means of transport

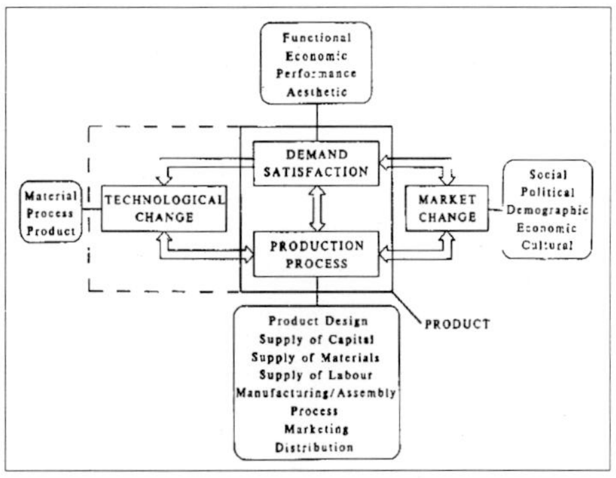

Model of active forces in creation of a product.

for social or political purposes. Such a see-saw process could take hundreds of years. Early railways present, in more senses than one, a faster example. The demand for the first commercial railway, the Stockton and Darlington line, was limited to providing improved transport to Stockton for coal from the Auckland coalfield. Although steam locomotives were used from the start, much of the transport on the line was horse drawn. The venture was a great economic success and reduced the price of coal in Stockton by one third in one year and one half in 18 months. This success changed the economic market for railway construction, vastly increasing demand from investors and entrepreneurs anxious to be in on such profitable ventures and raising the performance demands on steam locomotives. The capital investment in railways rose from the original £100,000 in 1825 to £76 million 20 years later. Equally, from an initial speed of 15 mph on the Stockton and Darlington line, by the end of the same period a Gooch Iron Duke locomotive on the Great Western Railway had achieved a speed of 78 mph.

I have dwelt on this point at some length before introducing the position of 'Technological Change' on the model because it introduces an important concept. The satisfaction of a demand can alter the society which is making the demand so as to alter the demand itself. Or more simply put: people are never satisfied when they get something new and always want something better.

Now, where does technological change fit into all of this? Technological Change, that is technological innovation, invention or discovery, can originate from within an industry or a firm, or from somewhere quite independent – hence the dotted line indicating its possible location within an industry. It can, as the circular box on the left shows, be a change in the materials available, or a change in the process of manufacture or use – for example production-line factory organisation or a change in the products available such as a new computer for distribution analysis. Obviously, as the lower arrowed link shows, all of these can have an influence on the production process. The production process can itself stimulate technological change, indeed create its own demand which craves satisfaction, and hence the two way arrow. For example, a poor supply or increased cost of a material may stimulate a company to innovate and develop the same product but made with different materials.

Now, demand satisfaction can also stimulate technological change. If a demand is inadequately satisfied due to limitations in the production process, such as unsuitable design or deficiencies in marketing, then technological change can be deliberately stimulated to allow the demand to be satisfied. So Du Pont, recognising a demand for low cost, sheer, stretch resistant ladies' stockings deliberately set out to develop a suitable synthetic yarn by employing W H Carothers to undertake research.

But, can technological change directly affect the satisfaction of a demand? At first sight the answer must be, yes (and it has the added advantage of making the model diagram neater). We must, however, go back to our definition of technology. It is not a *thing*, it is an *activity*. This activity may *produce* things but, at heart, technology is a skill, manipulation, use of tools, or process of manufacture which amounts to the *activity* of producing or modifying something. Such artefacts or products, be they buildings or buttons, satisfy a demand for an object or service or facilitate an activity. In order to do so they must be *produced*. Technological change can only make itself felt through the production process. So, in the case of nylon it may appear that the technological change or innovation directly satisfied a demand. This is not the case.

The nylon itself has to be manufactured by a chemical process and it is the *process* that employs the technology, not the product. The product is the end result of a technological process – the manufacture of nylon – and the manufacture of nylon is undertaken by the chemical industry.

It has taken a long time to explain this model but its significance is that it locates the role of technology, or technological change, in society. It demonstrates that society is *not* led by new developments in technology. Society makes demands on its products and technological changes may or may not contribute to the satisfaction of those demands. If they do they will do so through the medium of an industry. Technology is *demand* led or, in commercial parlance, *market* led. If this model is correct, it must stand examination in relation to the functioning of individual industries. I will use two technology-dominated industries to test it out.

For all the *Vorsprung durch Technic* advertisements, the modern motor-car industry concentrates a great deal of effort in originating new cars and components in a carefully researched assessment of future market demand. The decision to introduce such cars as the Mini in 1956 and the Ford Sierra in 1975 were both taken as a direct consequence of an anticipated demand for economy or low fuel consumption vehicles following the Suez crisis and the oil crisis respectively. Technological innovations were introduced solely in order to achieve perceived market ends. The Mini, for the first time in the mass market, located the gearshafts in the crank case and also for the first time in mass production developed a rubber-sprung suspension system. All this was to enable Austin to produce a 10-foot car with 80 percent usable volume which was their perception of a market demand for small, economical cars. Equally, the tremendous research and development programme which was devoted to the bodywork design of the Ford Sierra was centred around the creation of a fuel saving aerodynamic car. Ford had decided in 1975 that fuel saving was to be a major public issue and a significant market force. As they had only recently developed a new engine and as light-weight body materials were too expensive, they were forced to undertake research in bodywork design as this was the only economic means of satisfying their perception of the market demand.

The micro-electronics industry is much younger and is, due to the rapid pace of technological change, generally considered to be technology led. In other words products or processes are originated and a market is created by their manufacture. I do not believe this is actually the case. In fact, I believe, that even an examination of one of the legendary micro-electronics technology-led markets demonstrates that the concept of a technology-led market is in fact incorrect. The key to understanding this is to put forward the right level of required market satisfaction. The rapid growth of pocket calculator sales with the introduction of the Sinclair calculator is generally put forward as an example of a market being created for a pocket calculator solely by its introduction. This is to misinterpret the initial demand. The demand was not for a micro-electronic pocket calculator but for a simple portable aid to everyday arithmetic. Up until then everyday arithmetic was undertaken generally and precariously in the head or awkwardly on scraps of paper. A demand for aids to calculation had existed for hundreds, if not thousands, of years. The abacus, medieval counter accounting, the slide rule, and the mechanical calculator all demonstrate the demand for arithmetic assistance. Sinclair recognised that recent technological changes allowed this to be provided conveniently and at an affordable price. Once the market had absorbed the new product their demands changed from functional demands to economic and performance demands centred on the product and the race was on to provide a *very* small and *very* cheap calculator.

This rapid oscillation between the satisfaction of a basic demand and the change in the market brought about by the product which satisfies that demand is generally mistaken for a market creation by a new product.

Sinclair did not, as we all know, always get it right. His skill with the pocket calculator was to pair one of a massive number of available technological changes with an existing market demand. The miniature television, on the other hand, although a great innovation has not found anything like the market that was anticipated by British and Japanese manufacturers.

These examples serve to demonstrate the fact that the existence of technological opportunities and innovations by no means guarantees their success. There are many, technological inventions available in the micro-electronics industry alone – particularly in software – but, I am told, of the large number of advertised examples in magazines such as *Computers Today* hardly any have any market potential. Even inventions which were considered to be of great importance at the time of their introduction, such as thin film memories and tunnel diodes have, according to Gerald Brook in the *US Computer Industry,* turned out to be unimportant.

There is no inevitability about technological change. The invention of something, however wonderful it may seem at the time, carries with it no guarantee of its adoption by the society in which it was invented. Historical examples are not always easy to find as an invention is a singular thing and its multiplication and consequent probable survival is a demonstration of its suitability to its market. We do, however, know that the structural arch was developed above ground and complete with voussoirs as early as 1400 BC in Egypt. It was not, however, widely adopted for structural purposes until some 1,200 years later. Equally, the zero system of numeration had been developed by the Babylonian civilisation as early as the sixth century BC, it was known to the Greeks but virtually ignored in spite of what seem to us overwhelming advantages. The system was not to enter into a dominant Western culture until the Middle Ages. Perhaps the most telling story is that of the Roman Emperor Vespasian who turned down his engineer's invention of labour saving devices declaring 'You must allow me to feed my poor commons.'

As there is no inevitability about the adoption and progression of technical change, it cannot be predicted. We have no means of telling which of the many thousands of new technological inventions produced every year will be of any use to a future society. The unpredictability and hence the very low chances of commercial success in undirected or 'blue sky' research in the computer industry, for example, restricts it to very few large firms. Even then IBM in 1968 decided that the value was not gained from results but from maintaining the company's status, helping with recruitment and slowing down the losses of personnel to other scientific groups.

Society is neither led by technology, nor can the rate of adoption or even the fact of adoption of technical change or innovation be anticipated. Technology is a slave not even to society but to the products required by that society. The idea of a building or product of the future is a played-out science fiction myth. Nothing produced today can be judged today as ahead of its time; such an idea depends on the vision of a positive and predictable future created by the inevitable progress of technology. The vision is false. Only the future can create a past which is ahead of its time by reviving that past. The Ville Radieuse was a product of early 20th-century socialism inappropriately foisted on the mid-20th-century welfare state. It is time we came to terms with the reality of our childhood fantasies – Dan Dare is not the pilot of the future but a Spitfire pilot in fancy dress forever fighting a small green Hitler.

I have tried to keep the analysis of technology fairly clear of architecture and in the realm of industry in general in order not to cloud the debate by all our architectural preconceptions. Some may protest at the lumping together of architecture with something so vulgar as the industrial world and the commercial product. But I have only followed the early Modernist intention to parallel architecture with the most up-to-date and symbolic industries of the century. I too have gone along with the view, which I believe to be correct, that architecture or the construction industry including architecture, in as much as it relates to technology rather than fine art, is in many respects similar to other industries.

I too believe that we can learn a great deal from other industries and their technological development. The lessons are not, however, always as symbolic and straightforward as the theories.

The motor industry, as I have already pointed out, is a very fertile field for symbolic comparison together with allied aerospace industries. The motor industry is, however, in many significant respects quite unlike the building industry. Fundamentally, the motor industry consists of a very few companies producing a very limited range of mobile compact products in very high quantity and in highly controlled conditions. The building industry, on the other hand, consists of a large number of different sizes and types of companies producing an almost unlimited range of immobile, bulky products in virtually single numbers and in highly adverse conditions.

One has, consequently, to be very wary of simplistic analogies between the two industries. Perhaps the silliest idea to grow out of this analogy is that of planned obsolescence in architecture which, we are given to understand, is successfully applied in the motor industry and will similarly allow more rapid design turnover, greater flexibility of use by ridding us quickly of obsolete products, opportunities for the speedier introduction of the latest technological changes, and even a more egalitarian society fostered by greater consumer choice.

Far from making buildings more flexible, temporary architecture removes from building one very important optional quality – the ability to be permanent. Any long-life building can be made temporary merely by demolishing it, while a temporary building abandons that option. Except in special circumstances, the whole idea flies in the face of users' wishes, something the motor industry would not dare even consider. A recent survey revealed that people in Britain expect a building to last 60 to 100 years. Furthermore the existence of older or obsolete buildings with their consequent lower rents in fact contributes to the flexibility of the economy as a whole by allowing new or peripheral businesses to operate in the wake of the highly financed companies. We all know the problem of the small specialist retail outlet and the new shopping centre.

Perhaps most significant of all, the whole idea is founded on a myth. There is no planned obsolescence in the motor industry. There used to be *design* obsolescence but that was a matter of styling – putting different trims or wings on each year – and was abandoned in the mid-60s. *Planned* or *product* obsolescence is not a considera-

Cartoon from Dan Dare.

tion in car manufacture. The reason is simple: as almost every motorist finances his purchase of a new car on the retained value of his old car, the new car business is inextricably linked with the used car business and loss of value due to timed obsolescence would not only remove too much capital from the industry but would deter purchasers – witness the Fiat rust scandal. Rusting, or body obsolescence, is not deliberate but is a negative product of design evolution in unit construction.

Following on from this, there is the very common desire from both clients and architects for the process of construction to bring itself technologically into line with other factory-based industries. While individual building elements are already well established factory produced products, the construction industry as an assembly process *cannot* put itself under controlled conditions similar to a factory. Not only is it virtually impossible to control the working environment of a construction site in the same way as the enclosed space of a factory, but on a site the operative must move to his task whereas the essential quality of factory flow production is that the *task* moves to the operative.

In fact, the Modernist ideal of factory-inspired production is largely symbolic. In spite of eager anticipation in the early part of the century and government subsidised attempts to adopt wartime factory techniques to construction after the war, the traditional building industry has – to the bewilderment and dismay of modern movement disciplines – remained firmly entrenched and the hoped-for world or all buildings made for and looking like machines seems as far away as ever. This is not to say that development of more efficient building techniques and components should not proceed, but there are important lessons to be learnt from other industries.

The Ford Sierra is an example of a cladding design exercise. The Sierra design was, for reasons I have explained, limited to the re-modelling of the body shell. The engine and many of the moving parts were already developed. Notwithstanding this relatively limited task, the time from the commencement of research and development to launch was about six years and cost $800 million. Towards the end of this time prototypes were exhaustively tested not only in the buying market (and with rather worrying results) but most significantly in the function of the new design. Environmental chambers were used to test the behaviour of the bodywork in different conditions and the car was run with a number of test models in normal road conditions for a year to 18 months and at distances up to 150,000 km.

This level of investment and research in what amounts to the cladding and fitting out of one small object explains why sales of a virtually identical product have to exceed one million. Although the comparison is not direct, it still makes the quarter of a million pounds budgeted for prototype production in the Lloyds Building – one very large object – appear miniscule. We should not be surprised to see major failures in new cladding systems, such as the superplastic aluminium on the Sainsbury Centre, which are designed symbolically to relate to modern systems, such as motor car panel assembly, without taking account of the complete process used for the development of those systems.

There are, it is true, opportunities for using so called 'soft moulds' to more economically develop small runs of industrialised buildings or building components. There is also much talk of a future 'easily-formable . . . supermaterial' from people like Future Systems. It would, therefore, be of some benefit to examine the development procedures for the most tractable high-technology product, computer software.

Post-war prefab housing.

I reproduce a diagram which Frederick P Brooks Junior published in *The Mythical Man Month*, a series of essays in software engineering. This diagram was designed to show why programmes at their initial creation do not reach the market as speedily and economically as the initial programme would tend to suggest. From the top left, the programme has to go through two independent processes before it is brought together into the bottom right box as a 'programming systems product', that is 'the truly useful object'.

In the vertical direction it becomes a 'programming product' by generalising the original product, thoroughly testing this product in action and to its limits, and finally setting up information so that it can be used, fixed and extended by anyone.

In the horizontal direction it becomes a 'programming system' by fitting it into existing interface systems, by setting its level of performance, and finally by ensuring that it fits with other system components in all expected combinations. Each of these processes costs three times the production of the original programme and, when brought together in a programming systems product, will cost nine times as much.

The architectural pursuit of a symbolic relationship with these industries and others like them is, unfortunately, only skin deep. I do not think that anyone in the profession really wishes to see the construction industry dominated by small numbers of large firms committed to selling vast numbers of anonymous, virtually identical products. In truth, no-one will see this state of affairs in spite of the fact that it is the logical end of pursuing a parallel course with the most up-to-date industries of this century. It is, however, regrettable that in pursuit of this symbol some of the problems of manufacturing industries seem to have been adopted without learning the corresponding lessons that are there to be learnt.

I would like to show you a very modern, High-Tech building. All its parts have been influenced by recent technological changes and it has responded to new demands from the end-user market or the construction market by improving comfort, decreasing heat-loss, lowering maintenance, easing construction by a reduction in labour, or speeding up construction by the use of prefabricated components.

Architecture and the construction industry can, indeed, learn much from other industries but we should proceed with care rather than with rash enthusiasm borne of glib theoretical comparisons designed to achieve symbolic results. We are fortunate in that we do not represent a unified manufacturing system but are fragmented into designers, component manufacturers, and assemblers. It is this that enables us to retain our status as fine artists – and long may it remain. But it shields us from the bitter realities of putting a product on to a competitive market and, while we may compare ourselves with sculptors and painters who often share our aspirations, we are also part of an industry which produces commercial products. The pursuit of our symbolic technological aims has, due to its persistent technical failures, brought us great discredit and rather than dismiss this as a necessary part of a learning curve we ought to realise that it has, in fact, led to a dramatic restriction on our artistic freedom by the forcible entry of the public through such institutions as the planning control system.

There does, however, remain one nagging question. Every parallel so far discussed has been a product for sale whereas architecture is rarely marketed as a manufactured product. There is, nonetheless, a built product that is sold in very much the same way as the Ford Sierra or the home computer: the speculative house. I am

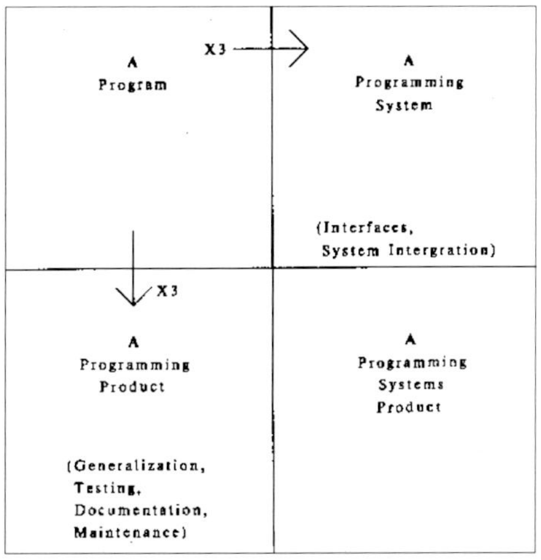

Evolution of the programming systems product.

sure that in common with myself you are all absolutely appalled by the design standard of these buildings and would blanch even at the word 'architecture' being used in connection with them. But the simple truth is that they are the product of a highly competitive market, as is demonstrated by the large companies' aggressive advertising, and their sales are a mark of their success.

The mystery is, how on earth can Sierra or Audi customers be seduced into buying something so patently false as this? To all of us educated in the design professions the quite common association of undisguised products of 20th-century technology with this ill-understood historicism is extraordinary. They seem a total mis-match and yet they take place in almost every drive and sitting room in Europe and America.

Rather than standing aloof and sneering at this, I believe that, like the common language philosophers, we should examine it and see what it will tell us. It is evidently a persistent phenomenon and so could it reveal something we have hitherto ignored?

Where does architecture and the construction industry differ from more popular technological products such as the car, the television, the telephone, the computer and so on? It is, above all else, in the age of the industry.

Architecture and construction are one of the oldest industries. The provision of shelter is one of mankind's most fundamental technological activities, second only perhaps to tool making. What we see on these houses is symbolic reference to past examples of that industry. This is, or so we imagine, something that does not exist in the motor-car industry, the micro-electronics industry and other more 20th-century manufacturing processes. And it is this contrast we find so marked.

But we have, largely for symbolic reasons ourselves, chosen particular industrial processes to represent the 20th century. The total operating technological system of the 20th century is not, however, solely composed of such newcomers to the scene. The railways are a phenomenon which owe their existence to technological changes in the 18th and 19th centuries but it is still one of the industries of the 20th century. The agricultural industry is still growing corn and rearing animals much as it has been for some 10,000 years, but it is still a vital industry of the 20th century.

It might be useful to examine a 20th-century industry which produces objects to facilitate as fundamental and historic a process as seeking shelter. The consumption of food seems a reasonable example and it has certain interesting parallels with the use of buildings. The means by which we eat, the use of plates and cutlery, are both functional and ritualistic. Much as the Western world uses crockery and cutlery in a way which is specific to its culture, so we use buildings in a manner specific to our culture. Such highly developed specific attitudes can only grow up in a long culturally developed relationship with the artefacts associated with the activity.

We usually eat off plates made of china in the West, what is known industrially as ceramic flatware. There is no necessity for the use of this material as in India, for example, metal eating dishes are held in higher esteem. The forms of plates and dishes that we use today are virtually identical to wheel-thrown vessels of five thousand years ago. These vessels are not, however, commercially wheel-thrown today, being slip-moulded, produced by a mechanical roller head process, or, more recently dry dust pressed.

In the 50s and 60s the ceramic industry was seriously concerned that it would enter into a decline due to the introduction of plastic crockery. There is no doubt

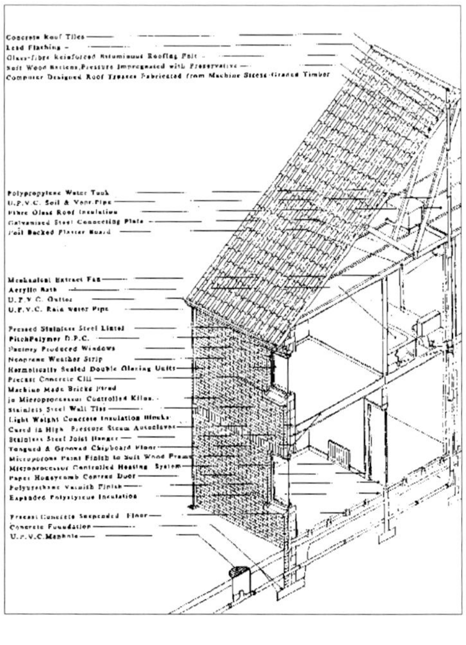

A modern High-Tech building.

whatever that plastic is in many respects a superior material for plates, it is cheap, lightweight, virtually unbreakable, made of a readily available raw material, colour-fast, and resistant to chemicals and heat. The promised revolution never occurred, the public just did not like the new material, eating was an aesthetic and ritualised affair not to be spoilt by something that felt wrong, however technically superior it may be.

There is, however, as far as I am aware no breast-beating by contemporary designers because they use this basic historic form and this superseded impractical material. There is no call, like that of Rogers, to 're-think our lifestyle' and go over to eating with radically re-designed cutlery and plastic crockery which expresses the spirit of the machine age. It is just that our mode of eating is taken completely for granted in much the same way as most ordinary people's mode of using buildings. An historic culturally conditional activity seems quite naturally to be associated with historic culturally conditioned artefacts.

All this, I believe, highlights an aspect of technological change rarely acknowledged. It is recognised in one discipline, although in a rather limited way. Archaeologists use the decidedly ugly work 'skeuomorph' to describe an object which retains features of an earlier object serving the same function but in a different material. Coincidentally the classic example is primitive pottery which was decorated geometrically to imitate the more familiar basketware. In architecture the obvious example is the Doric Order where reminiscences of timber construction were used as decorative features. Skeuomorphs are not just archaeological artefacts, early plastics were used to imitate wood and still do so to this day, the Morris Minor Estate car imitates the home conversions that led manufacturers to introduce estate cars.

Our example of ceramic flatware can be used to expand the concept of the skeuomorph into the society and the technology which produces it.

The origins of our methods of eating may have been to some degree practical but are largely forgotten and the ritual alone remains together with the means of carrying out that ritual. The skeuomorph, therefore, can be cultural beyond the mere imitation of a more familiar object. It is like the handshake which supposedly originated in a formal reassurance that neither individual was armed, or like the English predilection for suburban houses brought about to some extent by England's early advance in passenger railways.

It is perhaps most surprising to see that a skeuomorph can also be technical. Dust pressed plates can be any shape but they are pressed into a form which evokes a wheel turned product. This is not just a cultural or marketing pressure – cupboards, dishwashers, plate racks, table mats and so on are all produced to accommodate the same basic product.

This is a surprisingly common phenomenon. The English clay roof tile, for example, was almost certainly originally a fireproof substitute for a timber shingle and is, indeed, in terms of the best use of the material very inefficient – unlike Roman tiles or pantiles which were designed in clay from the start. Railways run on tracks which are set at a gage of 1432mm or 4ft 8.3/8in only because this was the gage on the horse-drawn railway at Killingworth Colliery where George Stevenson developed his first locomotives; Brunel's 7ft gage had to be changed to accommodate this narrower track in 1892 in spite of the fact it led to instability at higher speeds.

These are all, of course, relatively old examples of industrial skeuomorphs. It may be that this is just an historic phenomenon or the result of out-of-date misguided attitudes to design and that a more up-to-date and revolutionary concept of technology and society will do away with such restricting left-overs. Although architecture and, to a significant extent, the building industry are burdened with this inheritance, that could be said not to be a reason for accepting and thereby compounding such folly.

It will be revealing to examine the most recent and technologically rapidly moving industry to see if we can find evidence for such a clean sweep. In fact, in the computer industry we see just such phenomena not only in existence but in the process of developing. The personal computer uses the typewriter keyboard for normal operation and it has, for good marketing reasons, used the completely familiar and internationally accepted QWERTY keyboard layout. Paradoxically the QWERTY keyboard was designed in America in 1873 quite specifically to slow down the typist in order to avoid jamming the early type-bars. Of course, this requirement has long been obsolete and speedier keyboards have been designed but still the QWERTY keyboard remains with us and will do for many years to come due to interlocking generations of typewriter users going back to the 1870s. While the joystick and the mouse have improved the computer operator's flexibility not only does the keyboard look like remaining but there are signs that as the number of trained operators grows so the whole operating system interface – the words and mode of communication with the computer – are tending to resist change and move towards a standard.

We can observe similar phenomena in the motor industry but at a later stage. The internal combustion engine itself is, in principle, identical to those at the turn of the century and innovative and theoretically superior power units such as the Wankel engine are unable to establish themselves and develop their potential due to the entrenched position of the traditional engine and the vast and extended servicing system that surrounds it. Anomalies such as national differences in driving direction and random standards such as the three pedal layout from the 1930s are virtually impossible to change.

These tendencies are so widespread and such a familiar part of our everyday lives that, although in pure efficiency terms they can be frustrating, they have to be accepted. Indeed as they are both cultural and technical they form a natural part of society's relationship with the objects it has created. Rather than dismiss it, therefore, we should accept that it will influence not only the way we respond to products and, by the same token, architecture, but also the production process.

The principle that products carry with them the history of their evolution both in their technological development and in our use and perception of them, does explain the common feeling that a building or a piece of cutlery or an item of furniture can have a distinctly historical character but sit happily alongside a television, or a personal computer, or a motor car which have no references of such antiquity.

In a practical sense this serves largely to reinforce my non-revolutionary view of technological design in the building design and construction industry. Culturally I think it foolish, even immoral, to attempt to overturn such a natural and persistent aspect of society's way of responding to the products of its industries. To do so in the name of a false analysis of the industrial process itself is even more foolhardy and to do so in the name of cultural superiority is even more morally suspect.

This is, however, not intended to be a debate on moral issues. My purpose is served by drawing attention to this phenomenon throughout an industrial and, therefore, technological system. This does not amount to a plea to fossilise our production processes but an attempt to identify one of their inescapable but generally ignored constituent parts and thereby to undertake change not only in the most efficient way, but also in the least destructive and disruptive fashion. Industry and its technological changes do not operate independently of society, have no self-generated 'calculus of efficiency' or have goals any different from those of the society in which they operate and the, unfortunately called, skeuomorph phenomenon is a very real demonstration of how cultural attitudes interlock with our technology.

Where does all this take us? Two principles have emerged: the first is that comprehensive technological change only becomes probable when a significant demand can be met in a manner which improves the satisfaction or decreases the cost of satisfying that demand. Or, more crudely but simply: new technology helps you do what you *want, better* and *cheaper* – and that's all. The second principle is that artefacts carry with them the history of their evolution both in their technological development and in our use and perception of them – the skeuomorph principle.

The first principle de-mystifies the blind and omnipotent god of relentless technological advance. It should neither be worshipped nor even respected by profanity. The god does not exist. Its disciples have clung to their vision of an approaching millennium where the great god will banish all ills and we will bathe in the light of pure progress unencumbered by the burdens of our sordid history. For almost a century this lonely fraternity have sought in vain to convert the masses while forming themselves into a powerful visual sect in an otherwise orthodox society. The results are disastrous. An architecture discredited and increasingly circumscribed and a growing popular culture floundering rudderless in a sea of taste. Like Aristotle's helmsman, we are responsible for the loss of the ship by our absence from the helm.

If we can recognise that technological change serves not the adherents of this sect but society at large and does so not according to some vision of a new world but according to the everyday and even mundane desires of this society, then we can free ourselves from the overpowering passion for imposing our visual revolution on a world that does not want it. The destruction of a vision, however false, can also be the destruction of a source of inspiration. I hope that the second principle – the skeuomorph principle – will give a theoretical framework for entering into the everyday conception of the products of our society. If inspiration can be gained by a release from the apocalyptic fantasy of the machine aesthetic and an entry into the popular accommodation of historicist and contemporary design then both architecture and public taste can move together towards a better future.

I would like to conclude with a poem which is not only an important historical document from the first century BC but also an eloquent expression of a simple unity between an historic culture and new technology. The poem, by Antipater of Thessalonika is one of the earliest records of a water mill:

> Cease from grinding, you women who toil at the mill; sleep late, even if the crowing cocks announce the dawn. For Demeter has ordered the nymphs to perform the work of your hands, and they, leaping down on the top of the wheel, turn its axle, which with its revolving spokes, turns the heavy concave Nysarian millstones. We taste again the joys of the primitive life, learning to feast on the products of Demeter without labour.

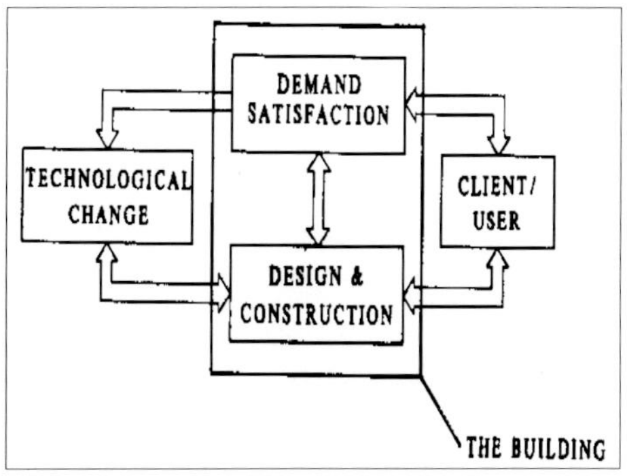

The active forces in the creation of a building.

A DECADE OF ARCHITECTURAL DESIGN

Modernism & High-Tech

Ada Louise Huxtable: On Modern Architecture

Has modern architecture really failed? Or are we loading onto it our perceptions of another kind of failure – something far beyond the architect's control? I believe that we are addressing a much larger theme – the failure of a moral vision and the breakdown of ideals of a society in transition. What we have lost is what sociologists and psychologists call our 'belief systems' – those commonly held convictions that guide our acts and aspirations. No society can function without them. Those articles of faith have been behind everything from architecture to social policy in our time.

These systems of belief were surely extraordinary. From the end of World War I to the 1960s, we believed devoutly in social justice, in the perfectibility of man and his world, in the good life for all. The Bauhaus taught that the machine would put beauty and utility within the reach of everyone. We believed that the world could be housed and fed; that we could bring order to our cities; that misery and hunger are not eternal verities. We joined hands and sang 'We shall overcome.'

We also believed that everyone had a right to beauty, and that aesthetic values equalled moral values. What was useful was beautiful and good, and what was good was good for all of us . . . Architects sincerely believed that health and happiness were the natural corollaries of the right way of building; they even believed that human nature could be conditioned or changed by the right physical environment . . . The architect was to be central to these aesthetic and social solutions – inextricably linked – of age-old problems, and the gratification of new expectations.

In retrospect, the hopes and beliefs of this century have been both admirable and naive, but they have also been humanitarian to an extraordinary degree. Perhaps we in the advanced countries have come as close to genuine civilisation as we ever will, if we define civilisation as the unselfish preoccupation with the betterment of the human condition at the highest level of shared experience and universal concern.

* * *

Architects are discovering the umbrella. Released from a restricted and reductive aesthetic, they are dazzled by possibilities that are as old as time. An older generation sees the new directions as heresy; a younger sees them as the creative reopening of the limits of design. In every case, the source is being transmuted into something different. The approach is erudite, romantic, and fiercely intellectual – even if it is not always the kind of thing that keeps us warm and dry.

All of this is part of something deeper; a search for meaning in a way to re-establish architecture's ties within human experience, a concern for architecture in the context of society. This is no longer seen just as the right to safe and sanitary dwellings and workplaces, but as the provision of a special quality of life. That is as large an ambition as anything that concerned the early modernists; it may be an equal trap. But it is a return to a basic understanding that architecture is much more than real estate, shelter or good intentions; it is the recognition of that extraordinary mixture of the pragmatic and the spiritual that is the tangible vehicle of man's aspirations and beliefs, the lasting indicator of his civilised achievements.

Norman Foster, The Millennium Tower, Tokyo, Japan.

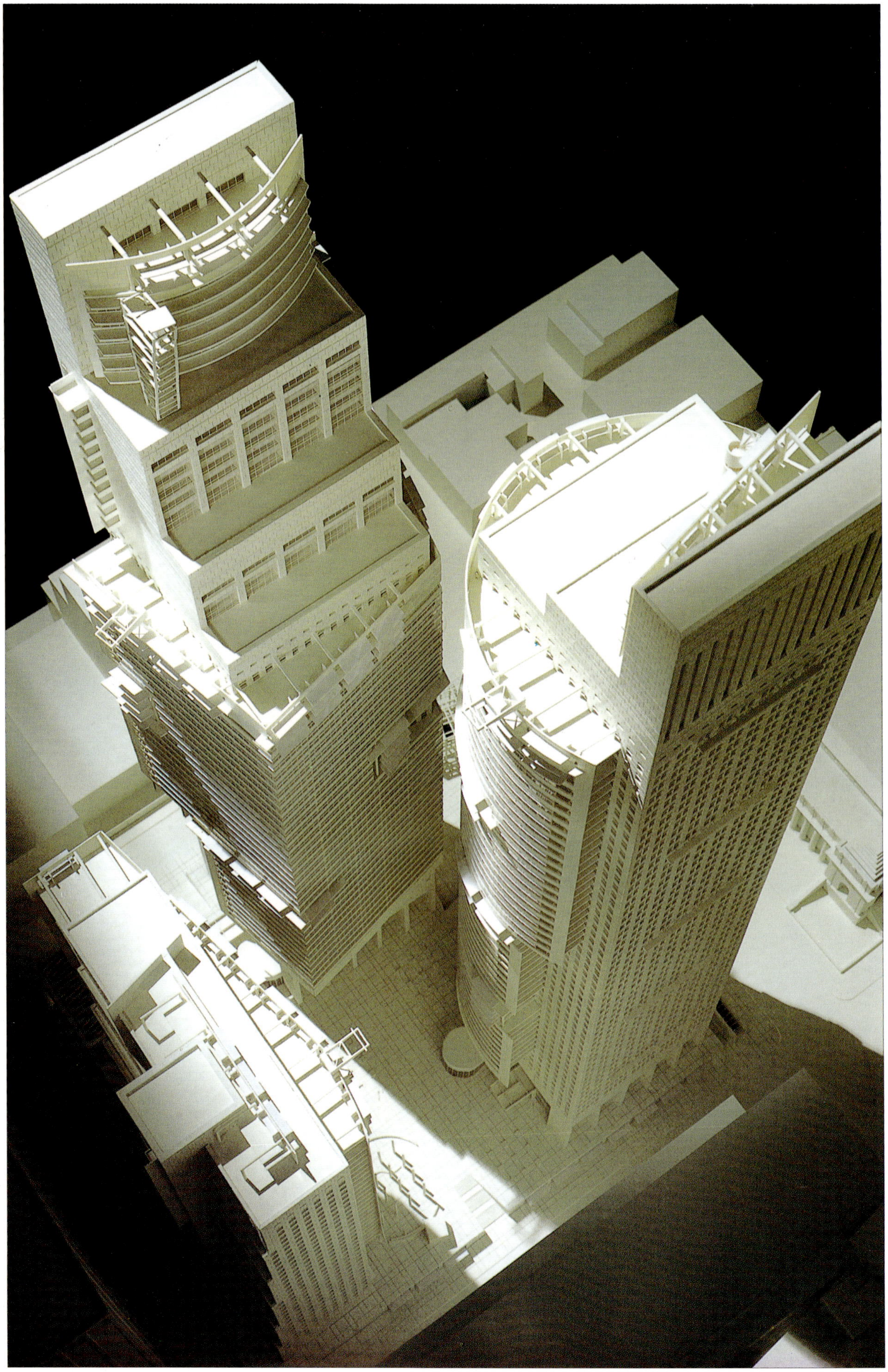

A DECADE OF ARCHITECTURAL DESIGN

Richard Meier

Richard Meier was born in Newark, New Jersey in 1934 and attended Architectural School at Cornell University in Ithaca, New York. He opened his own firm six years after his graduation in 1957. Soon afterwards, his design for the Smith house in Darien, Connecticut, which was completed in 1967, brought him international acclaim as an extremely talented interpreter of the so-called 'Five Points' of Le Corbusier. As he himself has described his renewal of that direction: 'We now assume the tectonic and spatial authority of the Modern Movement, (but) for me technology is no longer the subject of architecture, but simply the means. Architecture is the subject of my architecture . . . what I seek to do is to pursue the plastic limits of modern architecture to include a notion of beauty moulded by light. My wish is to create a kind of spatial lyricism within the canon of pure form. In the design of my buildings, I am expanding and elaborating on what I consider to be the formal base of the modern movement . . . The great promise and richness of some of the formal tenets of Modernism have almost unlimited areas for investigation . . . I work with volume and surface, I manipulate forms in light, changes in scale and view, movement and stasis.'

Throughout his career, Meier has steadfastly continued his search for what he calls spatial lyricism in a consistent, yet highly innovative way, demonstrating the remarkable variety that is possible in the formal vocabulary that he chooses to work within. As it was with earlier masters of the Modern Movement, space is the primary focus of that vocabulary, with its infinite potential to speak to the users of Meier's buildings. Movement through that space is always widely varied in his work, and yet carefully considered. The definition of the inner volume by natural light and structure is always in the best tradition of the International Style, and yet Meier also still manages to retain his own personality.

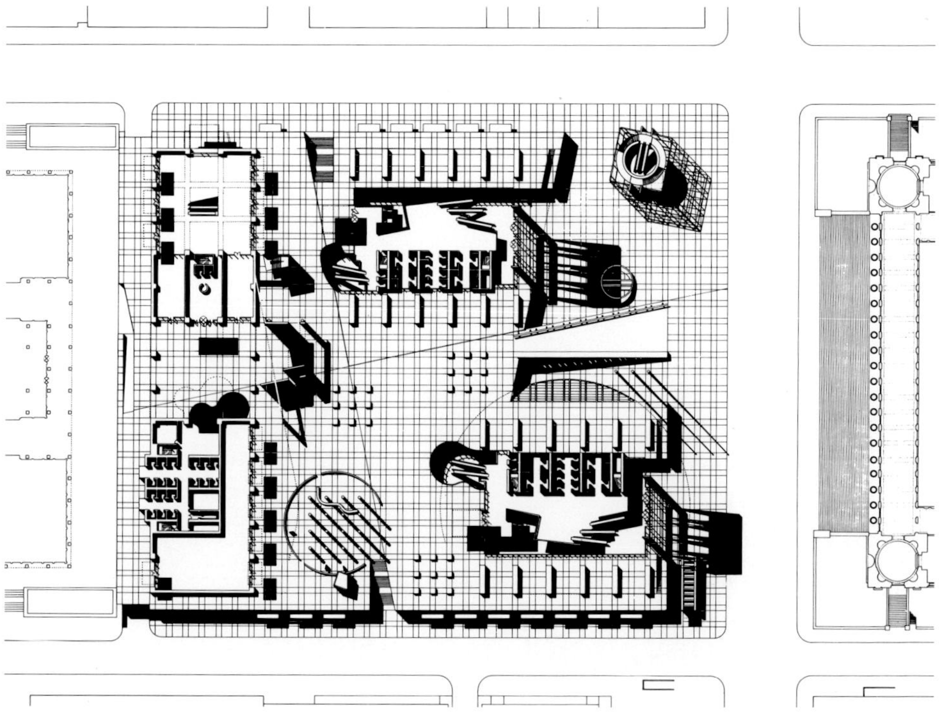

While Meier has not designed many high-rise towers, he has managed to introduce many fresh ideas into a difficult typology whenever he has the opportunity.

OPPOSITE & LEFT: Madison Square Garden Towers, New York, New York.

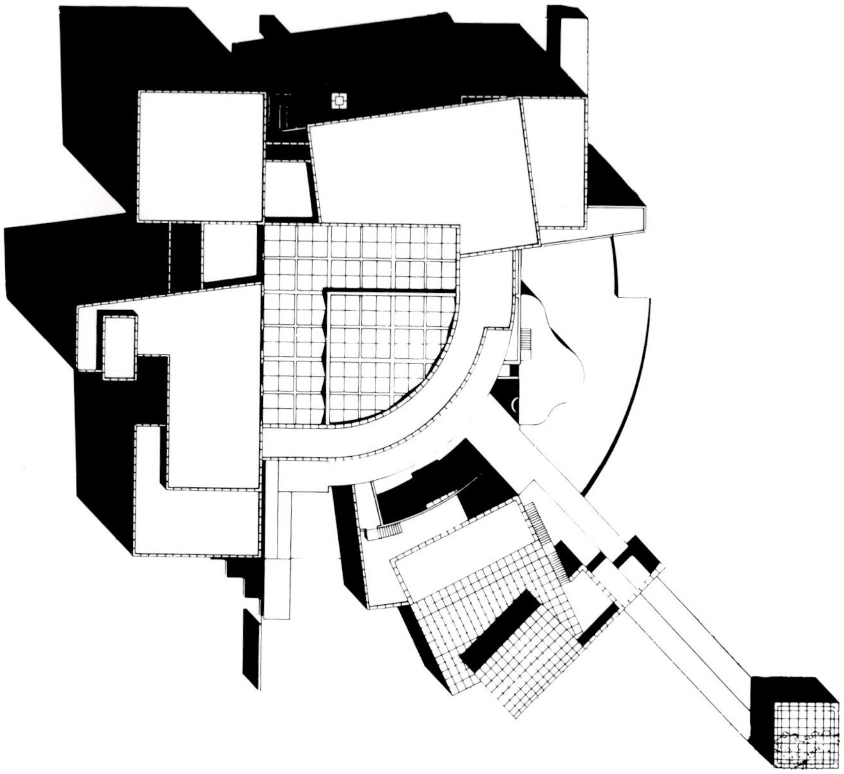

A DECADE OF ARCHITECTURAL DESIGN

The curvilinear shape of the Atlanta Museum pays homage to the Guggenheim by Frank Lloyd Wright, with circulation patterns through the exhibition space being the main generator of the form.

ABOVE & LEFT: The High Museum of Art, Atlanta, Georgia.

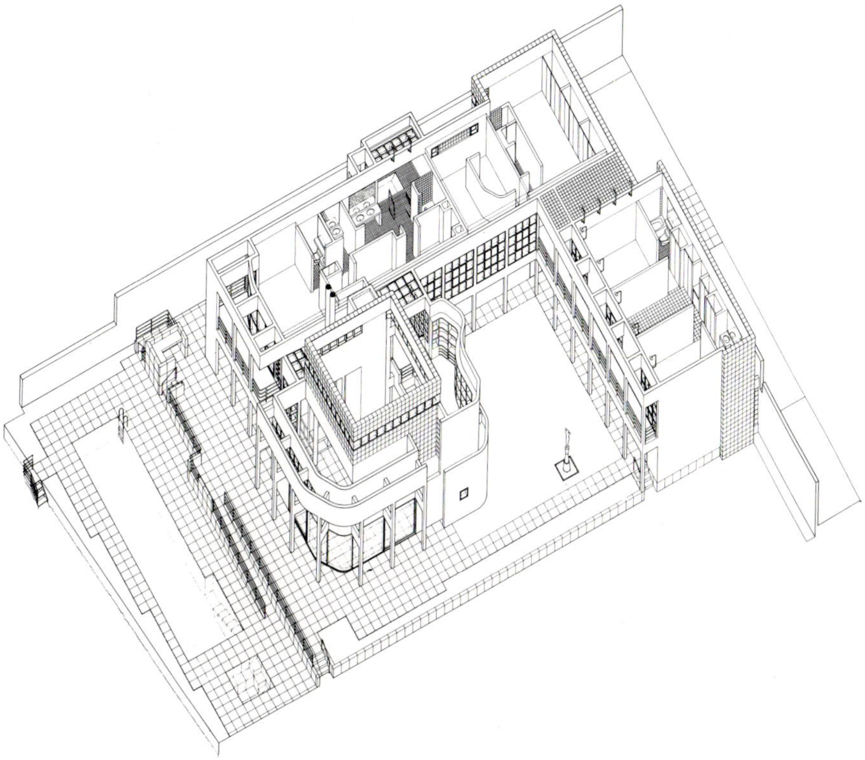

RICHARD MEIER

The white surfaces that have become a hallmark of Richard Meier's work provide an ideal background for subtle changes of light at different times of day.

ABOVE & LEFT: Ackerberg House, Malibu, California.

A DECADE OF ARCHITECTURAL DESIGN

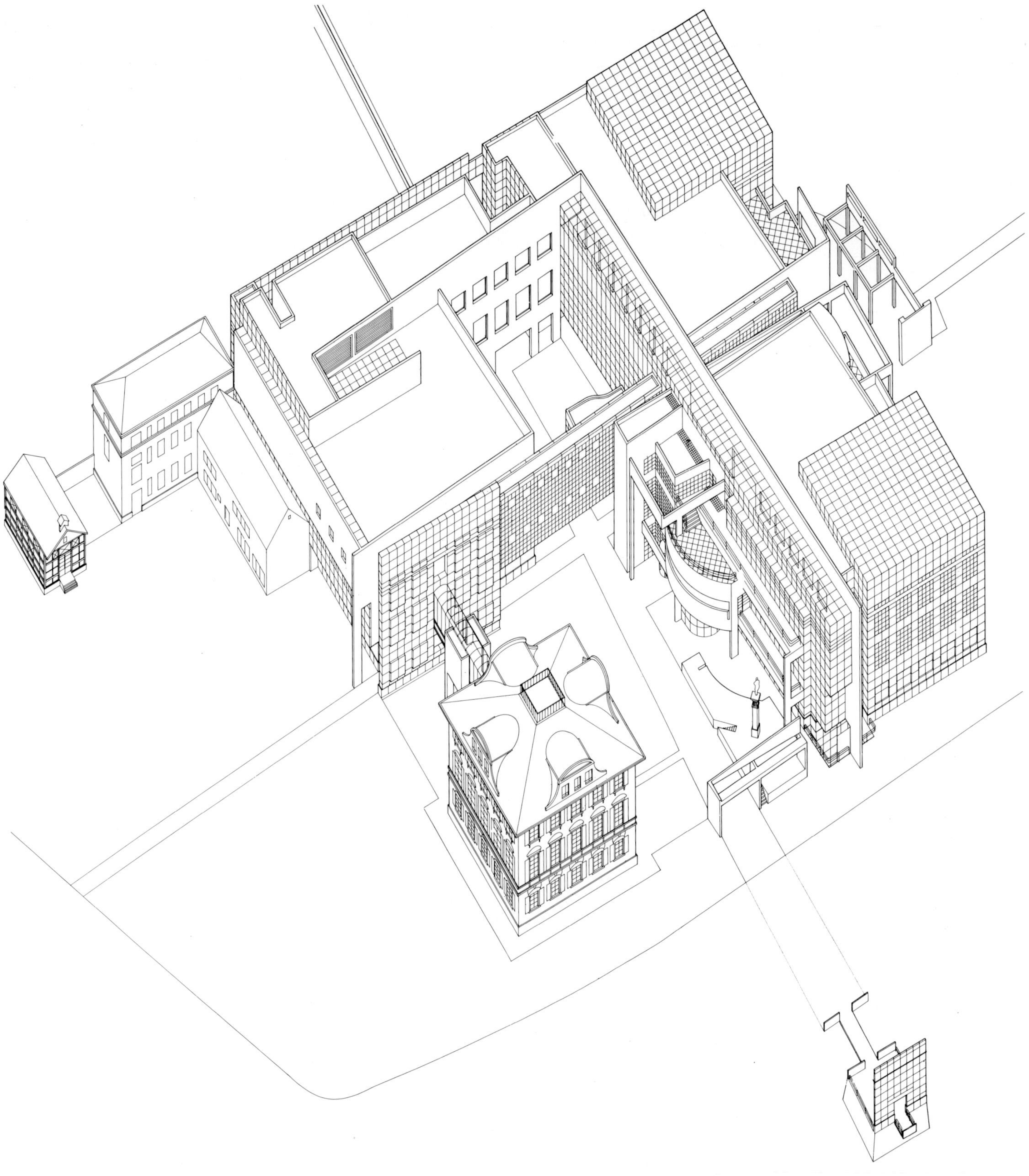

RICHARD MEIER

While a literal representation of context is never appropriate in Meier's chosen vocabulary, an abstraction of that context has provided a far more effective way of linking his architecture with its surroundings.

OPPOSITE: Ackerberg House, Malibu, California.
ABOVE: Museum für Kunsthandwerk, Frankfurt, Germany.

A DECADE OF ARCHITECTURAL DESIGN

Tadao Ando

In direct contrast to the Modern Masters who would initially seem to have inspired Tadao Ando because of his amplification of the basic nature of such materials as concrete, he is not intentionally functionalist, but looks for the meaning of architecture in another, highly individual way. In trying to supersede functional requirements, Ando hopes to discover the true sense of Modernism, and while this may initially seem to put him in company of others like Peter Eisenman, who agree that the true essence of Modernism has yet to be fully explored, the contrast between the spaces that result could not be more different. The first, basic concern in Ando's work is tectonics, because he feels that the way materials go together is the beginning of architecture. As he has said of his work:

'I believe three elements are necessary for the crystallisation of architecture. The first is authentic materials, that is, materials of substances such as exposed concrete or unpainted wood. The second is pure geometry, as in the Pantheon. This is the base or framework that endows architecture with presence. It might be a volume such as a Platonic solid, but it is often a three-dimensional frame, because I feel the latter to be in keeping with pure geometry. The last element is nature. I do not mean raw nature but rather domesticated nature, nature that has been endowed by man with order and is in contrast with chaotic nature. Perhaps one can call it order abstracted from nature: light, sky, and water that have been rendered abstract. When such a nature is introduced into a work of architecture composed, as I have said, of materials and geometry, architecture itself is made abstract by nature. Architecture comes to possess power and becomes radiant only when these three elements come together. Man is then moved by a vision that is possible, as in the Pantheon, only with architecture.'

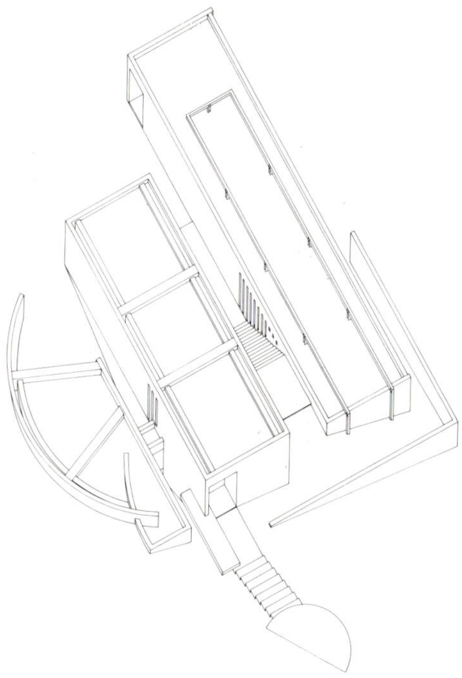

In his minimalist approach to the creation of space, Ando reduces architecture to its essence, and heightens the inevitable contrast between the natural and the man made. Against the neutral background of an unadorned concrete wall, an exquisitely made chair, or vase full of flowers can be more fully appreciated as the work of art that it really is. In such a distilled environment, things as ordinary as a window screen take on an entirely new level of meaning, becoming a lace-like filter between inside and outside space, rather than simply a utilitarian object.

OPPOSITE: Chapel on Mount Rokko, Kobe, Hyogo.
LEFT: Theatre on the Water, Tomamu, Hokkaido.
ABOVE & OVERLEAF: Koshino House, Ashiya, Hyogo.
SECOND OVERLEAF: Rokko Housing I, Kobe, Hyogo.

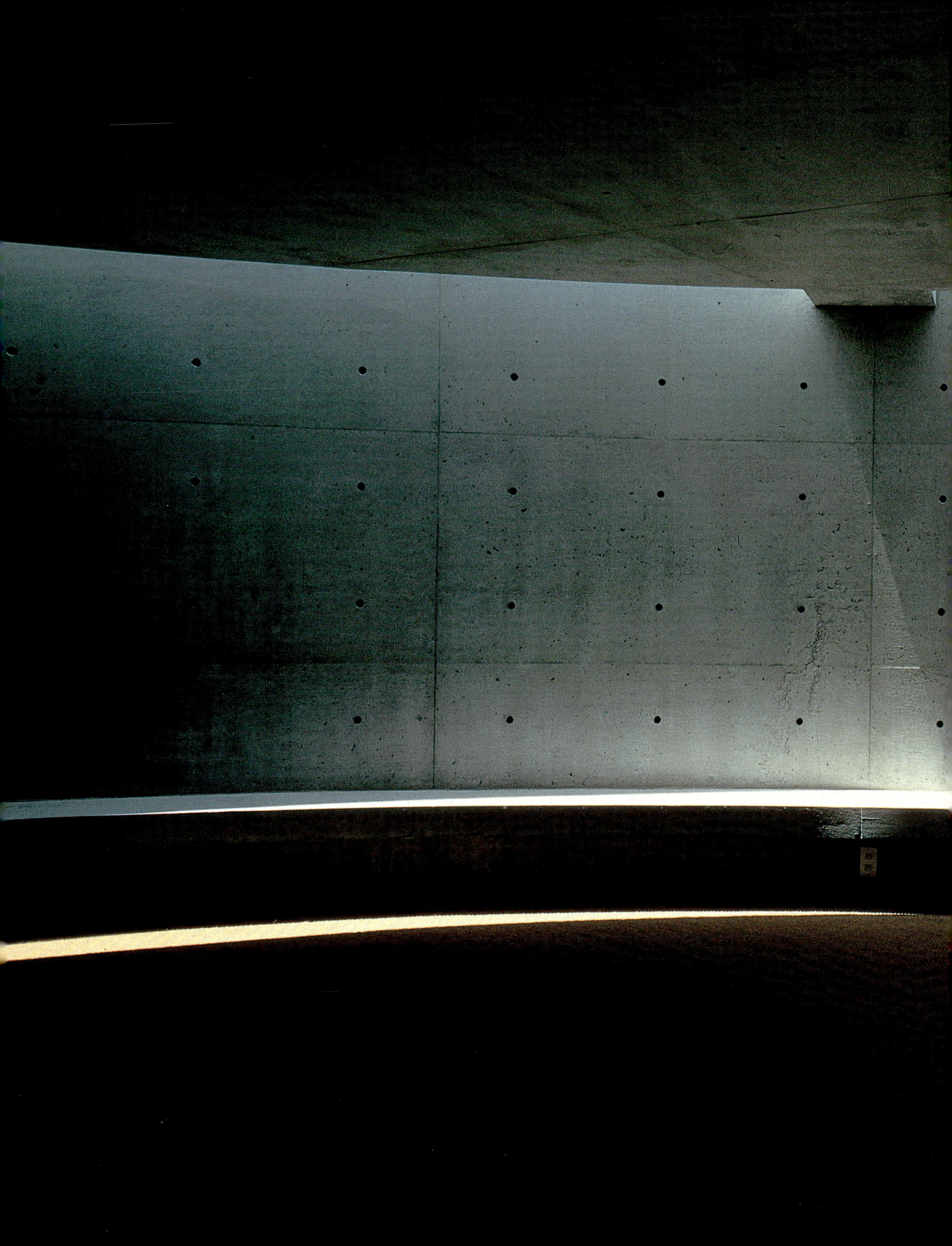

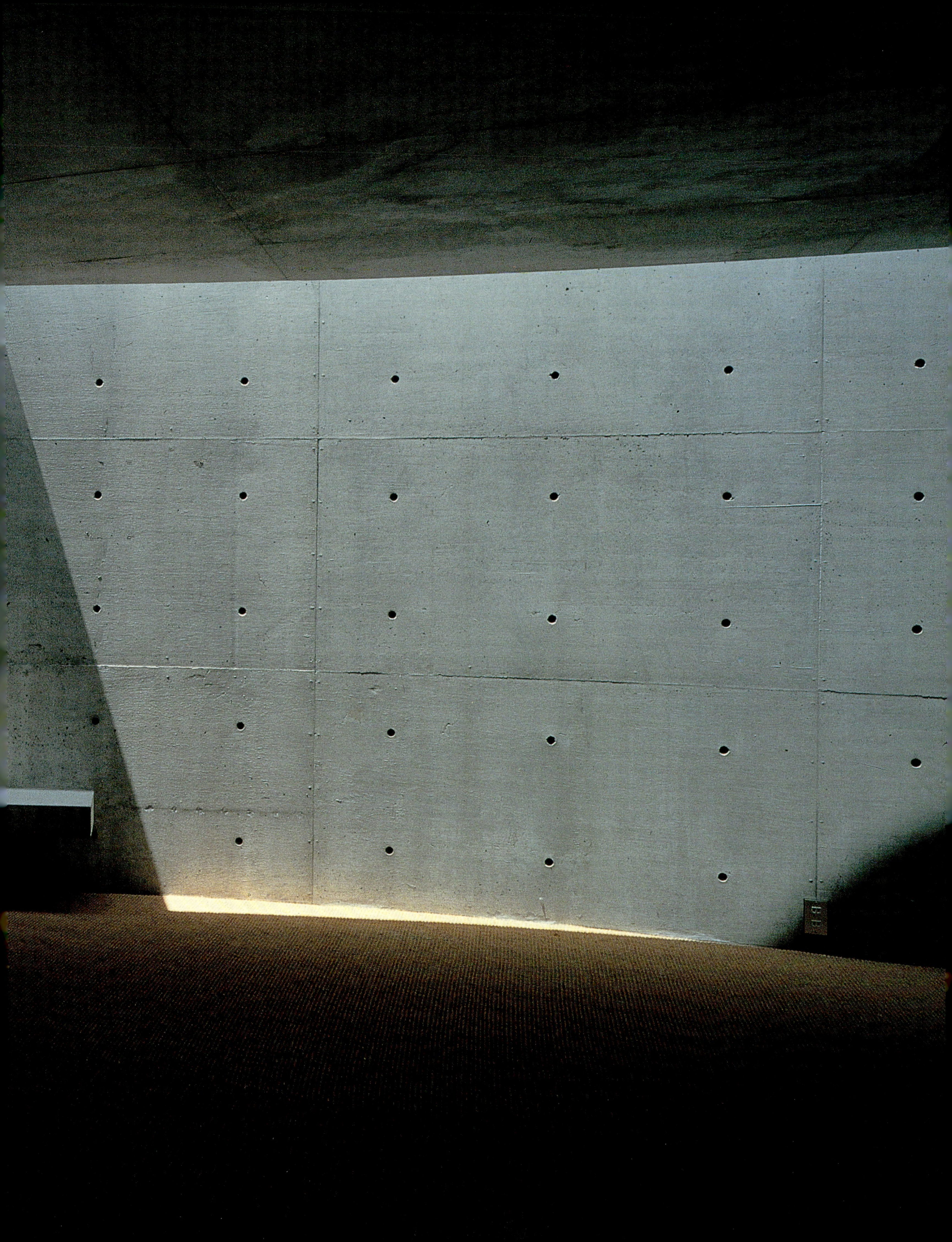

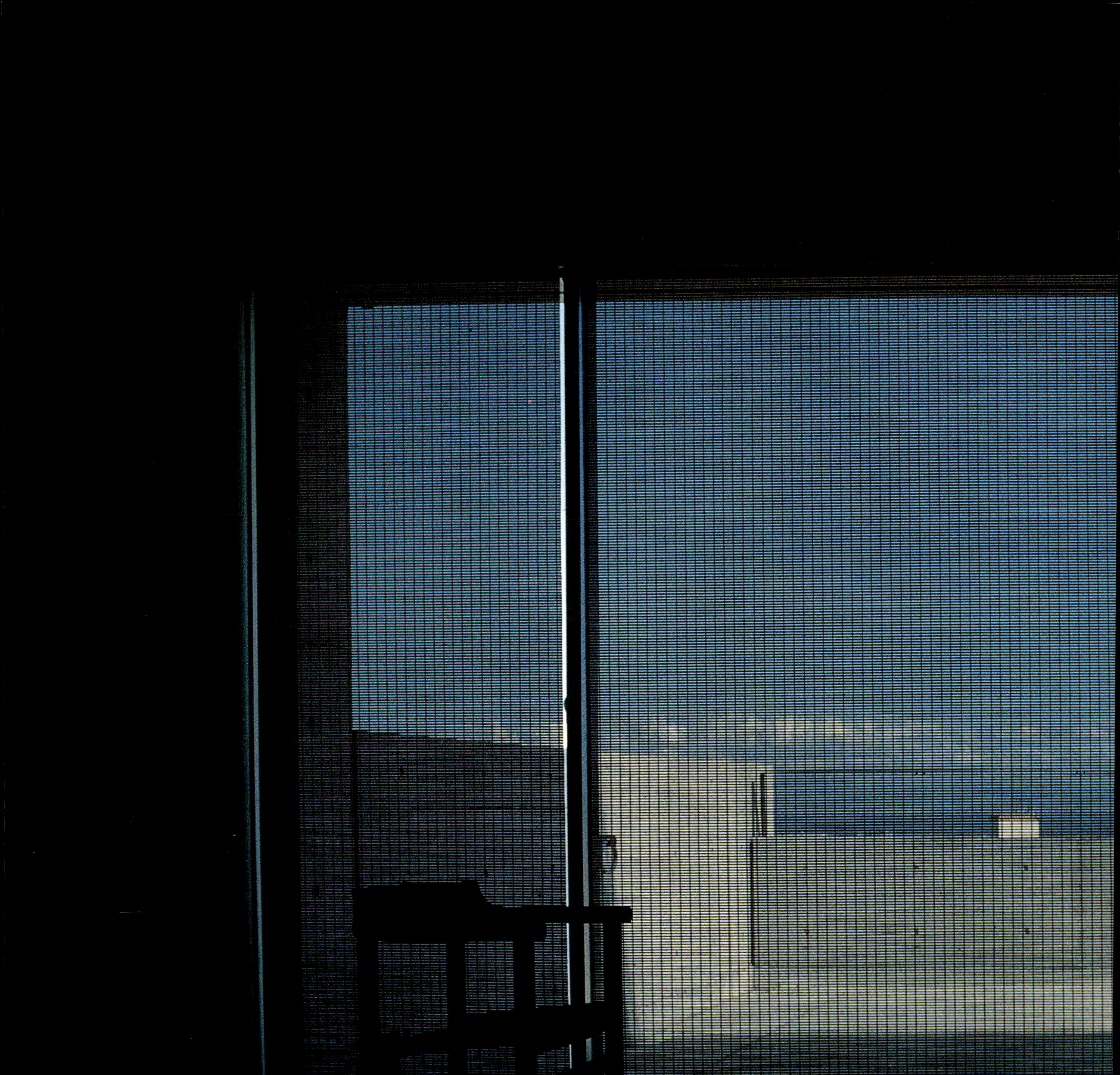

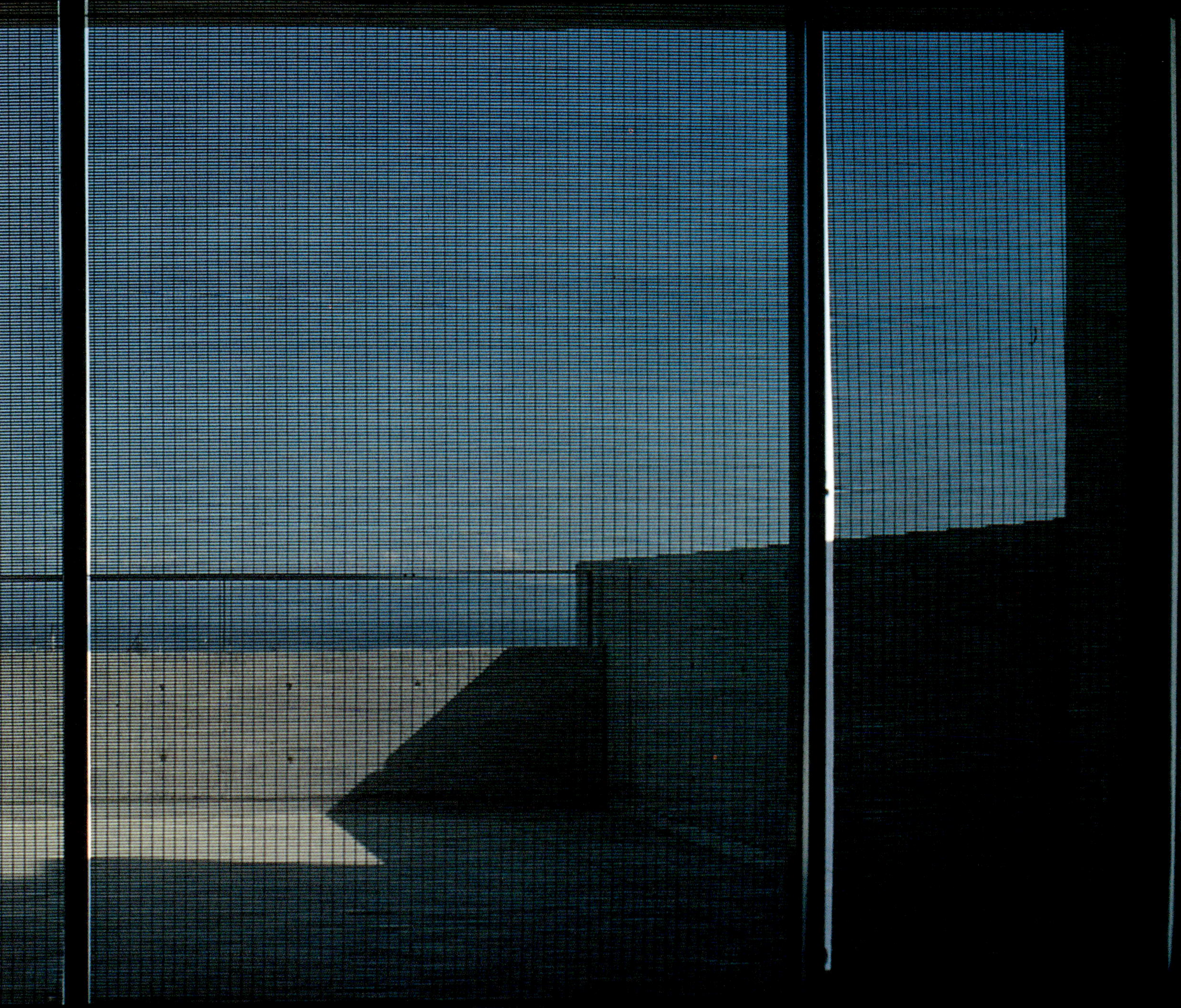

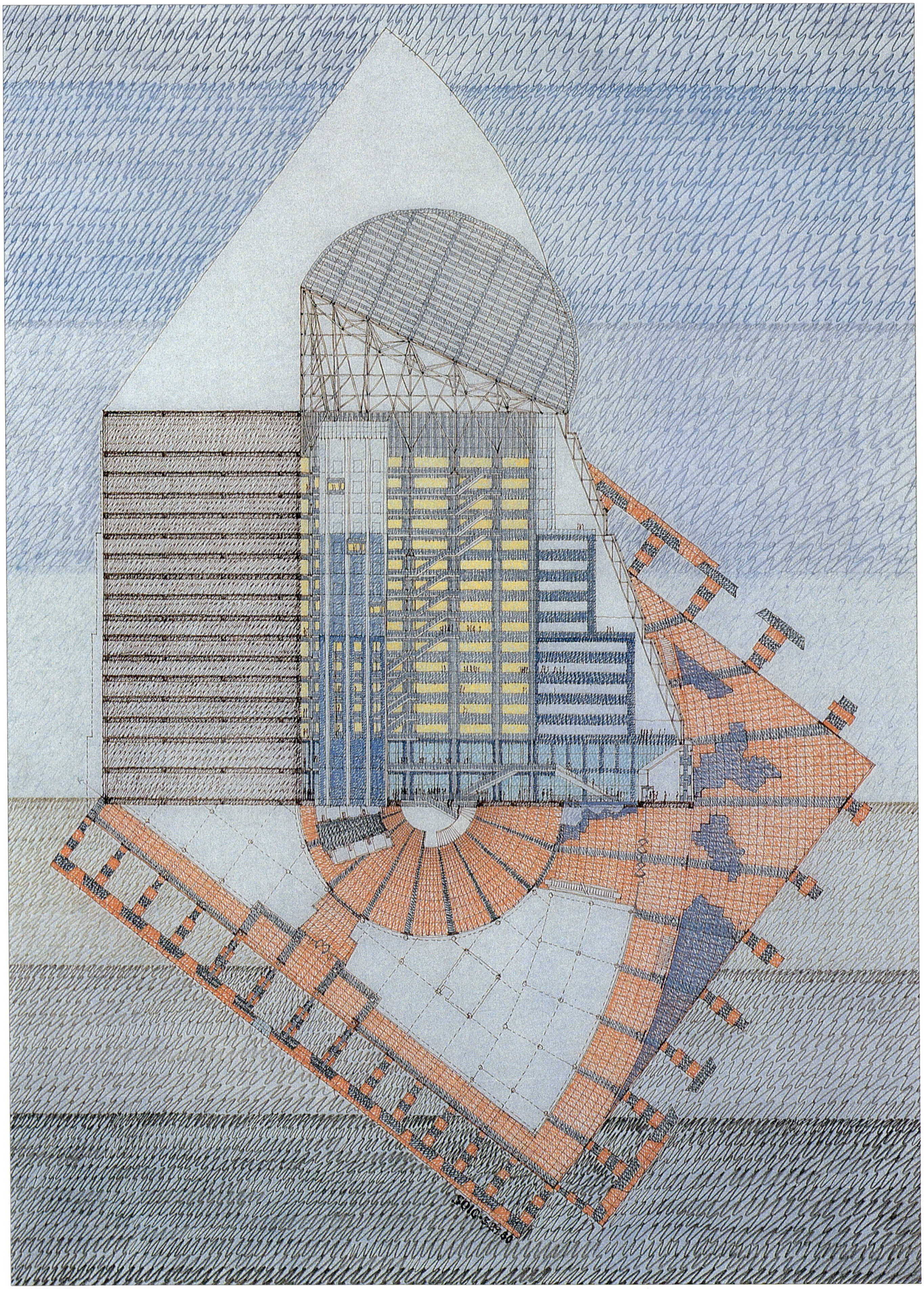

Helmut Jahn

When Louis Sullivan said that a skyscraper must above all, 'be a tall and soaring thing,' he couldn't possibly have foreseen what Helmut Jahn would do to this relatively new typology. While he has certainly had considerable experience in designing other kinds of buildings, it is the skyscraper with which Jahn has now become most closely identified, and in which he seems to have found the perfect medium of expression. Having begun his career as a strictly Miesian functionalist, and a true believer in the need for a rationalist basis to design, Jahn has since been converted to the ranks of those architects who have been seeking to return the skyscraper to its earlier, anthropomorphic division into base, middle and top. Such division itself is also perfectly rational, from a physiological point of view, given the inability of those walking or driving down the concrete canyons of any major metropolis today to fully comprehend a tall tower from bottom to top. Using his extraordinary graphic facility, Jahn is able to quickly explore formal options that he feels are most appropriate to each client and context. He also manages to sustain the tricky balance demanded in a seemingly contradictory compositional exercise that requires both the linking and separation of a complex, tripartite form. When layered over such pragmatic, commercial requirements of floor area ratios and rental return per square foot, these considerations make the skyscraper an extremely difficult design problem to deal with and begin to hint at the degree of Helmut Jahn's skill in doing so.

Jahn's graphic skill, which seems to be incongruous with his obvious love of technology, allows him to explore many formal options and avoid the mechanical coldness endemic to most High-Tech architecture.

OPPOSITE: State of Illinois Center, Chicago.
FAR LEFT: Chicago Board of Trade Addition, Chicago.
LEFT: Humana Project for Louisville, Kentucky.

A DECADE OF ARCHITECTURAL DESIGN

Fumihiko Maki

While one of the original founders of the Metabolist group in Japan in 1960, Maki's interest in social issues and his subsequent studies of what he characterised as the 'collective form' of urban infrastructure soon became tangential to the principles of that group. Even he, however, had to surrender eventually to the relentless, consumer-driven forces that have now made Tokyo so illegible; and his most recent work is less concerned with relating to context than it is with creating an orderly world of its own. As he has said in describing the idea behind the Spiral Building, for example, 'The days when there was an immutable style . . . are past . . . the classical urban order having collapsed, any work of architecture that, in a sense, internalises the city and functions on its exterior surface as a mechanism of transmission will . . . symbolise today's image of the city – an environment that is fragmented but that constantly renews its vitality precisely through its state of fragmentation.' In the Spiral, then, and to a lesser extent his Kyoto National Museum of Modern Art, Maki not only comments on the disintegration of the city, but also on the Modernist iconography that was a part of an earlier, naive belief in an architect's ability to control effectively urban growth. In both cases, strong Corbusian forms are showcased behind open structural frames and piloti are used to indicate circulation patterns into and through both buildings. Shoji-like panels, which recall the most beloved symbol of Japanese architecture for the Modernists, are also used as billboard-like projections, in contrast to the shiny aluminium walls around them, just in case anyone might miss the connection he is trying to make.

If there is a final lesson in Maki's work, it may be that it is extremely difficult to classify, as the forms of his Fujisawa Gymnasium indicate. As with many architects in Japan today, style is continually subverted to accommodate new situations depending upon the current aesthetic priorities of each individual designer.

In his flawless echoing of both function and content, Maki may be one of the few to have now successfully bridged the gap that Modernism intentionally established between a building as object and its surroundings. The elevation of the Spiral Building that faces Aoyama Avenue, which is now Tokyo's most fashionable shopping street, is a complex ideogram that includes many elements abstracted from the heroic phase of Modernism.

OPPOSITE, FAR LEFT & LEFT: The Spiral Building, Tokyo, Japan.

A DECADE OF ARCHITECTURAL DESIGN

Itsuko Hasegawa

The relationship between man and nature has always been a consistently provocative theme in Japanese architecture, and the changes in the perception of nature that are now emerging in the work of many architects there deserves far deeper study. As Japan continues to industrialise, with all of the problems of rural migration and urbanisation that typically accompany that process, the traditionally close relationship with nature that has existed in the past has now been altered, leading to it's interpretive rather than literal inclusion in architecture today. In the work of Itsuko Hasegawa, that interpretation is ironically metaphorical, with the products of technology, which is the very cause of the separation in the first place, being used to mirror the natural world. In her design for the House in Nerima, for example, where a wave-shaped roof of corrugated aluminium joins several, disparate volumes under an all-encompassing form, perforated screens are used to recall hills and clouds, and the secondary roofs over each separate room also become 'moon viewing platforms', from which to appreciate one of the only natural features still left untouched by the urban sprawl of Tokyo other than Mount Fuji. At Bizan Hall, in Shizuoka, Hasegawa goes even further in her metaphor, using monitor roofs to create an actual, physical reproduction of the mountainside which the building has replaced. In each case, technology has not only become a replacement for the environment that it has destroyed, but is also intentionally moulded into a substitution for it. Such gestures, while admittedly made within a Modern idiom, once again highlight the difficulty of classifying the work of this, or any other architect in Japan today, because of the complex issues now brought into question by an entire society that, having reached the pinnacle of industrial power, now wonders if that achievement was worth the price.

For Itsuko Hasegawa, industrial materials not only provide an opportunity to enclose space in new ways, but also allow for an ironic recollection of natural paradise lost.

OPPOSITE: House in Nerima, Tokyo, Japan.
LEFT: Bizan Hall, Shizuoka, Japan.

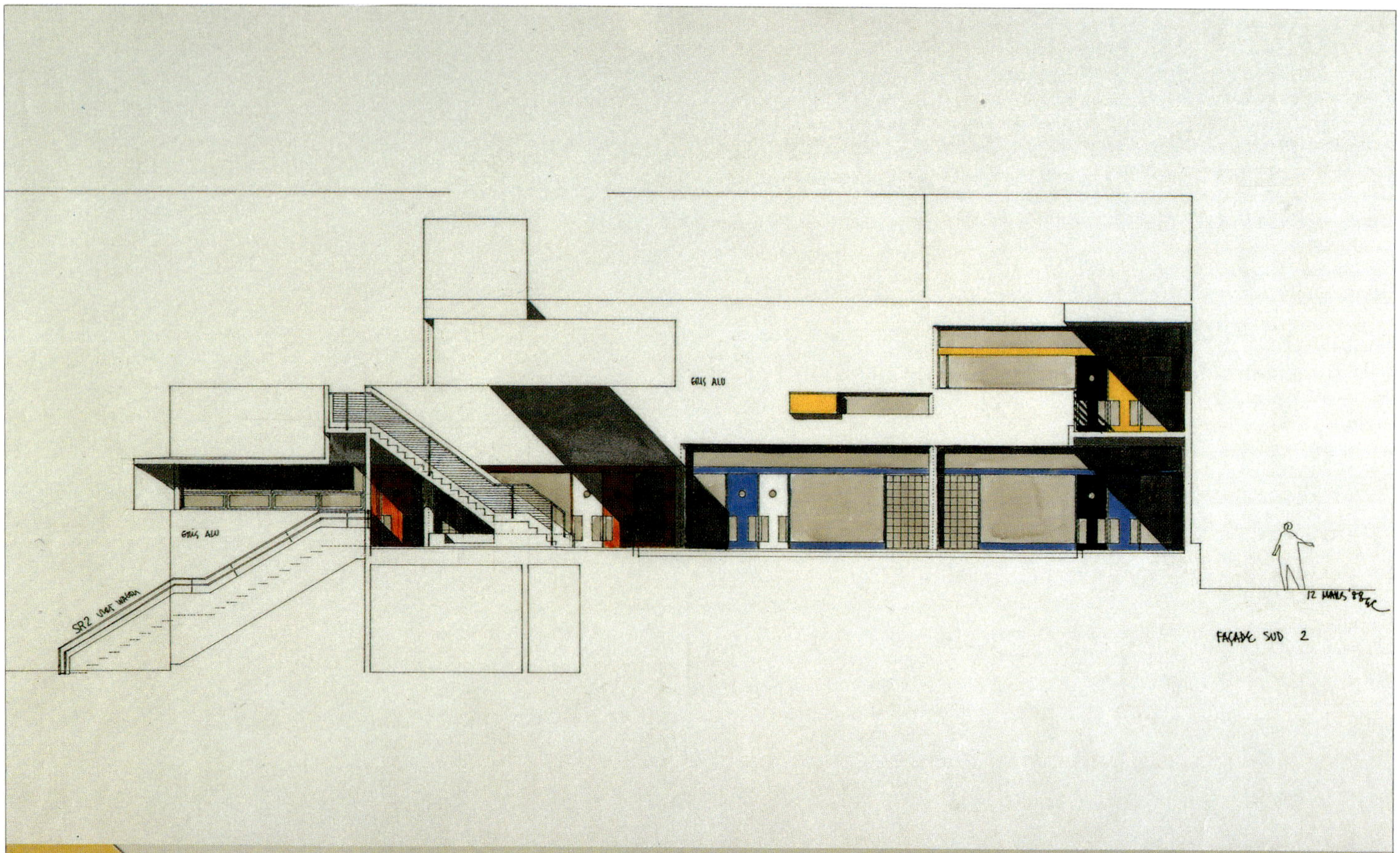

FAÇADE SUD 2

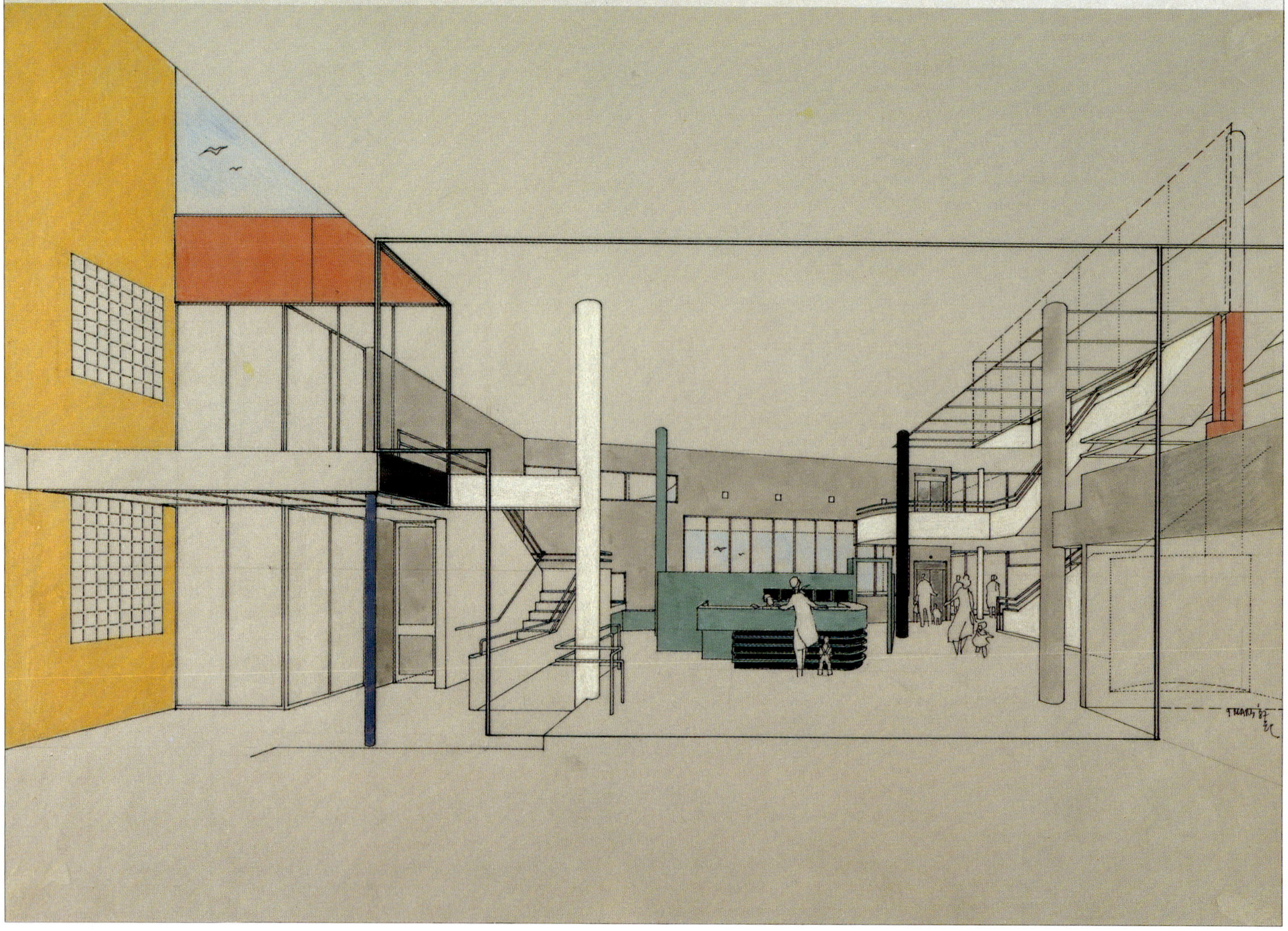

Henri Ciriani

In this design for the Maison de l'Enfance, or Childcare Centre, in Torcy, France, Ciriani reveals Modernist sensibilities that he is quick to acknowledge. In his description of the project, his intentions emerge even more clearly as he says:

'Between a large commercial centre located to the east, and a pedestrian esplanade located near the water and Val Maubuée on the west, one finds a residential quarter which forms a central, linear space, and it is in the middle of this that the Centre de la Petite Enfance was built in Torcy in 1989.

'The site is almost 45 metres on each side, and includes a five metre difference in level along the diagonal. It is limited on the east by a concrete parking lot, on the south by a 14-metre passage, and by a public square on the north.

'In this design, there was first of all the desire to affirm the presence of the building by establishing a north-east angle, which finally developed into a right angle, that allowed public access as well as volumetric reference to be established. There are three levels within one in this building which are all aligned with the square, these all open out to the south, thereby creating transparency and an architecture which is lit from behind. These three levels accentuate the scale of what is essentially a public building, making it assertively frontal in character, but this diminishes towards the east, to produce a void that marks the entrance of the Centre. The angular line remains opaque to affirm an anchoring effect, and progressively forms a cavity at each end that allows for escalating volumes. These are used to produce terraces and gardens that seem to be suspended in a diagonal frame.'

Colour and scale and structure are not only used to expand the high central space of La Maison de l'Enfance, but also to make it more reassuring to the children who use it.

OPPOSITE & LEFT: Maison de l'Enfance, Torcy, France.

A DECADE OF ARCHITECTURAL DESIGN

I M Pei

In his 40-year career, IM Pei has managed to have many buildings built, and each of them, while produced by a large organisation, has also clearly retained his own direction. That direction is undeniably modern, in the best tradition of the heroic phase of that movement, stemming from his background at the Harvard Graduate School of Design, and the influence of Walter Gropius and Marcel Breuer, in 1946. Such influence is most recognisable in his emphasis on the quality of space, and the importance of light, circulation and structure in defining it. His recognition of the exigences of each site, however, is particularly Late-Modern, and this is especially notable in such projects as the National Center for Atmospheric Research in Boulder Colorado, the East Building of the National Gallery of Art in Washington DC and the Fragrant Hill Hotel in Peking China. At Xiangshan, as Fragrant Hill is known in Chinese, this concern is even more visible and important, as this location, close to where the Dowager Empress had her summer palace in the final days of empire, and which was an encampment at the end of the Long March is redolent of associations with the past. His response to that commission is instructive of the degree to which his view of the modern aesthetic differs from its origins. While asked by the Chinese Government to provide a high-rise tower in the International Style, Pei responded with a sensitive low-scale scheme that uses courtyards and gardens to give a sense of intimacy to the hotel-rooms surrounding them. The reception atrium is roofed with the same space frame trusses used in the East Building and the overall design approach taken there has now set a precedent for a more regional attitude in public buildings in this country in the future. Similar concerns have also guided Pei in his proposal for the glass entrance to the Louvre, which, in spite of some early controversy, has now impressed many as the most logical solution to a design problem.

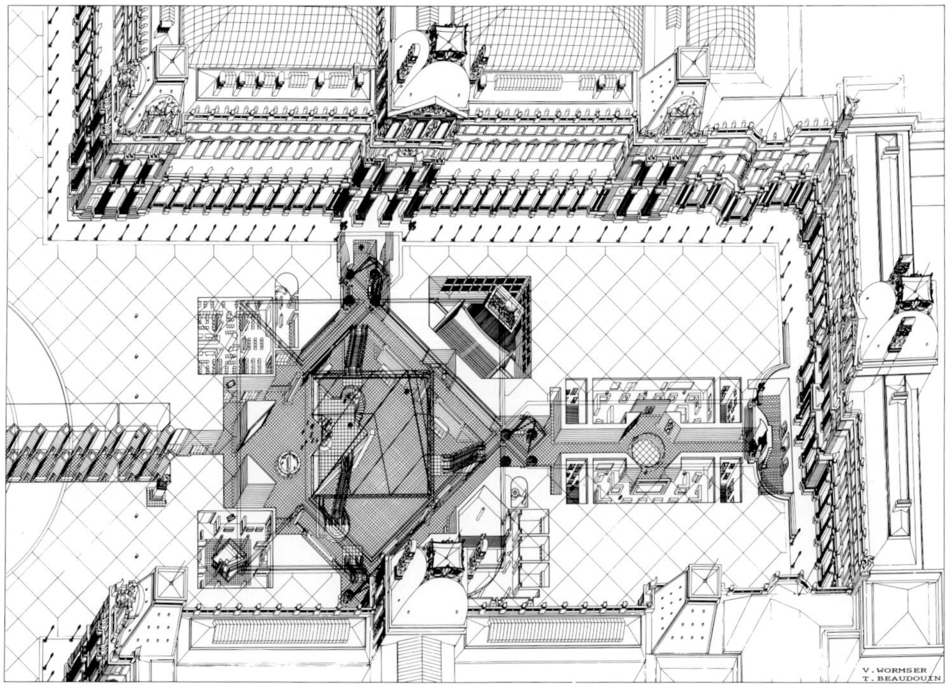

Acting as a hub for all of the various parts of museum, Pei's design organises what was a very crowded entrance, and provides badly needed space in a very unobtrusive way.

OPPOSITE & LEFT: Extension to the Louvre, Paris, France.

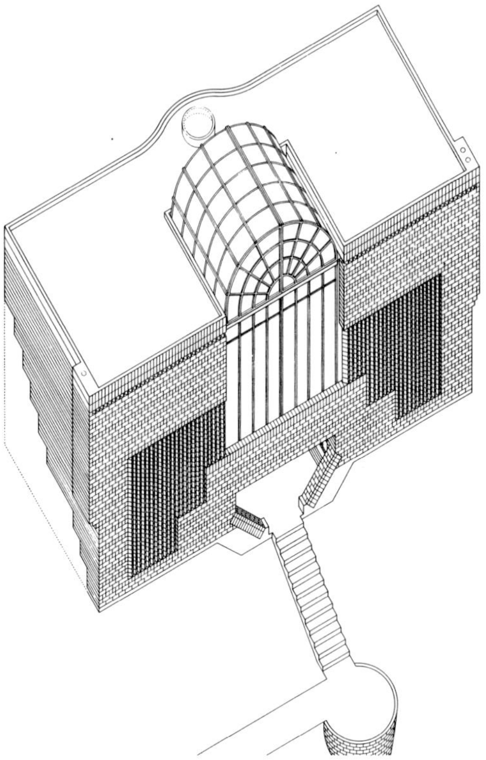

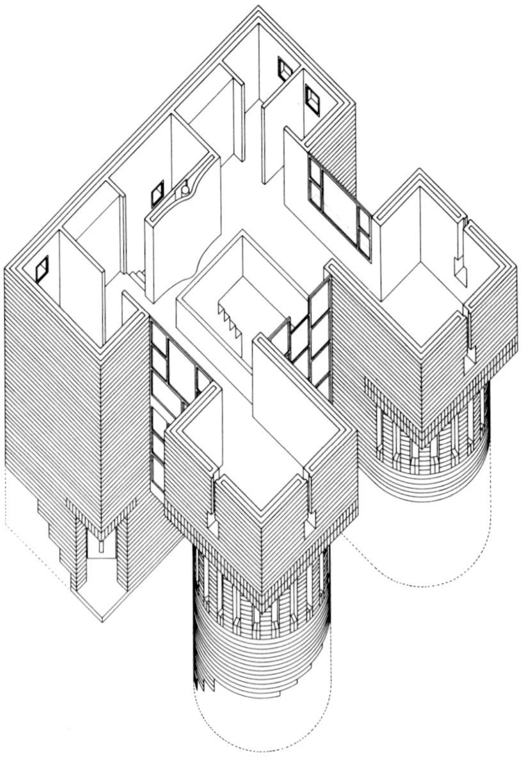

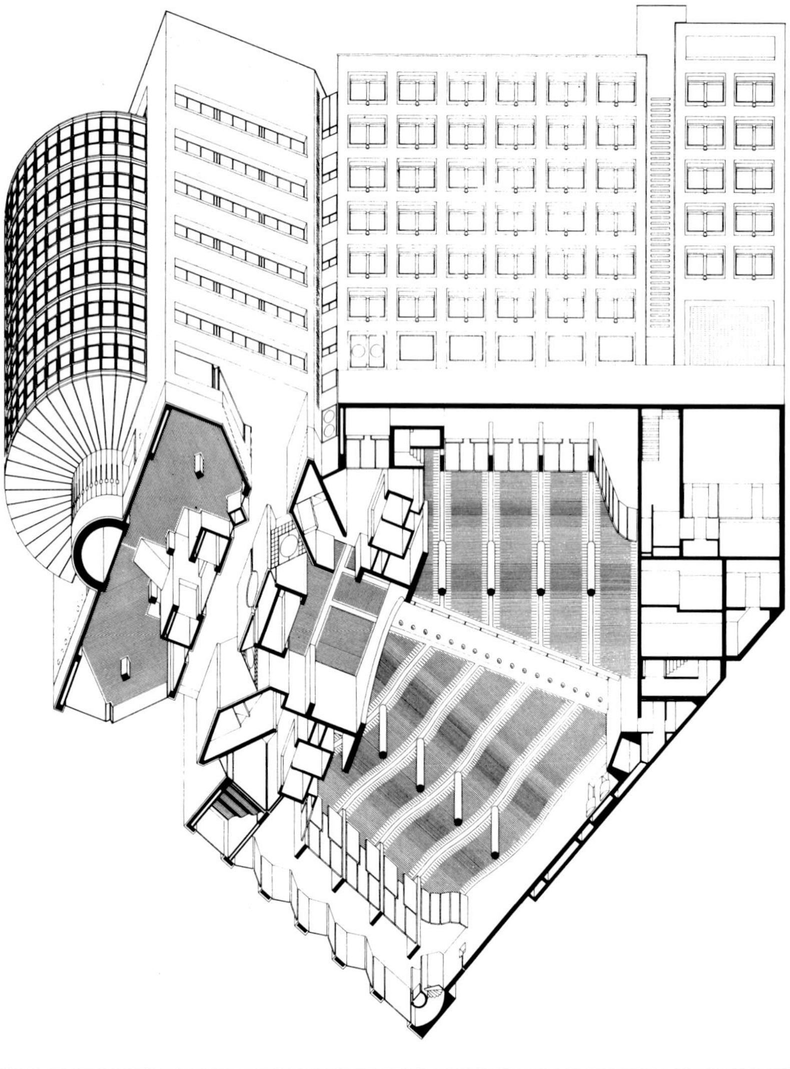

Mario Botta

There are five factors that can be consistently considered in the relationship between Mario Botta's architecture and its context. The first of these is an attempt to set up a reciprocal exchange between a given site and any addition to it. Part of this exchange, for Botta, includes emphasising the positive aspects of the site to the exclusion of extraneous elements. His objective, in this exclusion, is not to impose subjective meaning on the area to be built upon, but to bring out whatever intrinsic values already exist there. He calls this amplification 'building the site', and considers it to be as important as the programmatic imperatives of the structure itself. The second factor that is stressed in his work is an understanding of any territorial imperatives, and a study of the physical, psychological and symbolic impact that his architecture will have beyond the restrictions of unseen legal boundaries. Thirdly, Botta recognises that the geological character of each site must be fully understood, so that each landscape, can be truthfully expressed. Each site, no matter how neutral it may seem, has an individual morphology that must be recognised. Fourthly, this architect is very aware of history, believing that the best way to pay homage to the past is to be truly modern. Like Aldo Rossi, he has noted that all continuously valid architecture has always been able to not only survive changes of use, but also to adapt to them: he cites examples such as the Pantheon in Rome, which has served many different functions across time. His modernity is based on realism rather than technological or structural exhibitionism, and extends to a straightforward use of materials. Lastly, these combine to give his architecture a timeless, humanistic quality that must serve to qualify the Rationalist label that is usually applied to him and give it more depth.

While introducing a strict, geometrical order into his architecture, Mario Botta still relates that order to the individual territorial characteristics of each site.

OPPOSITE, ABOVE LEFT: House, Viganello, Italy; ABOVE RIGHT: House, Origlio, Italy; BELOW: State Building, Fribourg, Switzerland.
FAR LEFT & LEFT: House, 'Rotunda', Stabio, Italy.

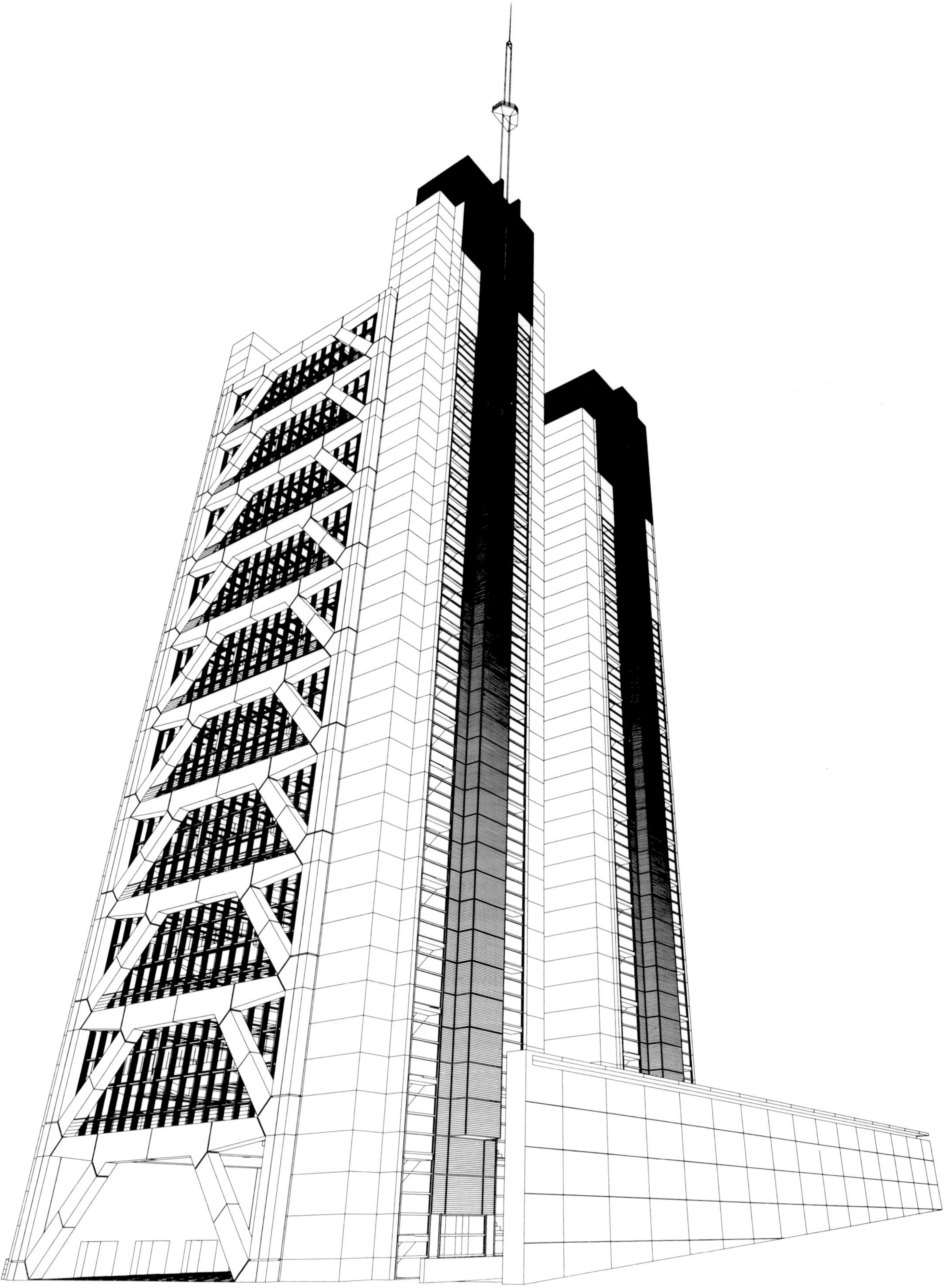

A DECADE OF ARCHITECTURAL DESIGN

Norman Foster

In his teaching, Louis Kahn was fond of using the analogy of Giotto's painting, saying that while the artist could afford to take the creative latitude of showing the wheels of a cart as being square to give an impression of how difficult it was for a donkey to pull it, an architect has no such option and must make them round. As an art as well as a science, architecture constantly straddles the question of how best to balance creativity and functionalism, and few have been able to reconcile this dilemma as successfully as Norman Foster. More often than not, that reconciliation is achieved in delightful ways, as in one of his earlier projects, the Willis Faber Dumas Building in Ipswich, Suffolk. Confronted with the seemingly insurmountable problem of relocating a corporate head office into the fragile fabric of a traditional English town, the architect managed to placate both local council and client by designing a building that reflects, rather than overwhelms its neighbours. Through deceptively simple strategies of detailing, such as the removal of scale giving elements of plinth, cornice and floor lines, and the introduction of nearly invisible glass clips, the building nearly vanishes during the day. At night, however, when the contextual rules change, interior lighting makes the glass skin itself disappear, revealing the inner concrete structure to passers-by. The litany of innovative ideas used here, as well as in other bench-mark efforts such as the Sainsbury Centre at the University of East Anglia in Norwich, or in the Hong Kong Shanghai Bank, consistently show that seemingly conflicting programme requirements need not necessarily result in the exclusionary attitude taken by the Modern Movement. Instead, Foster shows that enlightened attention to detail, as well as due consideration to the needs of all parties concerned with a design, can result in highly creative architecture that also works.

While there is always the feeling of the sleek beautifully crafted object in Foster's buildings, they remain sensitive to specific aspects of site and context.

OPPOSITE: The Century Tower, Tokyo, Japan.
LEFT: Stansted Airport, England.
OVERLEAF: Renault Distribution Centre, Swindon, England.

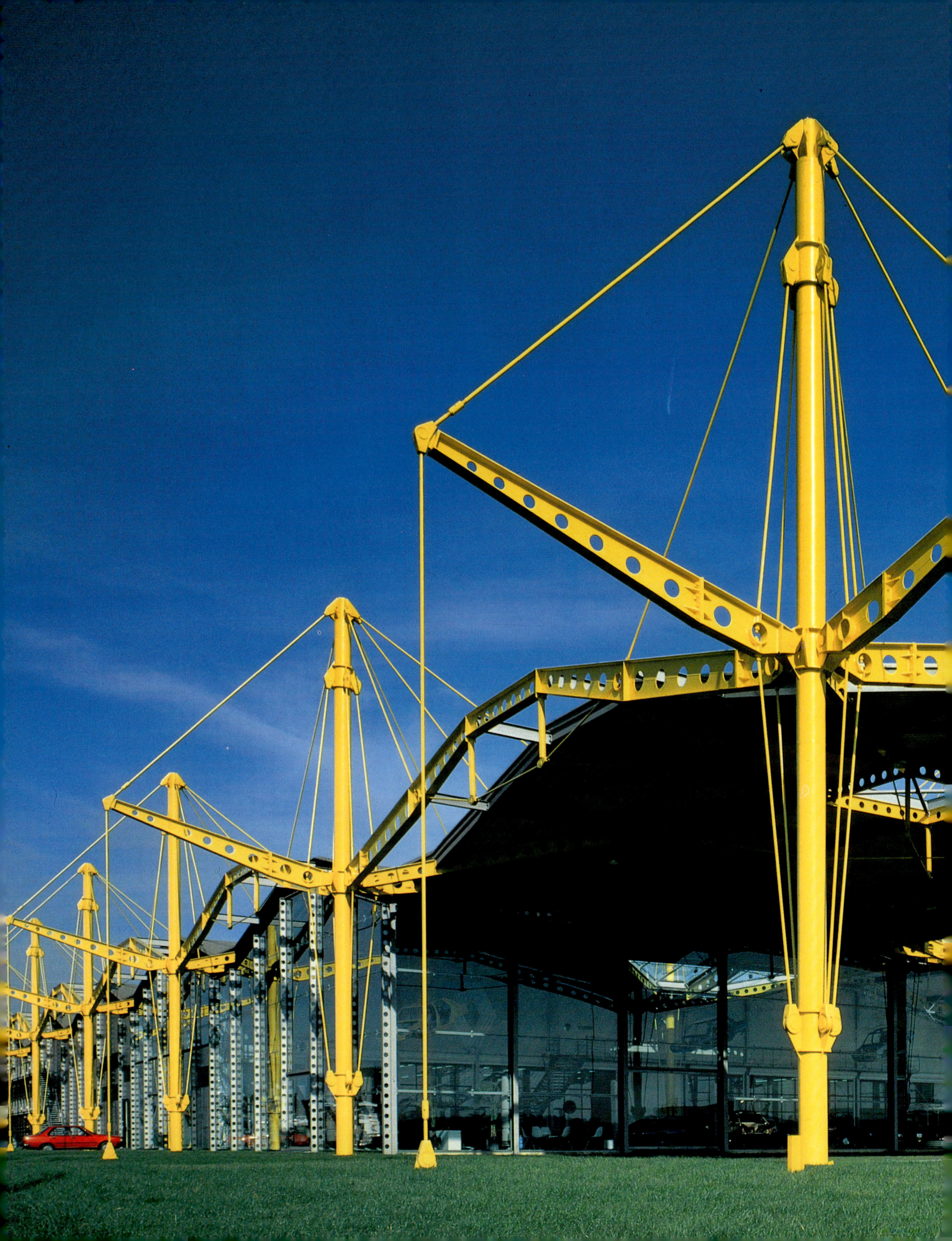

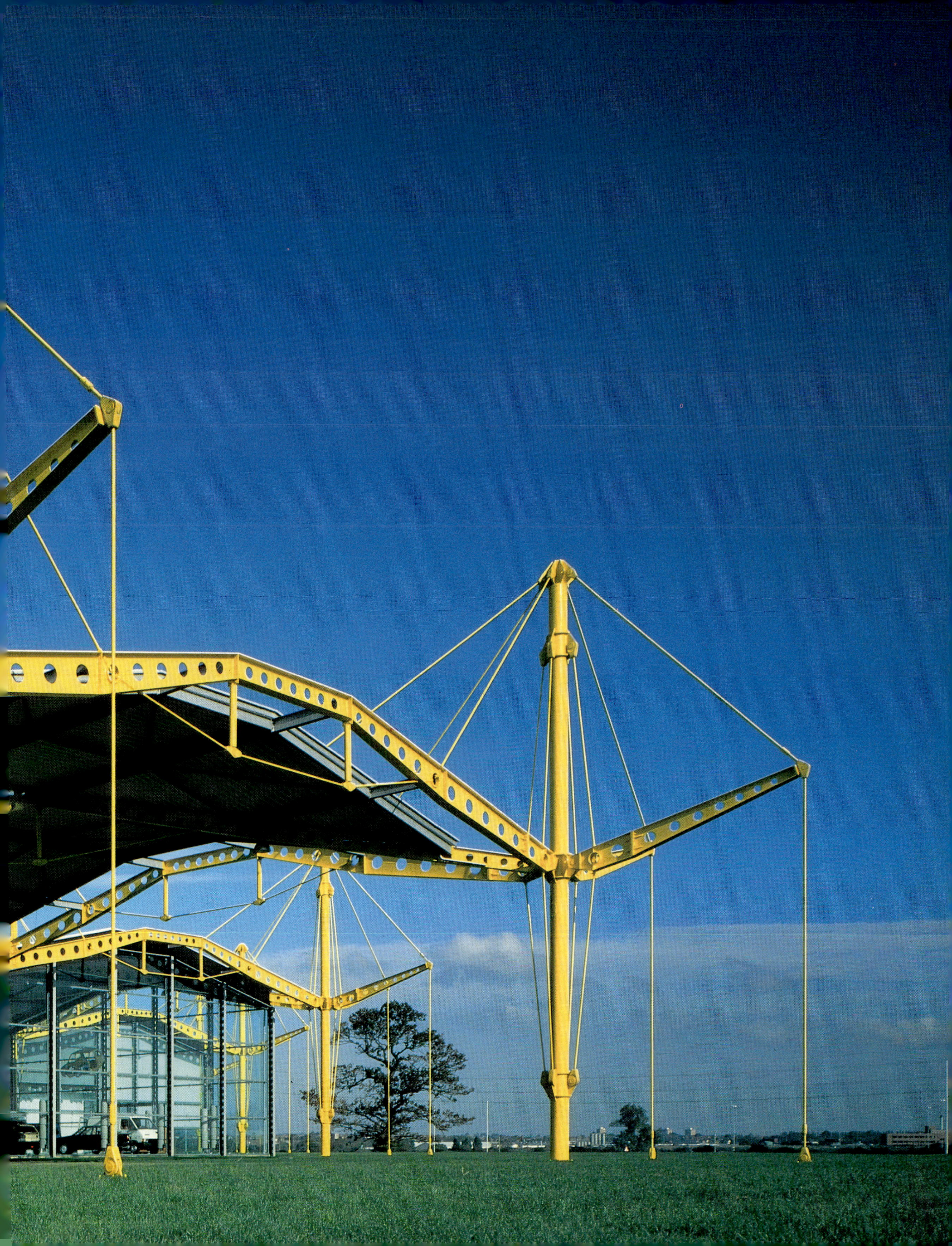

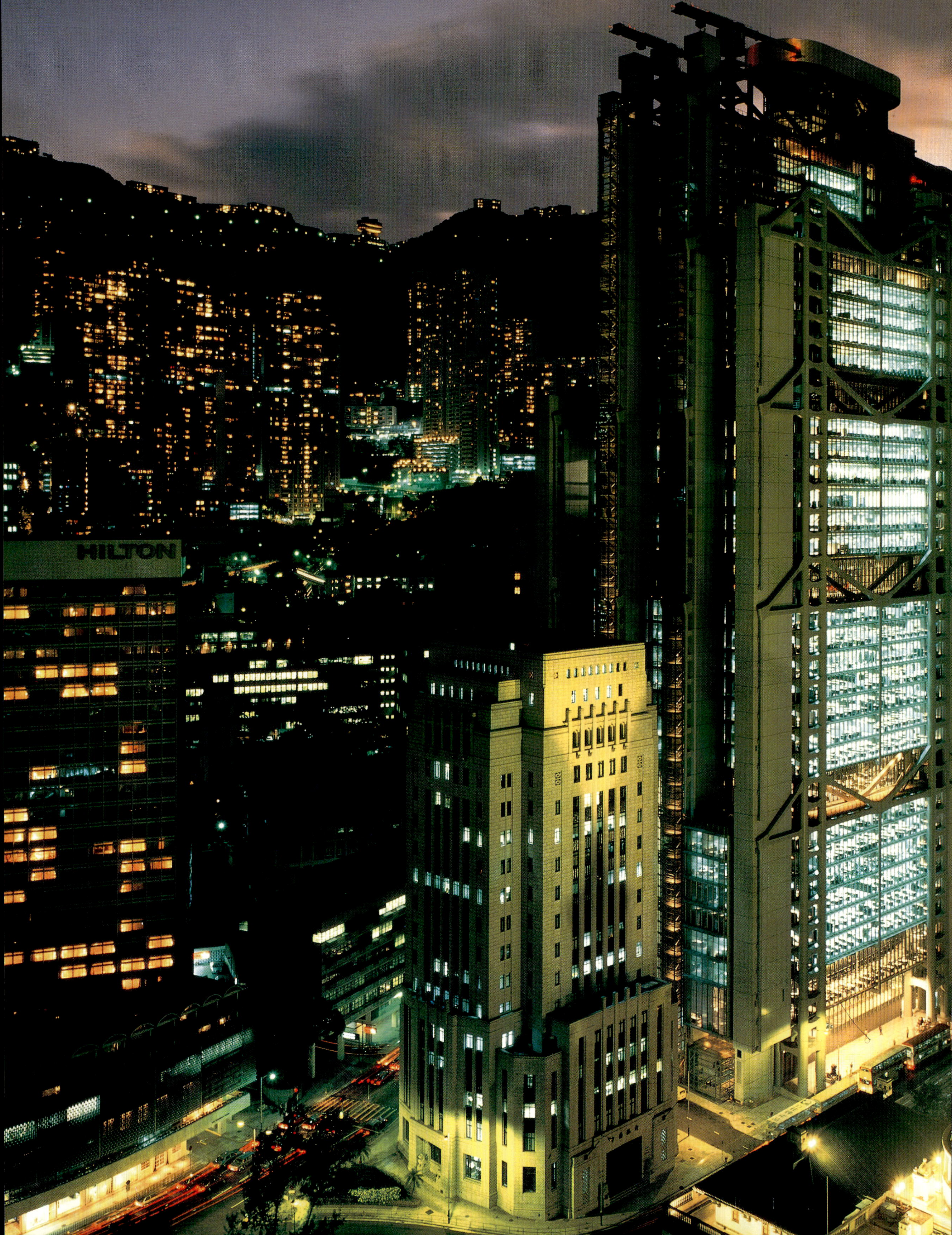
HILTON

NORMAN FOSTER

The fantasy of creating the highest building in the world, which also attracted Frank Lloyd Wright in his design for the Mile High Tower, is the ultimate Modernist dream.

LEFT: The Hong Kong Shanghai Bank Headquarters, Hong Kong.

A DECADE OF ARCHITECTURAL DESIGN

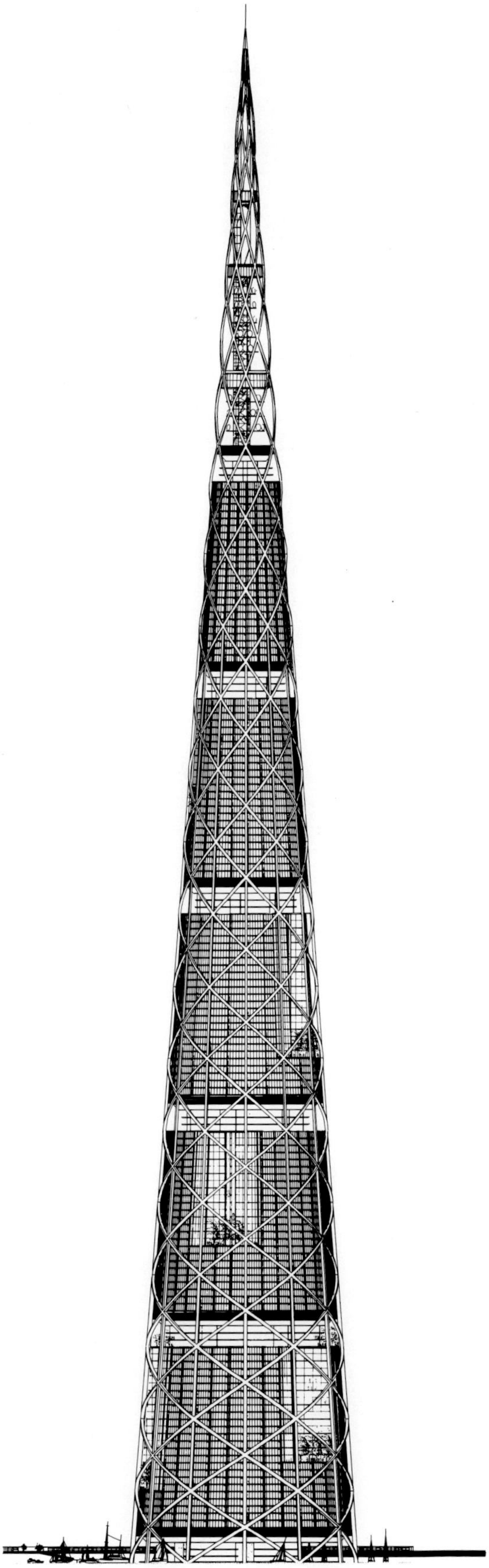

Exposed, accentuated structure, and zoned services which allow a more flexible interior are unshakable tenets of High-Tech dogma.

OPPOSITE & LEFT: The Millennium Tower, Tokyo, Japan.

A DECADE OF ARCHITECTURAL DESIGN

Richard Rogers

While an obvious proponent of High-Tech Architecture, Richard Rogers brings a refreshing degree of universality to a style that has otherwise been a highly visible symbol of Western, production oriented, consumer societies, and the ultimate expression of the machine aesthetic that has developed in them since the Industrial Revolution. This universality includes a commendable awareness of the global issues that should mitigate this aesthetic, including runaway population growth, and the concomitant environmental agricultural and economic problems that are associated with it. In addition to this awareness, he also has an historical perspective that is very rare, and which has allowed him to place his work within the technological traditions of the past. These traditions have included such diverse strains as Gothic architecture, which Rogers views as the most advanced use of the materials available when it developed. In this case, Notre Dame Cathedral becomes a logical ancestor to the Pompidou Centre in Paris and questions of context take on an entirely new dimension. In spite of chronological differences, each building attempts to stretch material, skin and structure to the utmost, in order to create a flexible internal space, and therefore each belongs to the same tradition. When viewed in this way, architecture for Rogers becomes an appropriate extension of the maximum resources available at a certain place and time, and High-Tech becomes the only alternative in the industrialised world. He has noted that the technological capabilities of that world continue to expand at an unbelievable rate, bringing what he has termed a second industrial revolution, especially in computers and biotechnics. Because of his universality, he is able to look upon this second revolution not only as an opportunity to enhance his aesthetic, but also as the means by which architecture, in general, can finally achieve the Modernist vision of serving society in the widest sense, by incorporating all aspects of contemporary society.

Contrast with, rather than sympathy to the past is characteristic of High-Tech architecture in the hands of Richard Rogers.

OPPOSITE: The Lloyds Building, London, England.
LEFT: The Pompidou Centre, Paris, France.

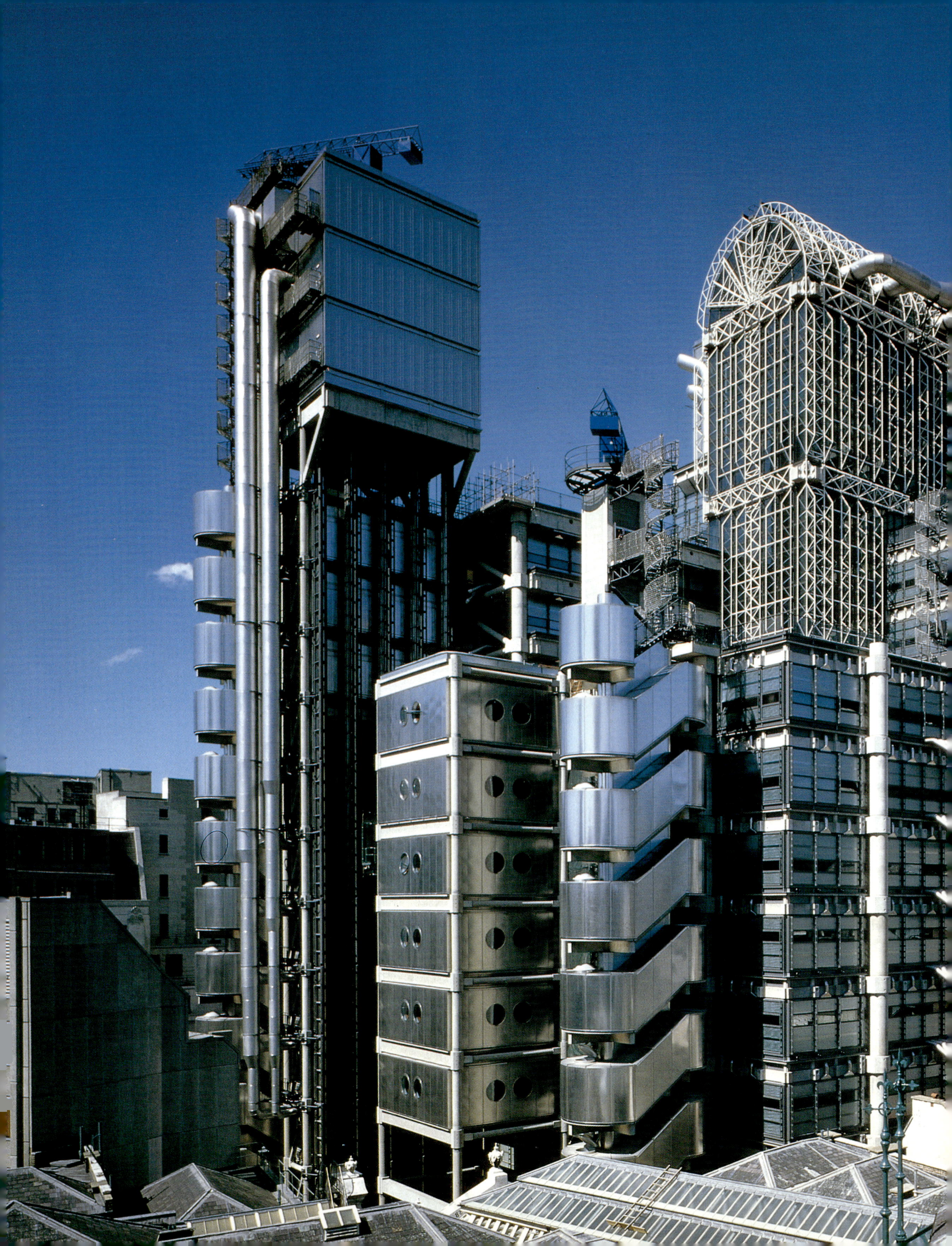

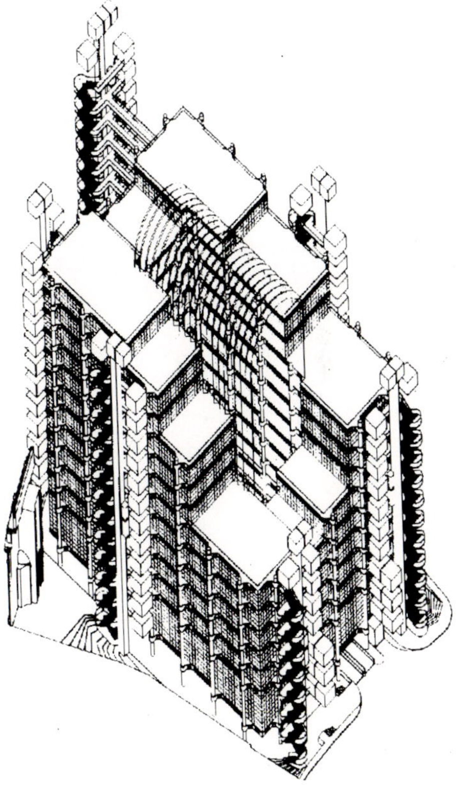

RICHARD ROGERS

Historical sources, such as Gothic Cathedrals, massive stone *Palazzi*, and St Pauls Cathedral have provided inspiration through the audacity of their achievement.

OPPOSITE: The Lloyds Building, London, England.
ABOVE: An early version of the Lloyds Building, London, England.
OVERLEAF: Inmos Factory, Newport, Gwent, Wales.

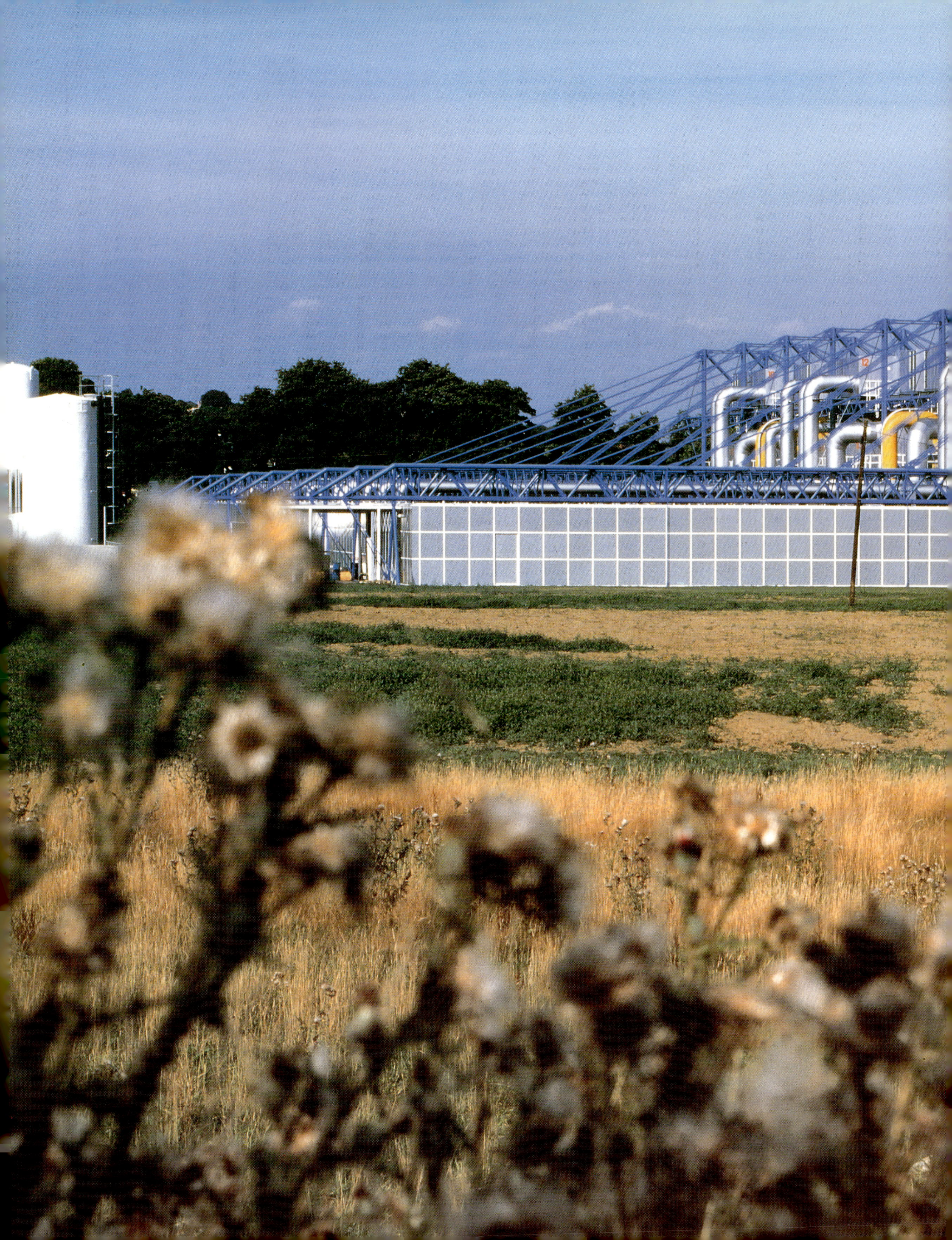

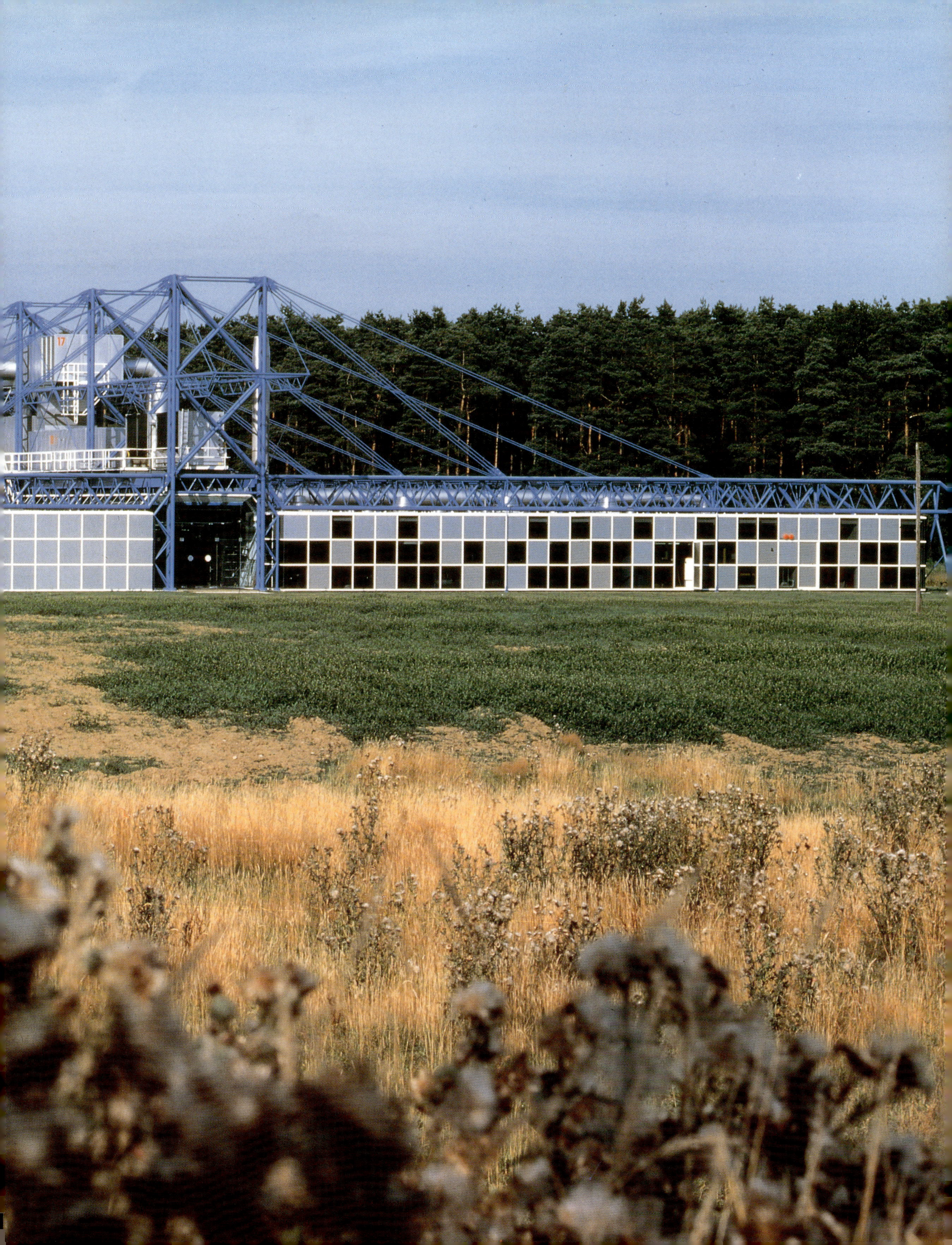

A DECADE OF ARCHITECTURAL DESIGN

Cesar Pelli

Always looking to the parameters of each new commission for clues to a design concept, Cesar Pelli is obviously very pragmatic in his attitude toward his work, seeing limits as a positive, rather than negative aspect of creativity. While such a belief may initially seem to make him a strict functionalist, he looks for the possibilities within each problem, rather than dwelling on finding solutions to strict programmatic requirements in each case. In his constant references to 'an architecture of life', Pelli also accepts the temporality that is its *corollary*, and expresses that acceptance in his preference for glass as a building material. His mastery in the use of that material, in the way it is detailed and joined, is a hallmark of his work, and has consistently remained so since his early days at DMJM as well as Gruen associates in Los Angeles. With it, he constantly explores the possibilities of lightness and transparency that fascinated the Modernists in the first, visionary phase of that movement, and which made the early crystalline projects of Mies van der Rohe so compelling. By constantly refining the detailing of this glass skin, Pelli has perhaps come closer than most to finally achieving that initial Modernist vision and with the addition of colour, he has managed to expand it. In the Museum of Modern Art Gallery expansion and Tower, for example, both his choice of colours and his application of them are intended as a commentary on the reticence of the International Style to accept the potential of that medium. In the first and second phases of the Pacific Design Centre, as well as in the Canary Wharf project, that commentary has been dramatically expanded to reflect all of the vitality inherent in each, individual context, and has provided fresh proof that Pelli is very close to his goal.

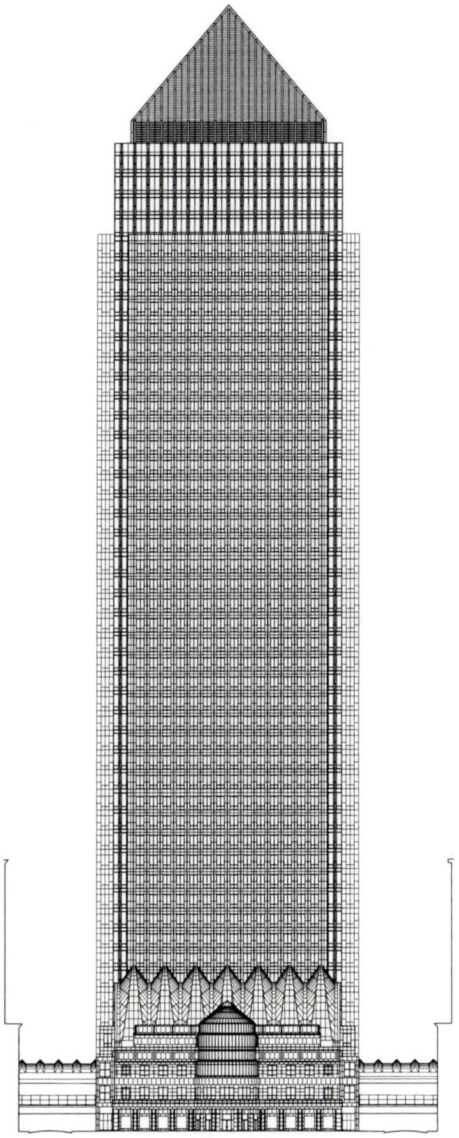

Pelli's town at Canary Wharf has provided a dramatic focal point for the Docklands development zone and has become a symbol for the regeneration of the entire area.

OPPOSITE, LEFT & ABOVE: Canary Wharf, London.

A DECADE OF ARCHITECTURAL DESIGN

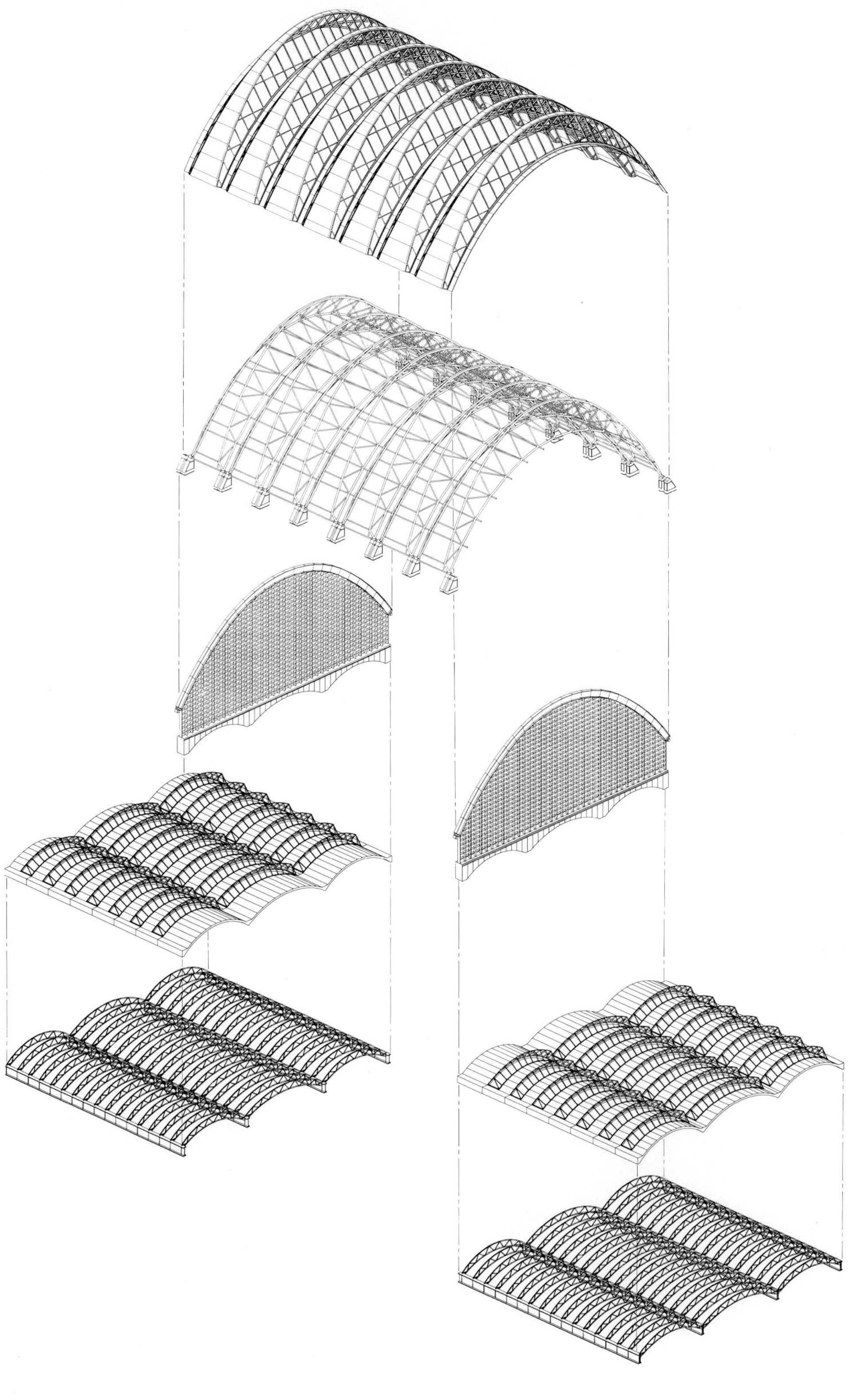

CESAR PELLI

The three towers of Battery Park, with their intentionally tripartite division into base, middle and top, compose well as a group, yet each have a personality of their own. Reflective glass tends to reduce the scale of this tower and alleviate the feeling of claustrophobia that is so characteristic of Manhattan.

OPPOSITE: World Financial Center, Battery Park City, New York.
LEFT: Canary Wharf, London.
OVERLEAF: Pacific Design Center, Los Angeles, California.

A DECADE OF ARCHITECTURAL DESIGN

CESAR PELLI

A DECADE OF ARCHITECTURAL DESIGN

Michael Hopkins

The work of Michael Hopkins is a direct extension of his experience with Foster Associates, where he was a partner in the 1970s. He and his wife Patricia formed their own firm in 1976 and from that point on, their direction might best be characterised as inspired functionalism. The Schlumberger Cambridge Research Centre, completed in 1985, is one of Hopkins' most memorable examples of this direction to date; state of the art tent technology has been brilliantly adapted to a function with which it would not normally be associated, giving the final building the sense of inevitability that is the hallmark of all great architecture. By fully utilising the translucency of teflon-coated fibreglass fabric, which was first developed by Geiger-Berger and Dupont in collaboration with Skidmore, Owings and Merrill in the Haj Terminal Project in Saudi Arabia, Hopkins has managed to accentuate, rather than obliterate the natural fall of the site, creating an expressive Hi-Tech building that is uncharacteristically sensitive to its setting. The teflon fabric also contributes a great deal to the environmental comfort of the Schlumberger labs, because of its high reflective and insulative capabilities, making it the ideal material of choice for an architect who wishes to give technology a human aspect. Hopkins goes a bit further in expressing the idea of thinness here, using trusses and cables in a way that make a fabric with a tensile strength akin to steel seem like skin, and the structure look like the exoskeleton beneath it.

The Mound Stand at Lord's involved the refurbishment of terraces and the provision of a new structure to seat more than 500 spectators. The teflon fabric which is used once again here is in complete sympathy with existing conditions. The architect chose to work within the restrictions of a seven-arched brick colonnade, built in 1898 by Frank Verity, and while functional considerations such as the retention of excellent sight lines to the existing Cricket pitch were of pre-eminent concern, an awareness of the past again makes this a unique example of the game.

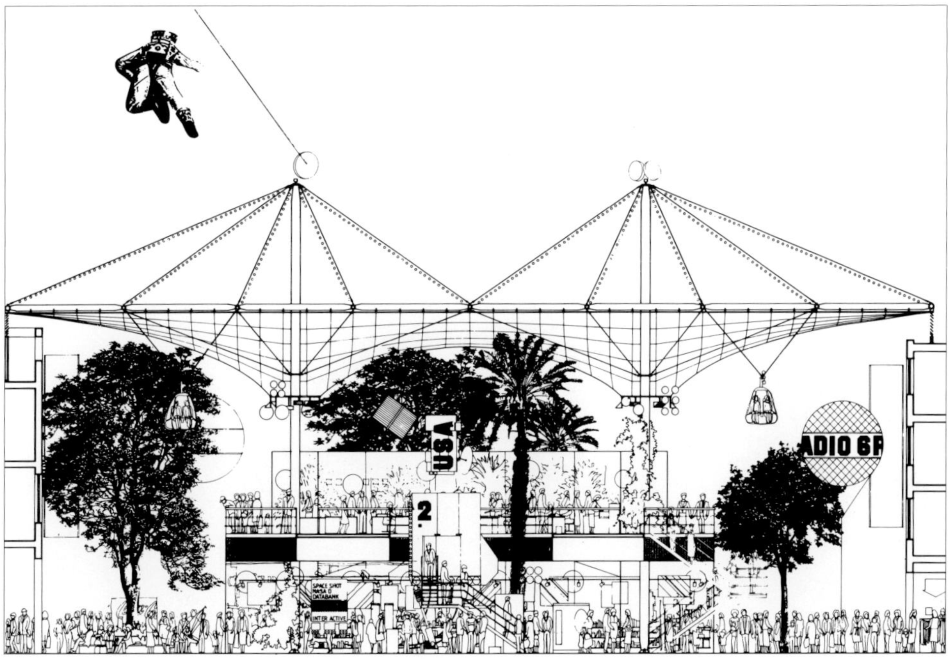

Recent breakthroughs in membrane technology make teflon coated fibreglass the material of choice for Michael Hopkins Partners, because of its translucence, lightness and flexibility.

OPPOSITE: Mound Stand, Lord's Cricket Ground, London, England.
LEFT: Town Square Enclosure, Basildon, England.
OVERLEAF: Schlumberger Research Centre, Cambridge, England.

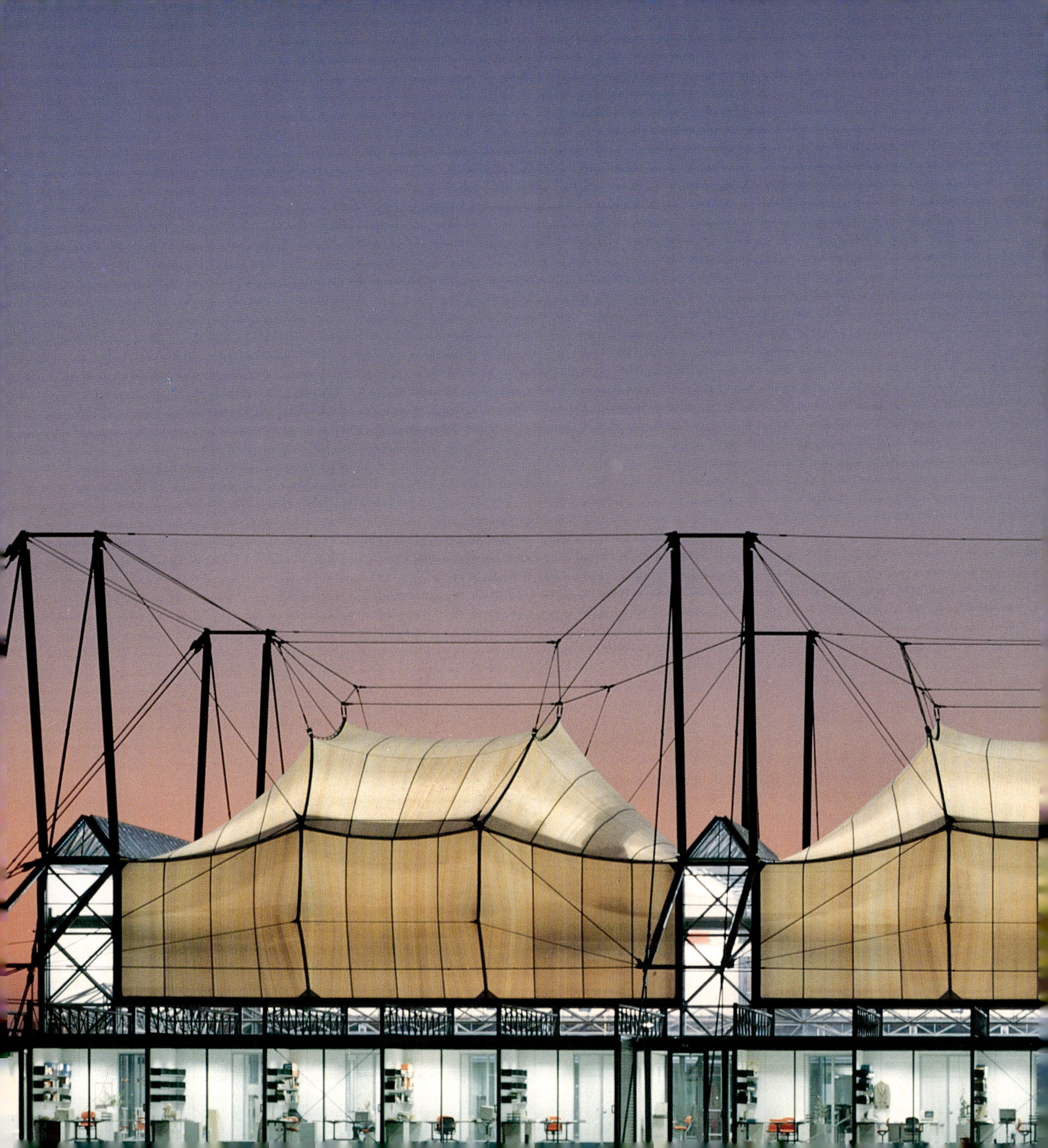

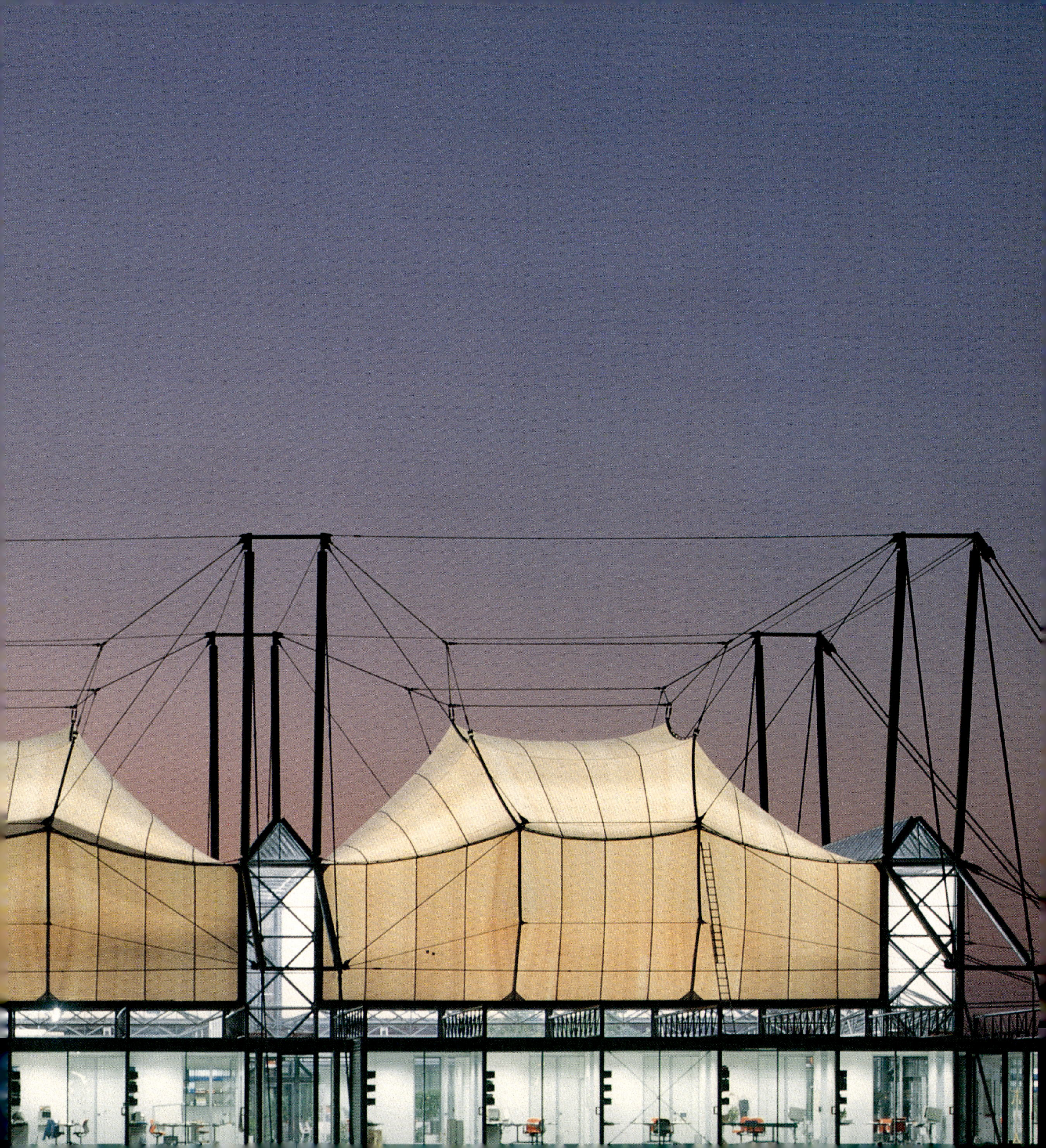

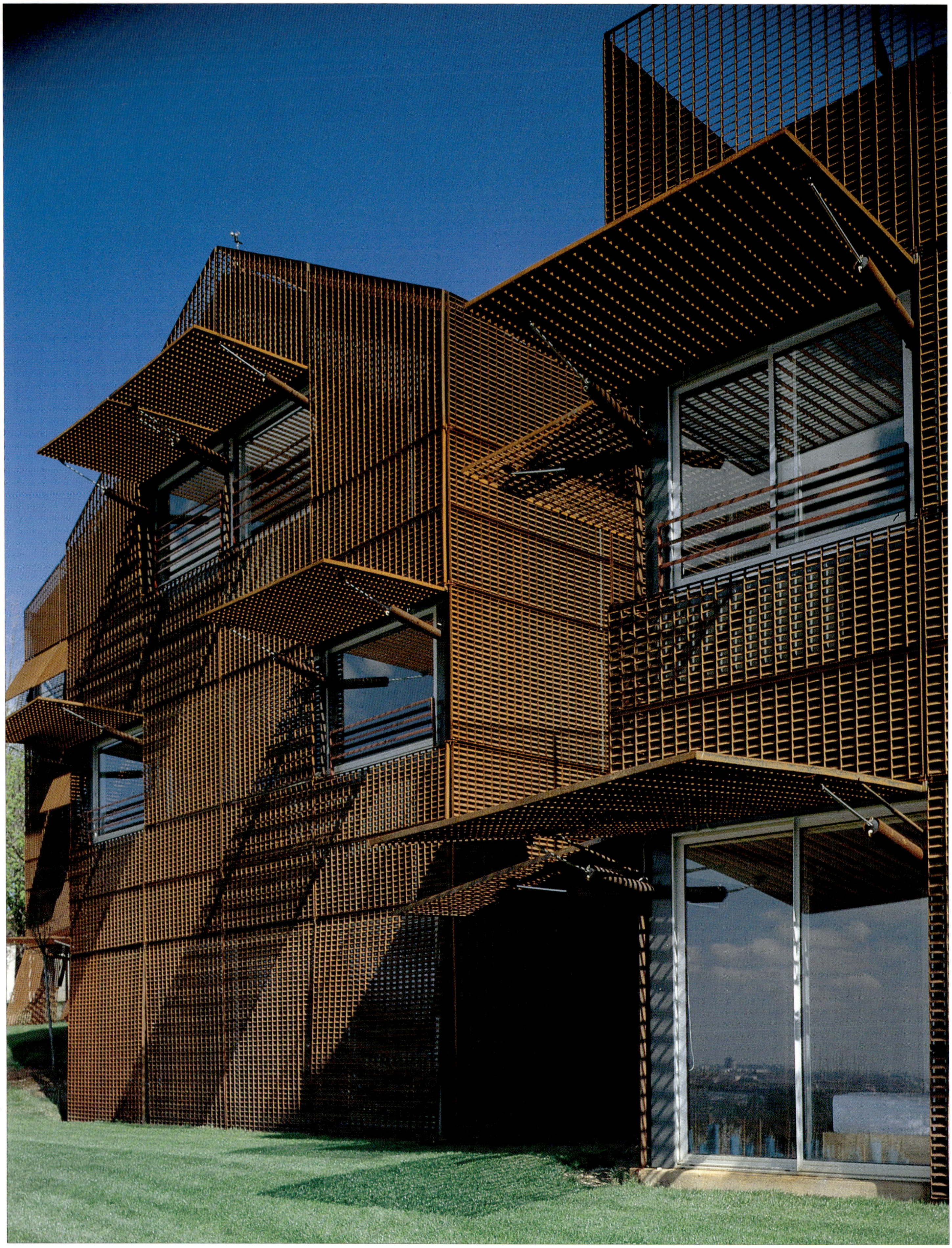

Jean Nouvel

Frequently, young architects who go on to receive international recognition can identify one project as a turning point in their career, and for Jean Nouvel, the Institute of the Arab World must be that project. In a seminar following his having been given the Aga Khan Award for this building in Cairo on October 15, 1990, Nouvel spoke with passion and deep conviction about his design, which he began by describing as a symbolic bridge between East and West. In addition to setting up what Nouvel called 'a dialogue between two cultures,' he noted that the Institute, which is near the Cathedral of Notre Dame in Paris, is also a gateway between the old and new parts of the City. For this reason, the plan of the building divides logically between a curved, scimitar-like section precisely fitted to the river Seine on the one hand, and a rectilinear block which makes the transition to the most recent orthagonal city grid on the other, appropriately separated by an open courtyard in the middle. In its precise and polished modernity, the Institute not only fulfils its intended role as what Nouvel calls a 'Parisian artefact' but also admirably satisfies its function as a showcase of Arab culture, presenting many tantalising references to that tradition. In addition to the pristine calm of the perfectly square courtyard, which Nouvel had originally wanted to grace with a fountain of mercury, there is the spiralling 'Tower of Books', which recalls the famous minaret of Samarra, as well as a technologically brilliant rendition of the traditional wooden mushrabiyya screens used throughout the Middle East as a device for controlling sunlight and privacy in the past. The southern façade of the Institute is clad with over a hundred photo-sensitive panels that activate these spectacular, shutter-like screens and they along with thin alabaster slabs, create an 'interplay of transparencies' that is finally as kaleidoscopic as the Arab World itself. With his design for the Institute of the Arab World, Jean Nouvel has not only shown great technological virtuosity, but also sensitivity toward a culture that has, until now, not been translated well.

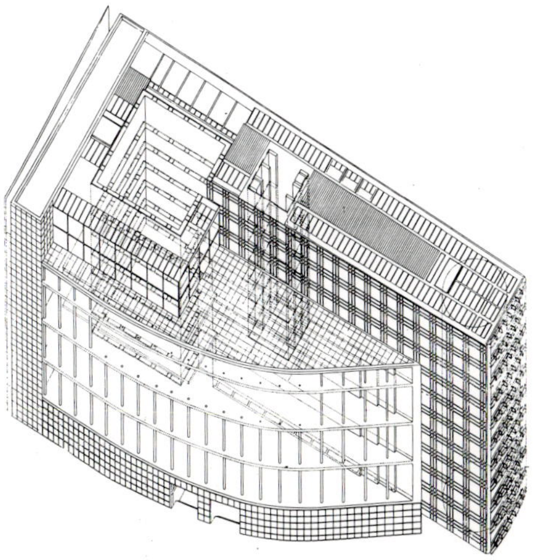

Nouvel's regional sensibilities are not confined to the urban context alone, but have shown up in smaller projects as well.

OPPOSITE: Hotel Saint James, Bordeaux, France.
LEFT & ABOVE: Institut de la Monde Arabe, Paris, France.

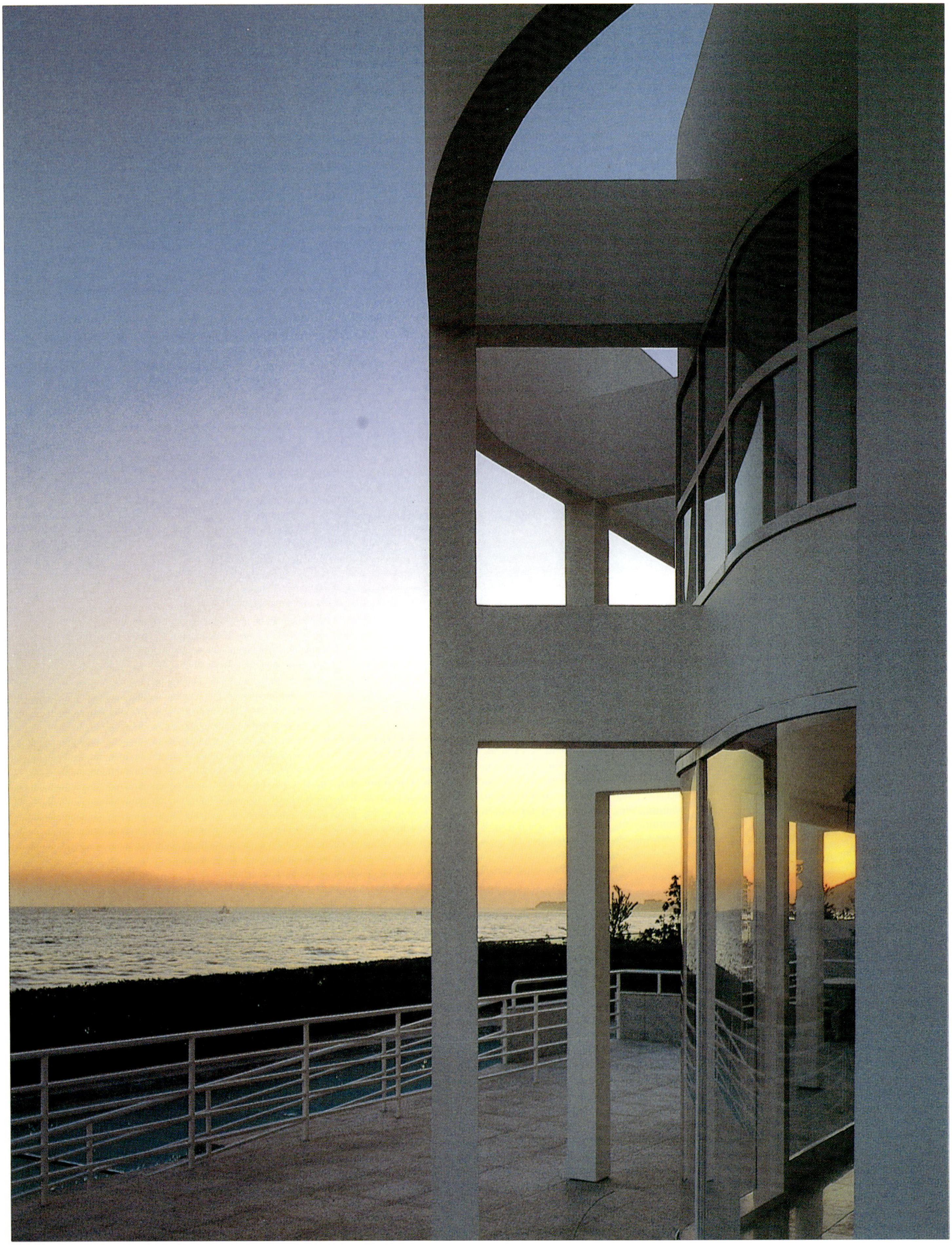

Richard Meier
The Subject of Architecture

The Modern Movement questioned the prevailing attitude of slavishly recreating the past. It yanked architecture out of the padded yoke of popular opinion, out of the comfortable despair of the banal. It changed the way we look and think about architecture so that ideas about place, use, materials and technology are related to ideas about *form, proportion, light* and *scale*. In striving to broaden the morphogenetic field, technology became paramount. But, it is as if in their love affair with the machine, with the cool light of the purely rational, they lost touch with the sensual, the ground of our aesthetic being. The heroic mind overwhelmed *its own* spiritual vision, for when the idea of the machine replaces the idea of the mind's eye and the architect's hand, there comes that deep alienation of man from his environment. Whereas the Modern masters seemed to our eyes to be too rigidly identified with the idea and potential of mass production, of industrial man, this is now a fact of life, simply one of a number of resources at the architect's disposal. We now assume the tectonic and spatial authority of the Modern Movement, each new miracle of building holds only limited fascination. For me, technology is no longer the subject of architecture, but simply the means. Architecture is the subject of my architecture.

Abstraction in architecture continues to be one of the most powerful legacies of the Heroic Period. It continues to provoke us to invent and to elaborate on ways to geometrically organise and interpret human activities. Distinct and completely evolved plastic systems such as De Stijl, Purism and Constructivism each embodied the thought that architecture was important and dealt with aspects of the machine and the poetry of space. Today, the most compelling extension of that impulse towards abstraction is Deconstructivism. I feel akin to the embrace of the purely sculptural. I applaud the evocative focus on intellectual commitment. However, the nature of their inquiry and the quality of their objects *inevitably* collide with my concerns for the particularities of scale and place. There is no place for the physical in the Decons' intriguing network of forces. The web of their universe exists in a mind clearly alienated from the hierarchy and order essential to habitation. Nonetheless, I defend the validity and vitality of their speculation on the unreal.

In the design of my buildings, I am expanding and elaborating on what I consider to be the formal basis of the Modern Movement. What the 20th century did was create the ability to crack open an otherwise classically balanced plan. The spirit of the 20th century is allowed to go in and out through that crack, so that the experience of being in the building is not static, but everchanging. This 20th-century fissure made possible by the free plan, the free facade, the separation of structure and skin, the whole formal basis of the Modern Movement, fostered a new kind of volumetric exploration, one that still seems to hold many possibilities.

The great promise and richness of some of the formal tenets of Modernism have almost unlimited areas for investigation.

Richard Meier, Ackerberg House, Malibu, California.

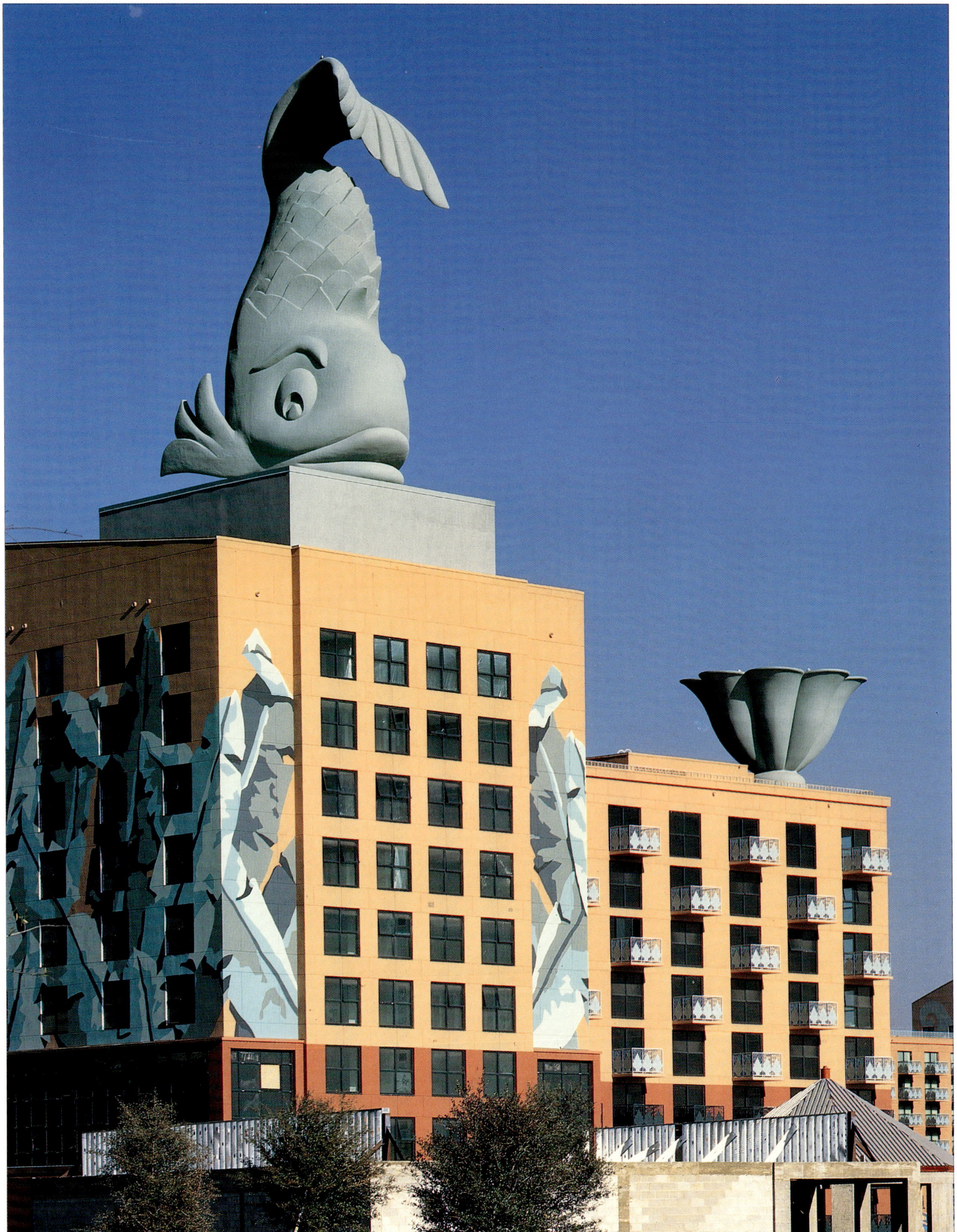

Post-Modernism

In his book *Post-Modernism: The New Classicism in Art and Architecture,* Charles Jencks has reflected on this style in part, by saying:

'After more than 20 years the Post-Modern Movement has achieved a revolution in Western culture without breaking anything more than a few eggheads. It has successfully challenged the reign of Modern art and architecture, it has put Positivism and other 20th-century philosophies in their rightfully narrow place, brought back enjoyable modes in literature without becoming populist and slowed, if not halted altogether, the wanton destruction of cities. In at least one city, San Francisco, it has instituted positive laws for growth. This revolution has cut across film, music, dance, religion, politics, fashion and nearly every activity of contemporary life and, like all revolutions, including planetary ones, it entails a return to the past as much as a movement forward.

'Contrary to common belief Post-Modernism is neither anti-Modernist nor reactionary. It accepts the discoveries of the 20th century – those of Freud, Einstein and Henry Ford – and the fact that two world wars and mass culture are now integral parts of our world picture, but doesn't make from this entire ideology. In short, as its name implies, it acknowledges the debt to Modernism but transcends this movement by synthesising it with other concerns. Anyone who has come under the sway of Post-Modernism owes allegiance to two quite different pasts – the immediate and the more distant one.

'The prefix 'post' has several contradictory overtones, one of which implies the incessant struggle against stereotypes, the 'continual revolution' of the avant-garde – and hence, by implication, the fetish of the new . . . In fact Lyotard's argument in *The Post-Modern Condition* stems from that of Ihab Hassan's advocating ultra-Modernism. Fearing the 'death of the avant-garde' which for the last 20 years has been so widely reported by Irving Howe, Hilton Kramer and other writers (evidently a malingering last act), Lyotard intends to give it a large jab of experimental adrenaline. He needn't bother: 'The *Late*-Modern Condition', as his book should have been called, is alive and economically flourishing in most of the world's galleries, corporate headquarters, and university literature ('Deconstructionist') departments. The Hong Kong and Shanghai Bank is there in all its wealthy splendour to celebrate, if not support, it. Late-Modernism – will go on thriving as long as technology changes, the youth need counter-challenges and fashion rules consumer society; ie from now on. But Post-Modernism is something different, based on further connotations of the prefix 'post' which stress that it comes 'after' not before Modernism. As implied it's a reweaving of the recent past and Western culture, an attempt to rework its humanist tenets in the light of a world civilisation and autonomous, plural cultures. The way this new tradition has grown slowly and fitfully out of Modernism and away from Late-Modernism shows amusing similarities with previous movements.'

Michael Graves, Dolphin Hotel, Walt Disney World, Florida.

A DECADE OF ARCHITECTURAL DESIGN

Michael Graves

Largely through the graphic power of his images and the effective superimposition of many different levels of symbolism in his work, Michael Graves has had an enormous influence on the architectural profession during the last decade and his seemingly limitless imagination indicates that that influence will undoubtedly continue for some time to come. In seeking to create what he has called 'metaphorical landscapes', Graves has consistently managed to combine highly diverse sources in a way that not only provides a commentary on the culture in which he works, but also continuously reinvents it. In these 'landscapes' he has also effectively used colours to either extend his metaphors, or to make a direct connection with natural elements in the Classical manner, creating in the process a polychromatic replica of the context surrounding his buildings. Having expanded his design vocabulary nearly 15 years ago to include the anthropomorphically-based architecture of ancient Greece and Rome, he has also opened up an entire area of vernacular influence that had previously been closed to him, and has been able to transfer his knowledge of the past into regional commentary. On larger projects, such as the Portland and Humana buildings, or the more recently completed Dolphin and Swan Hotels at Walt Disney World, this Classically-based, tripartite division and an instinctive use of colours changes have served to make his architecture more humane, indicating that the highly individual language that he has now developed does not suffer through changes in scale.

The Humana Building in Louisville, Kentucky, continues the ideas first used in 'Portlandia', using extended vertical scale and incorporating set-backs from the street and a loggia base to a much greater extent. As a result of the initial controversy raised by the Portland Building scheme when it was first introduced, the pavilions on the roof, as well as the long, stylised garlands at the sides were revised in the final version.

OPPOSITE & ABOVE: Humana Medical Corporation Headquarters, Louisville, Kentucky.
LEFT: Portland Public Service Building, Portland, Oregon.
OVERLEAF: Dolphin & Swan Hotels, Walt Disney World, Florida.

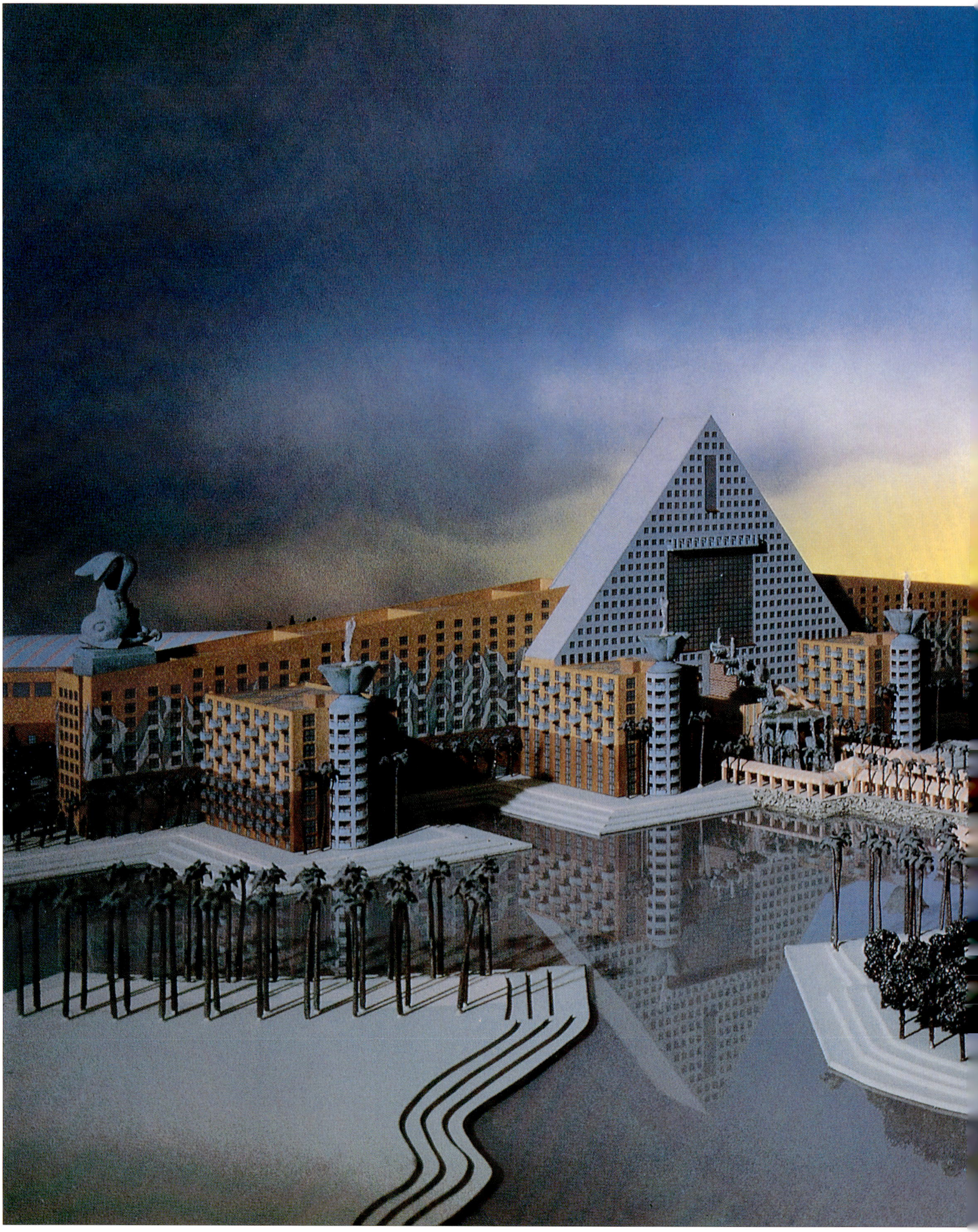

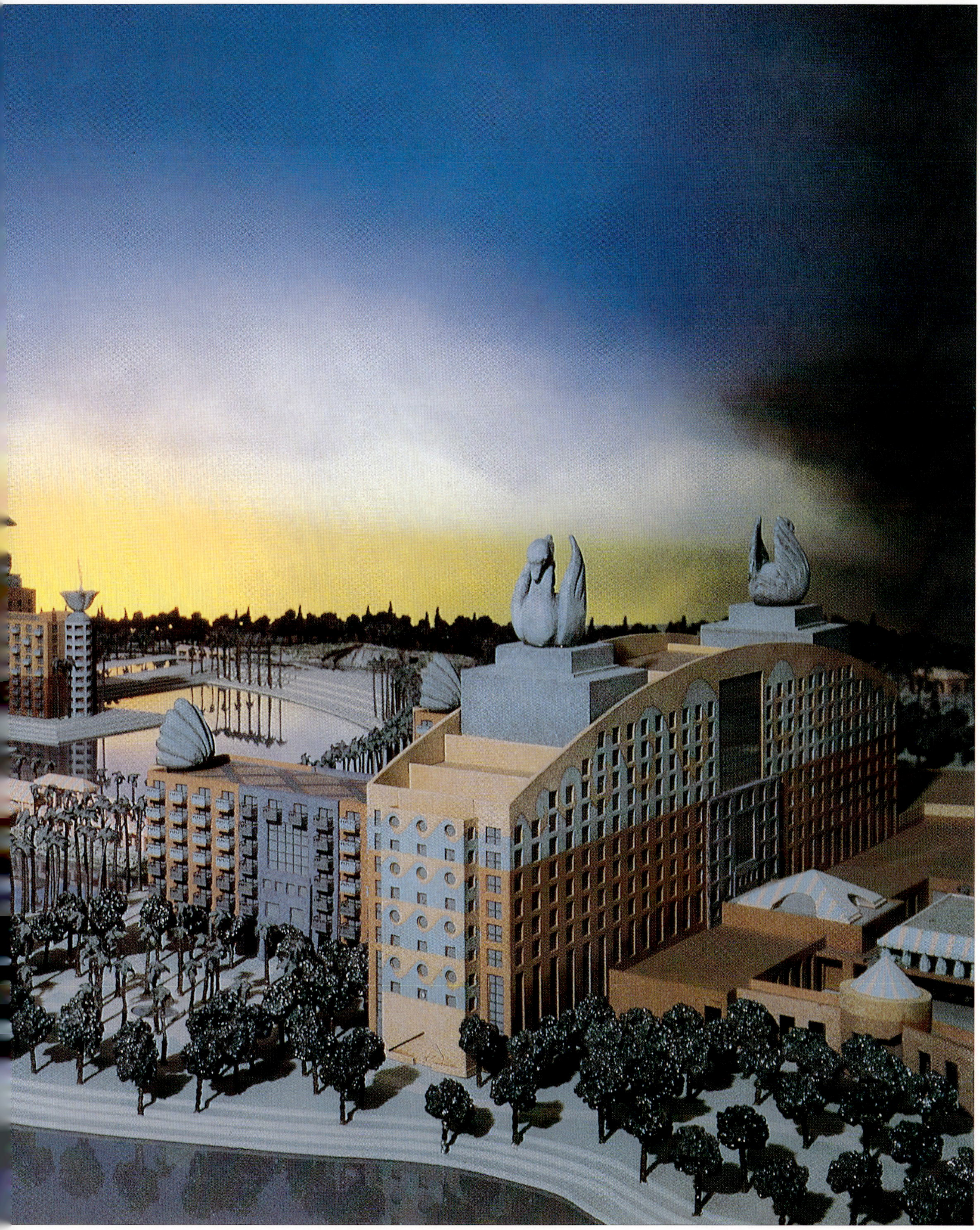

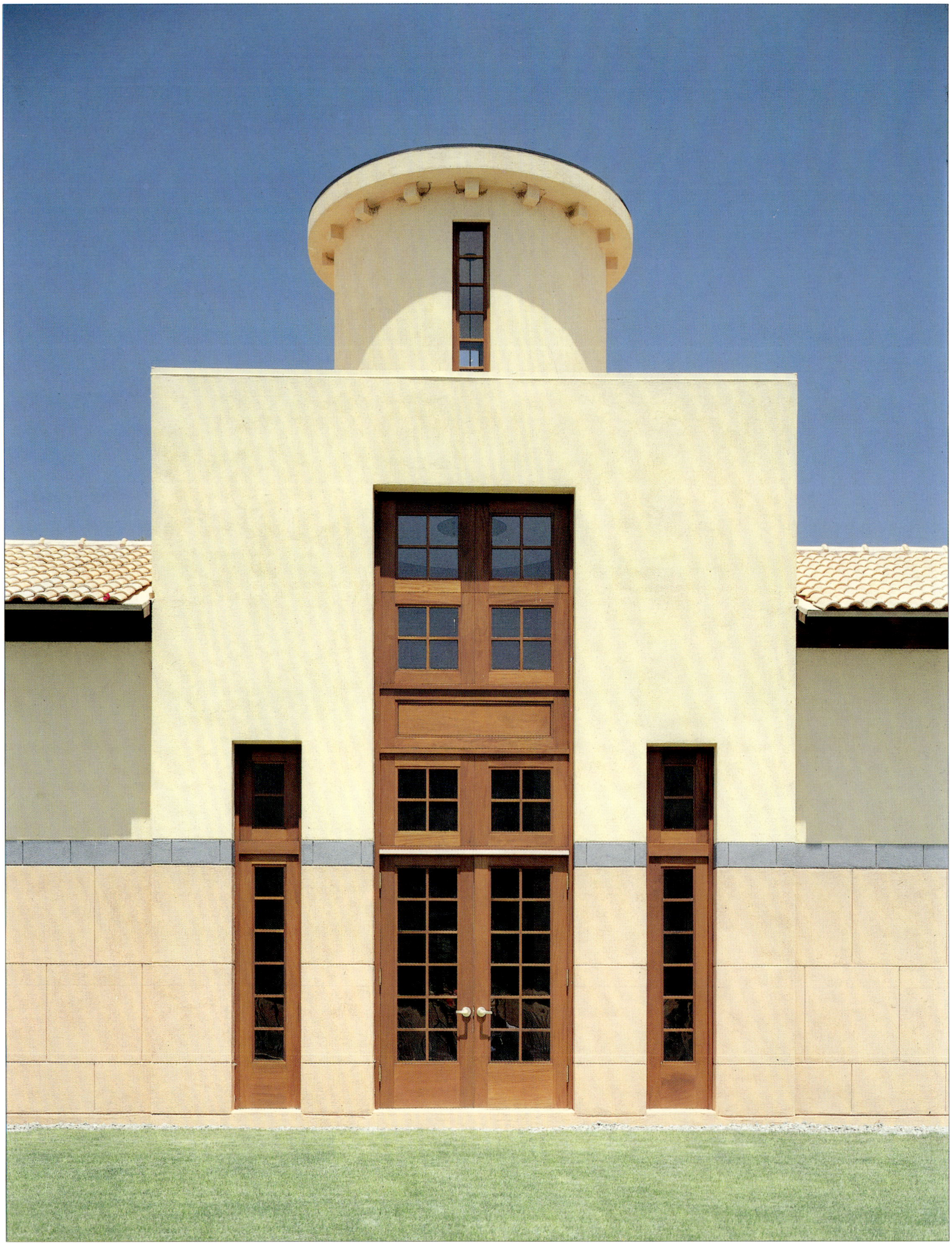

Buildings at Clos Pegase Winery were positioned so as to separate the public and private parts of the site.

OPPOSITE, CENTRE & BELOW: Clos Pegase Winery and Residence Calistoga, Napa Valley, California.
ABOVE: Swan Hotel Walt Disney World, Florida.

A DECADE OF ARCHITECTURAL DESIGN

Robert Venturi & Denise Scott Brown

Without exception, all of the issues that have been central to the architectural debate of the last 25 years can be traced through the buildings and writings of Robert Venturi and Denise Scott Brown. Beginning with the Vanna Venturi house and *Complexity and Contradiction in Architecture*, Robert Venturi sent shock waves through the Modernist establishment that are difficult, for those who enjoy the stylistic freedom that he made possible, to appreciate today.

Denise Scott Brown began a professional collaboration with Robert Venturi in 1960, and they were married in 1967. In describing the firm's approach to urban problems in a recent *Architectural Design* article entitled 'Paralipomena in Urban Design', which also gives an insight into the general approach they have taken, she says the: 'strains of thought in our work have been recognised by few architectural historians and critics, because most lack the cross-continental and inter-disciplinary span to do so. Also, the high-profile critics are interested primarily in built work: they are not drawn toward social thought and they avoid difficult images . . . where social planning ideas have been explicitly discussed in our writing, as they were for example in *Learning from Las Vegas*, they have been ignored. We consider these ideas, nonetheless, vital to our architecture and believe that, to the extent they are omitted from the discussion of our work and thought, our architecture is misunderstood. Our *Learning from Las Vegas* research project and our South Street community planning project were conducted at the same time. Therefore we smart to hear our ideas on popular culture described as 'cynical populism', and to read that our architecture is lacking in social conscience. The techniques of deferring judgement that we recommended in *Learning from Las Vegas* were just that, techniques. Their aim was to make subsequent judgement more sensitive.'

An encyclopaedic knowledge of history has informed Venturi's work, giving it a depth of source that goes beyond the scale of a particular project.

OPPOSITE: House on Long Island Sound, Stony Creek, Connecticut.
BELOW: Trubeck and Wislocki houses, Nantucket Island, Massachusetts.

A DECADE OF ARCHITECTURAL DESIGN

ROBERT VENTURI & DENISE SCOTT BROWN

In addition to historical sources, which are used with great care, context also plays an important part in the VSBA approach.

OPPOSITE, ABOVE & BELOW: House, Seal Harbour, Maine.
ABOVE & BELOW: House, Northern Delaware.

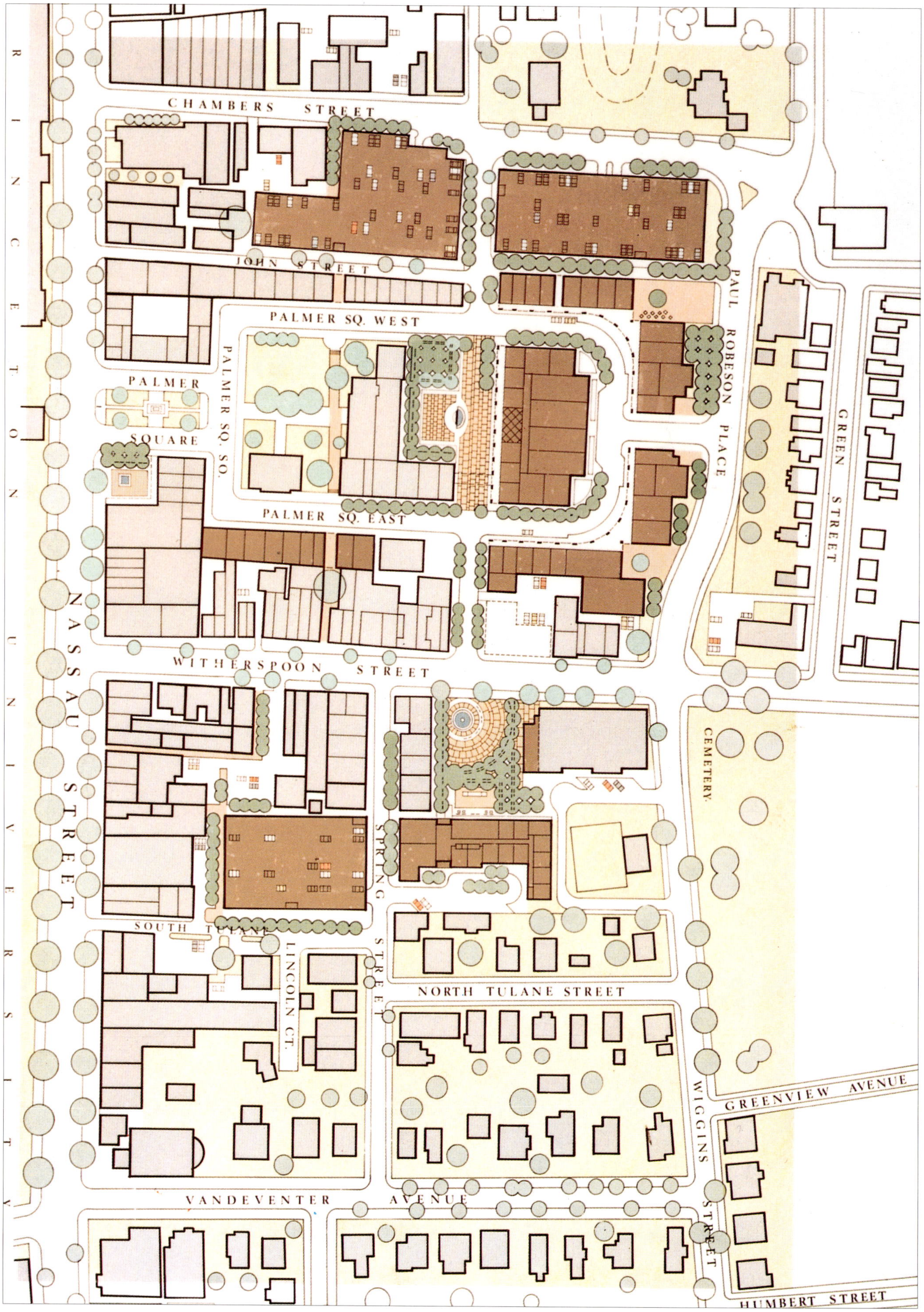

A DECADE OF ARCHITECTURAL DESIGN

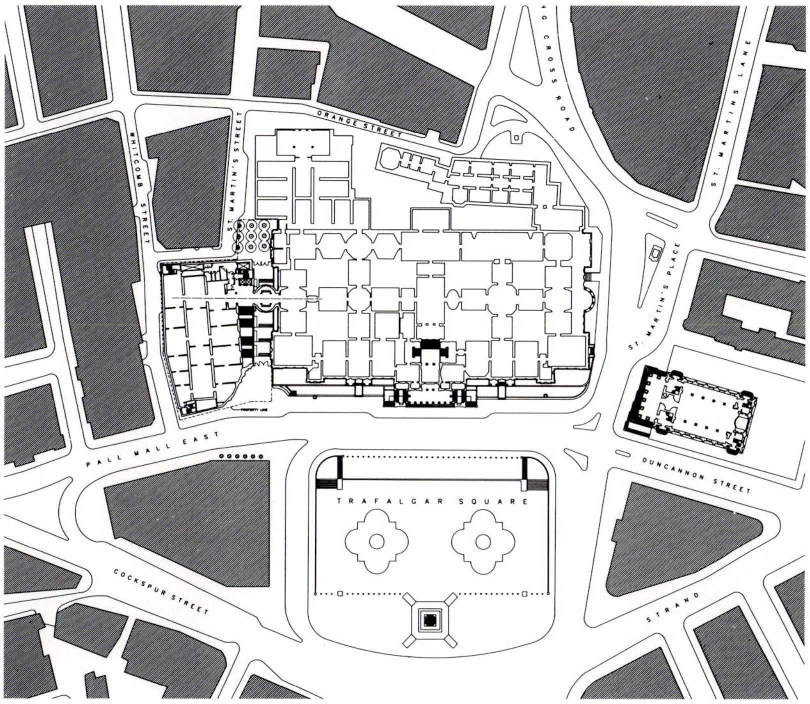

ROBERT VENTURI & DENISE SCOTT BROWN

In both *Complexity and Contradiction* and *Learning from Las Vegas*, Venturi and Scott Brown have argued for diversity rather than simplicity in the built environment, and the separation of symbol from form.

OPPOSITE: Urban design study, Princeton, New Jersey.
ABOVE & BELOW: Extension to the National Gallery, London, England.

A DECADE OF ARCHITECTURAL DESIGN

O M Ungers

OM Ungers was born in Kaisersesch, West Germany, in 1926; and studied architecture at the Technical University in Karlsruhe. He opened his own practice in Cologne in 1950 and remained in Germany until 1970, when he moved to the United States. Many influential projects have included the Ruhwald Housing Estate in Berlin, built between 1966 and 1968, and the Bremen University Scheme of 1976; as well as the Messe Skyscraper, Galleria and Architectural Museum, which are all located in Frankfurt. In his Tower project, as well as the Architectural Museum, there is an intriguing play of volumes and materials, hard and soft, and form within form, that separates Ungers from the Late-Modern aesthetic, giving his work a more symbolic content. In describing his view on this play of form, he has alluded to what Sörgel has called 'the Janus face of architecture', saying:

'The significance of interior space, the primary object of architecture, was played down to such an extent in the 19th century in favour of what was formal, stylistic, and decorative, that Schmarsow's perception of architecture as being, by its very nature, the shaping of space came almost as a rediscovery of architecture . . . In fact the real essence of architecture lies in the dual action of interior and exterior, form and space, enclosed and enclosing elements. It . . . has been described as the 'Janus Face' of architecture. Squares and streets take their form from the buildings which surround them, in the same way as walls and supports define the space within them. The interaction between interior and exterior, between structure and skin, is the principle which distinguishes architecture from all other art forms.'

In heightening this distinction, Ungers seeks to make form autonomous, and to do so, consistently chooses those shapes most easily comprehensible to both mental and visual image, in the belief that complete geometric systems reduce complexity, rather than contributing to it. In this way form is a combination of fact and an ideal image in the mind of the architect.

Contrasts between glass, steel and brick create oppositions that heighten the normal response to each material, into one of visual synergy. Formal geometrical repetition strengthens this linking.

OPPOSITE: Messe Skyscraper, Frankfurt-am-Main, Germany.
LEFT: Fair Hall, Frankfurt-am-Main, Germany.
ABOVE: Galleria, Frankfurt-am-Main, Germany.

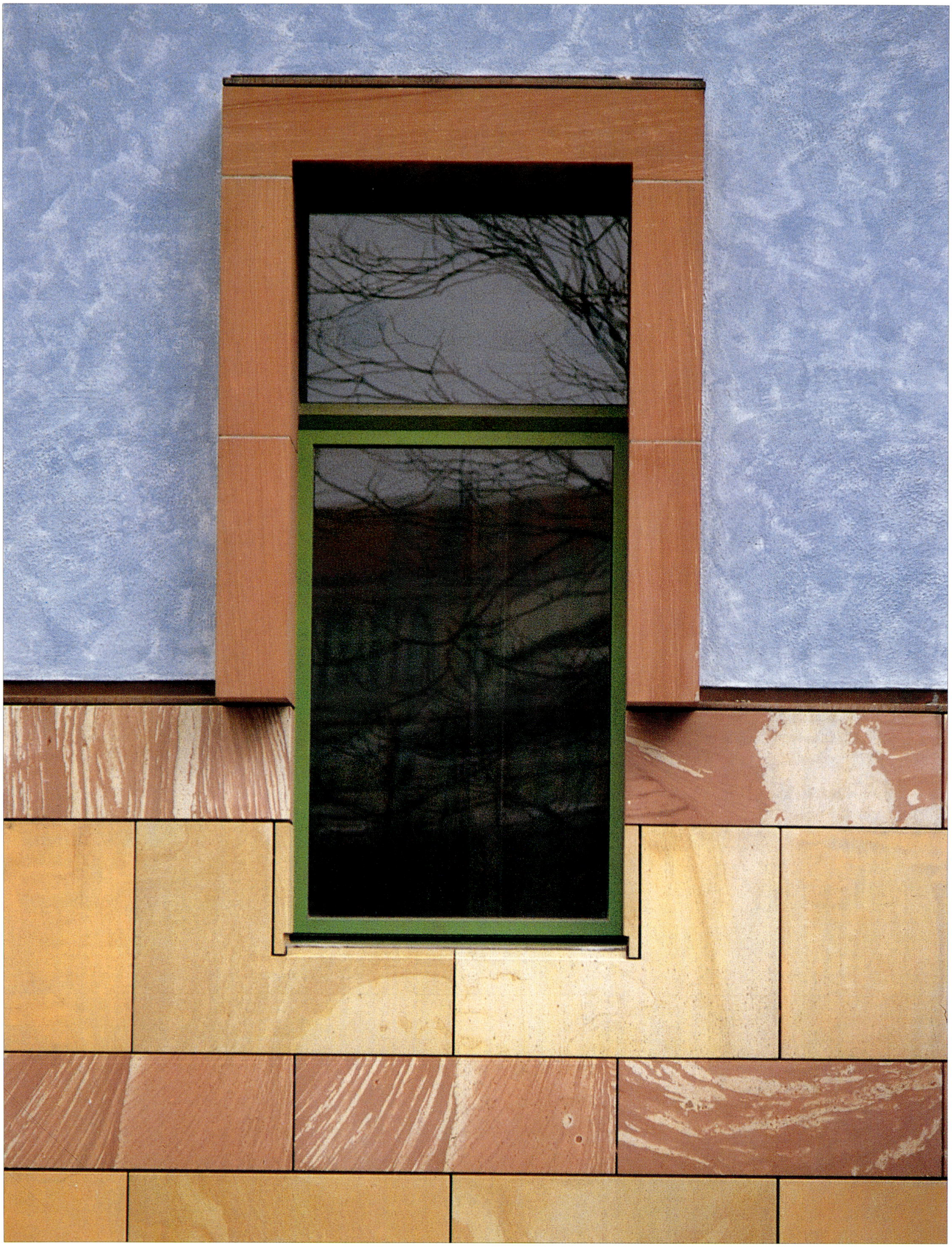

James Stirling

Though widely acknowledged to be the unofficial Dean of British architects, James Stirling has developed a considerable international following, who look forward to each new work with anticipation and delight. He, along with very few others, such as Robert Venturi and Philip Johnson, may be considered a truly transitional figure in architectural history, having not only survived great changes, but also having acted as a pivotal figure in making them happen. While his early projects, such as the Leicester Engineering and Cambridge History Faculty Buildings are virtuoso performances in the form-follows-function genre, and use steel and glass in the best Palm House and Crystal Palace tradition, his highly individualistic approach abruptly changed in 1970. Some may attribute the dramatic reversals evident in the Derby Town Centre Plan of that year to his association with Leon Krier, the contextual sensitivity evident there, as well as in the Dusseldorf Museum Scheme proposed five years later, mark a new phase in his career and in his architectural sensibilities in general. In both cases extreme care was taken to blend each project selflessly into a rather fragile, pre-existing urban fabric in such a way that they seemed an inevitable part of their surroundings, rather than intentionally alien to them. His Neue Staatsgalerie in Stuttgart, which made these intentions a reality, has proven to be extremely popular with the public, showing how far architecture has come in the 30 years since Leicester. As Stirling said in a talk given at Rice University, nearly a decade ago:

'I, for one, welcome the passing of the revolutionary phase of the Modern Movement . . . today we can look back and again regard the whole of architectural history as our background, including, most certainly, the Modern Movement, High-Tech and all the rest. Architects have always looked back in order to move forward, and we should, like painters, musicians and sculptors, be able to include representational as well as abstract elements in our art.'

Formal preoccupations have now changed from form-follows-function Brutalism to a more comfortable classically-based geometry.

OPPOSITE & LEFT: Science Centre, Berlin, Germany.

A DECADE OF ARCHITECTURAL DESIGN

Throughout Stirling's work, there is an appropriateness of massing and adaptation to programmatic relationships that has remained constant.

ABOVE: The Tate Gallery, London, England.
LEFT: Number One Poultry, London, England.

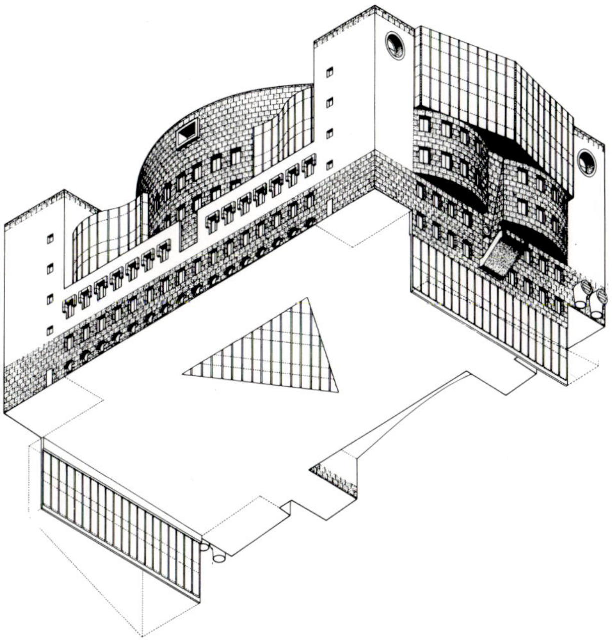

The use of colour and materials have tended to reinforce what the architect has called the 'casual-monumental' character of his latest public buildings.

ABOVE: Staatsgalerie, Stuttgart, Germany.
LEFT: Bracken House, London, England.

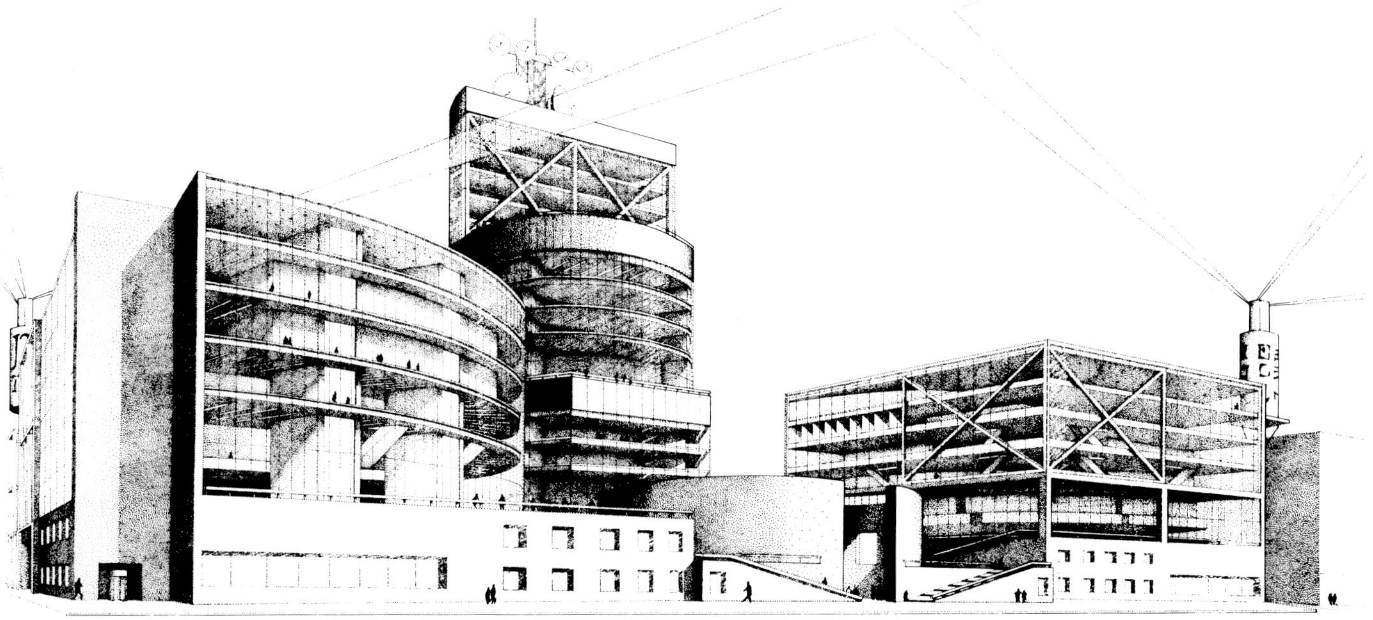

A DECADE OF ARCHITECTURAL DESIGN

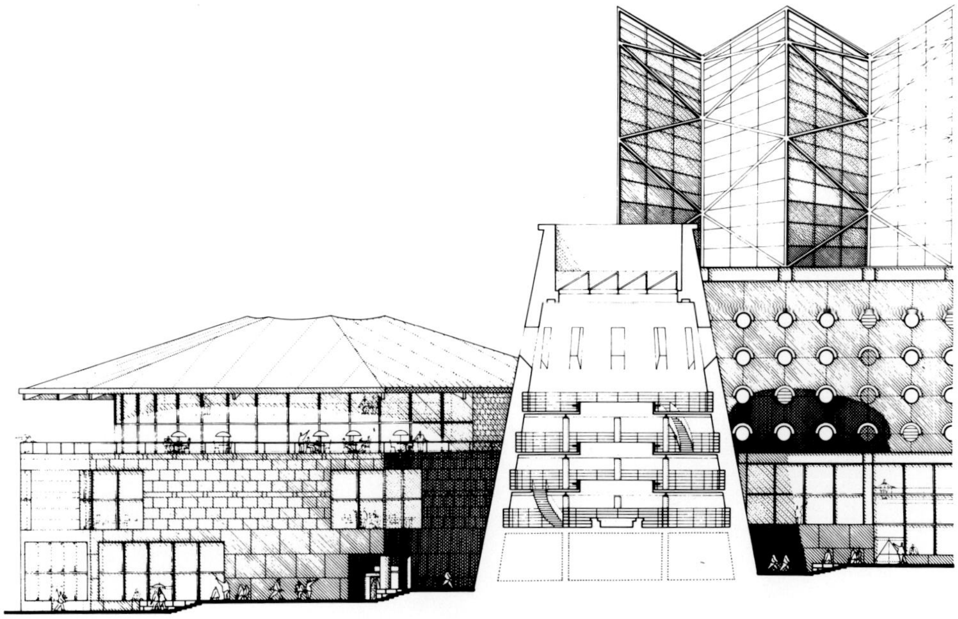

Beginning with the Derby Civic Centre and the Dusseldorf Museum Project, circular forms have continued to predominate to the exclusion of earlier, more aggressive elevations.

OPPOSITE, ABOVE & BELOW: Tokyo International Forum, Tokyo, Japan.
ABOVE & LEFT: Bibliothèque de France, Paris, France.

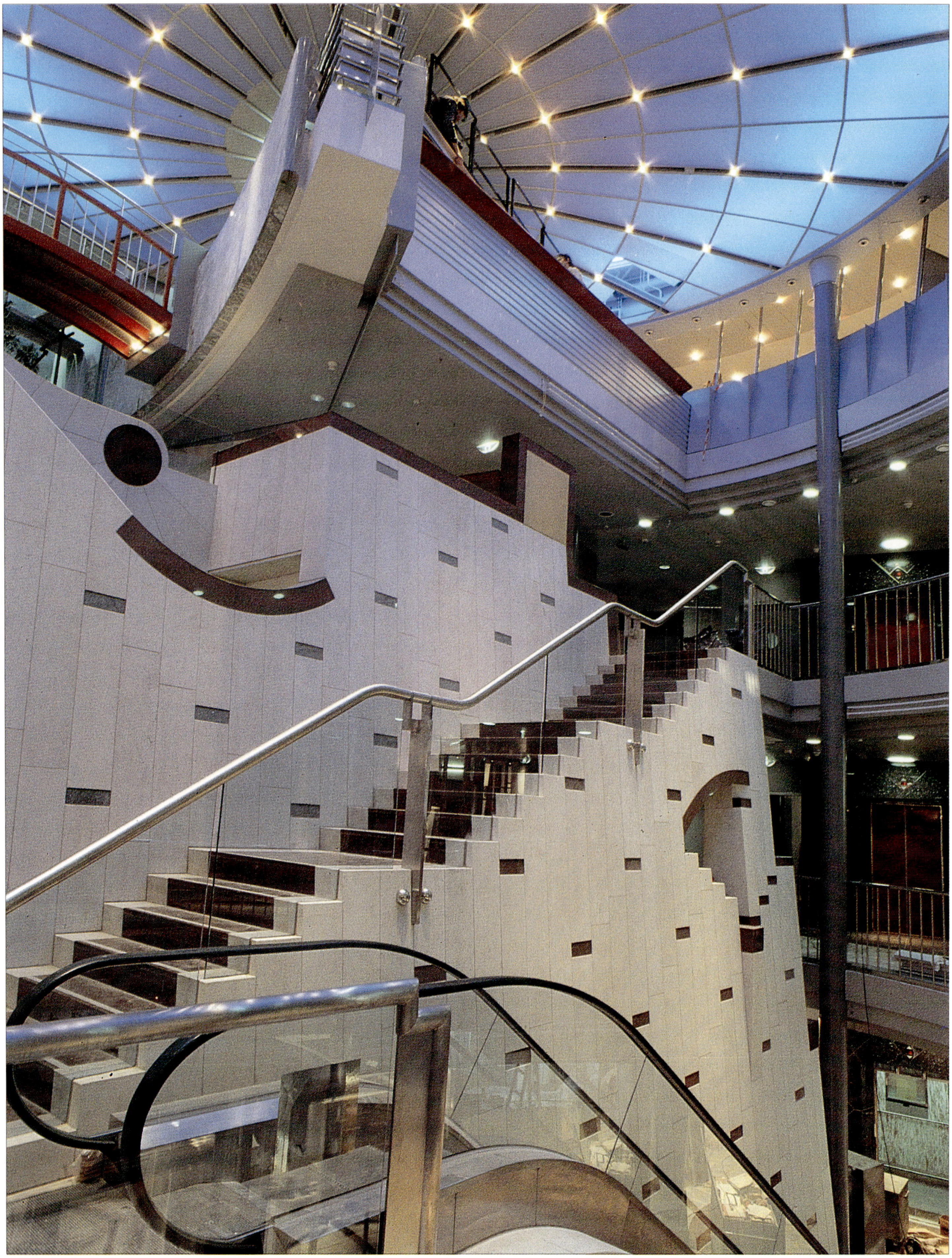

Hans Hollein

The completion of the Mönchengladbach Museum between 1978 and 1982, bridges the beginning of the decade represented here, and is also a bench-mark in the progress of one of its major protagonists. While previously best known for a series of small, exquisitely crafted efforts in Vienna, such as the Retti Candle and Schullin Jewelry Shops and the Austrian Travel Bureau, which were all finished between 1965 and 1978, Hollein had not, until Mönchengladbach, been given such a highly visible opportunity to work on a large scale. There has been a great deal of commentary in the past about what might best be called Hollein's 'Vienneseness', and his place within the tradition of Wagner, Hoffman and Loos as well as the Wiener Werkstätte and the Vienna Secession movement. His precise attention to detail, lapidary skill and uncanny ability to combine incongruous and luxurious materials together, which is most obvious in his commercial designs, would certainly seem to confirm that connection. At Mönchengladbach, however, there is a discernible loss of the distilled aesthetic control that is evident in Hollein's early work. In more recent projects, such as the Compton Verney Opera House that was intended for Shropshire, England, Hollein seems to have finally come to terms with the transference of his earlier sensibilities into a project of larger size. As he himself said in a description submitted as part of that competition:

'This array of buildings has been designed to enter into a dialogue with both the landscape and the existing historical setting around it. Size alone is not necessarily detrimental to integration into a landscape – as has been proven throughout architectural history . . . nor do small scale buildings necessarily blend better into the environment, especially when the basic typology of the building is a large object.'

While Compton Verney was admittedly intended for a rural rather than urban site, this latest design statement indicates Hollein's new awareness of scale.

The concept of the geological geode with it's plain exterior and crystalline centre is as persistent here as it is in that of Charles Moore, but Hollein's use of materials makes the contrast even greater.

OPPOSITE & LEFT: Haas Haus, Vienna, Austria.

A DECADE OF ARCHITECTURAL DESIGN

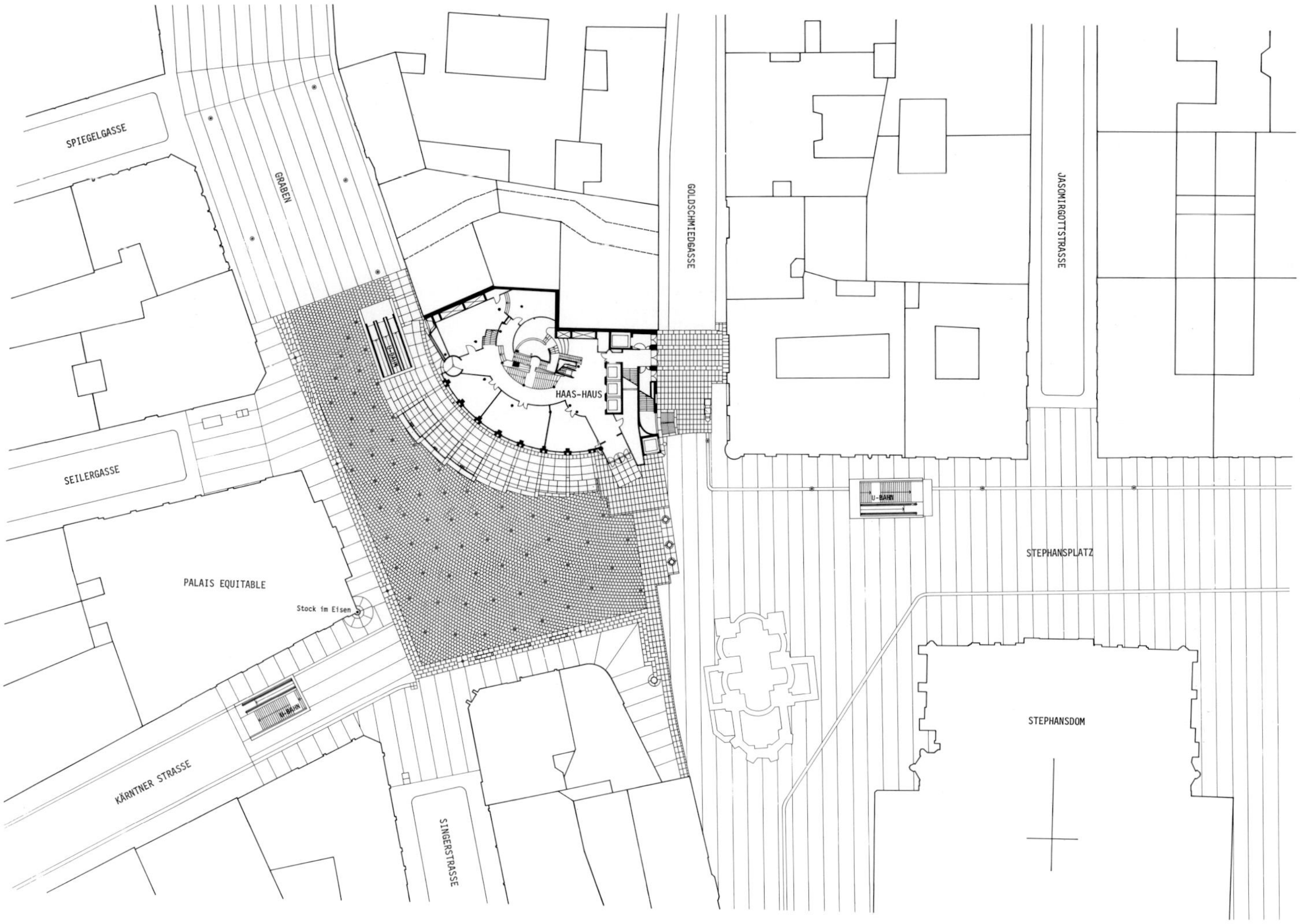

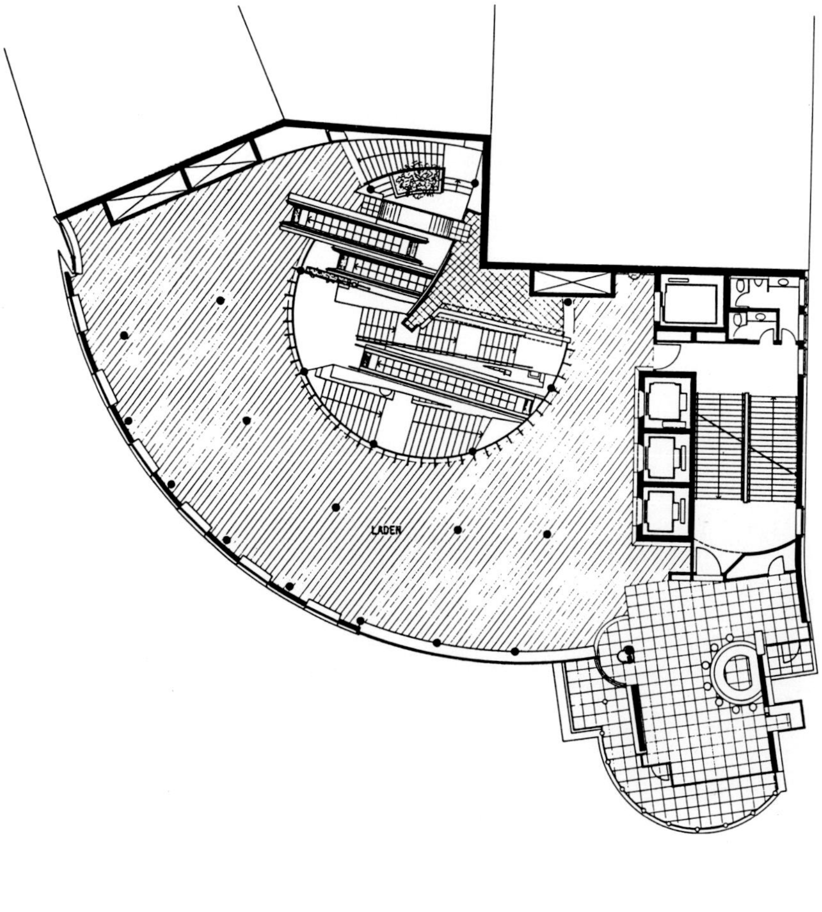

As Hollein has said 'Even if architecture is the creation of the spirit, it is also material. It is not only idea but also form, not only form but also fullness. It is present.'

OPPOSITE, LEFT & ABOVE: Haas Haus, Vienna, Austria.

A DECADE OF ARCHITECTURAL DESIGN

Ricardo Bofill

Over the last ten years, Ricardo Bofill and Taller de Arquitectura have focused their efforts in replacing the lamented urban spaces of the past into a series of highly controversial social housing projects. Beginning with les Temples et Les Arcades du Lac, in St Quentin-en-Yvelines, and carrying on through to Les Echelles du Baroque finished recently near Paris, those efforts have resulted in the use of a vastly overscaled classical idiom, paradoxically rendered in mirrored glass and pre-cast concrete. The common ideological denominator behind these, and six other projects completed in a similar style is to not only demonstrate that it is possible to provide people with 'exalted' surroundings, but also to show that technologically advanced construction methods can be applied just as easily to a classical or vernacular idiom as they can to a Modernist one. The contradiction, here, of course, is the use of historical allusion to achieve socially redemptive and therefore patently Modernist ends. While this contradiction continues to be hotly debated, Bofill's images imply more than the intention to simply glorify suburban life with a grand stage set; or to create a monumental reconstruction of an imperial past. The more substantial issue that he addresses is the appropriate tectonic response to people's aspirations, and to what extent those aspirations coincide with the architectural response being put forward today. Public housing is a particularly sensitive barometer for this issue, since solutions in this sector have not been noted for their popularity in the past. The positive response to Bofill's projects, by the people who actually use them, would indicate that conventional wisdom may benefit from a closer study of his methods.

Rigorous attention to detail in both the manufacture of and additions of colour to precast concrete have made Bofill's use of this material an example of the level of quality that it can achieve.

OPPOSITE: Les Echelles du Baroque, Paris, France.
LEFT: Le Viaduct Housing, Saint-Quentin-en-Yvelines, France.
ABOVE: Palace of Abraxas, Marne-la-Vallée, France.

A DECADE OF ARCHITECTURAL DESIGN

Terry Farrell

In his introduction to an Academy Editions Monograph on his work, Terry Farrell, quoting Isiah Berlin, notes that people can either be characterised as hedgehogs or foxes, with hedgehogs having a fixed game plan throughout life, and foxes surviving by continuous adaptation. Using that classification, Farrell is obviously one of the latter, having been flexible enough to have survived the vicissitudes of a practice that has sought to cater to, rather remain aloof from, the demands of the public. What remains to be seen, however, is if the architect who has been called 'Britain's premier Post-Modernist', can survive the changes in the movement with which he has come to be so closely identified. It is difficult to believe that his TV AM building, for which he is possibly best known internationally, and which has itself become one of the icons of Post-Modernism, is now old enough to have been built at the beginning of this last, turbulent decade. A fresh look at it now, however, serves as a reminder of Farrell's basic pragmatism in dealing with what was essentially a renovation of, and addition to an existing building. That pragmatism is certain to continue to serve him well in the future, for as Colin Amery has said of him: 'It is fair to say that Farrell is one of the very few architects who are popular with the public. I think that this is due to his sharing of their concerns. He is interested in the protection of the urban environment and a development of its contextualism in his new buildings . . . there can be no doubt about his willingness to acknowledge that the public is ahead of the profession.' That willingness is bound to make adaptation possible in the future.

Many of Farrell's projects, such as Midland Bank, Fenchurch Street and Charing Cross Station, are in highly visible urban settings.

OPPOSITE & LEFT: Midland Bank, Fenchurch Street, London, England.

A DECADE OF ARCHITECTURAL DESIGN

TERRY FARRELL

Crisp detailing of stone facing and coping, as well as integral jointing, are characteristic of a designer who has been called an 'architect's architect'.

OPPOSITE, ABOVE: Embankment Place, London, England; BELOW: Comyn Ching, London, England.
ABOVE: Embankment Place, London, England.
BELOW: Lee House, London, England.

A DECADE OF ARCHITECTURAL DESIGN

Charles Vandenhove

While Belgium continues to evoke images of traditional, intricately scaled urban architecture and unspoiled bucolic countryside, it was obviously one of the first European nations to suffer damage in World War II, and has not been spared the negative consequences of the growth that has occurred there since. While other architects, such as the Krier brothers, have been more visible and vocal in their proposals for a remedy to this destruction, Charles Vandenhove has been working quietly in his own way towards the same end.

There may be said to be three distinguishing features to Vandenhove's work. Firstly, he has successfully managed to extend the traditional language of the settings, in which he intervenes by raising the level of workmanship of conventional methods of construction rather than trying to reintroduce the crafts of the past. Through the use of such materials as pre-cast concrete, brick, cast-iron and bronze, rendered in a particularly fine hand, Vandenhove establishes a link with the past through the quality, rather than the authenticity of his details. This attention to precision leads into the second characteristic of his work, which is his invention of ornament, rather than duplication of it, to allow for adaption to contemporary production methods. This invention, as in the work of Charles Moore, also extends to the classical orders, which are revised as this architect feels appropriate, and used in a symbolic rather than conventional way. Thirdly, while Vandenhove sees no problem with using modern building techniques to recreate a traditional language, he resists the use of structure in the Modern sense, as in articulation of a single space. Instead, he uses it as a means by which to establish a continuity with other buildings nearby. In doing so he re-establishes the importance of order not only in a single, isolated instance, but throughout the entire city as well.

There is an ineffably timeless quality to Charles Vandenhove's architecture that makes it appear to be an extension of its surroundings, even though it does not slavishly copy them in style.

OPPOSITE: Zuid Singel project, La Haye, France.
LEFT & ABOVE: Maison de la Danse, Paris, France.

A DECADE OF ARCHITECTURAL DESIGN

Nigel Coates

In a recent radio interview in which his work was introduced as 'London's loss and Japan's gain', Nigel Coates praised the Japanese attitude towards the desirability of impermanence in architecture, as well as their receptivity to new ideas. Like several Western architects before him who have found the Far East to be the perfect catalyst for their own, previously unappreciated expressiveness, Coates has seemed to thrive within the ambiguous atmosphere of Tokyo, where the permanence and solidarity of the past has been replaced by the pragmatics of property developers realistically looking to capitalise on quick turn over. In response to this constant state of flux, Coates has had to become very philosophical about the potential life span of his designs, which he looks upon as 'situations' rather than buildings. As such, they are as temporal as the chance encounters that take place within them, exciting while they last, but haphazard and quickly forgotten. This philosophy of a contemporary 'sensibility' also extends to Coates' attitude towards architecture as an idea rather than an enduring monument, with what he likes to call 'the built phase' as only one brief episode in the life of that idea. Sometimes these ideas provide ironic commentary on temporality such as 'the Wall', which seems an incongruously permanent addition to a constantly changing city. Just because it is so noticeably stable, the Wall quite effectively raises questions of coincidence, and is also a simulacrum, revealing the lie of its presence on the street by its form. Coates has expressed the wish that his work in Japan will ultimately bring him more opportunities to build in Britain. While it undoubtedly will, it will be interesting to see if his ephemeral approach, so appropriate to Japan, will travel well, or will have to be adjusted to the increasingly conservative architectural atmosphere in his homeland.

Reminiscent of the Martian mood of *Total Recall*, Coates' ad-hoc combinations of materials verge on the surreal.

OPPOSITE: Bohemia Jazz Club, Tokyo, Japan.
LEFT: Caffé Bongo, Tokyo, Japan.

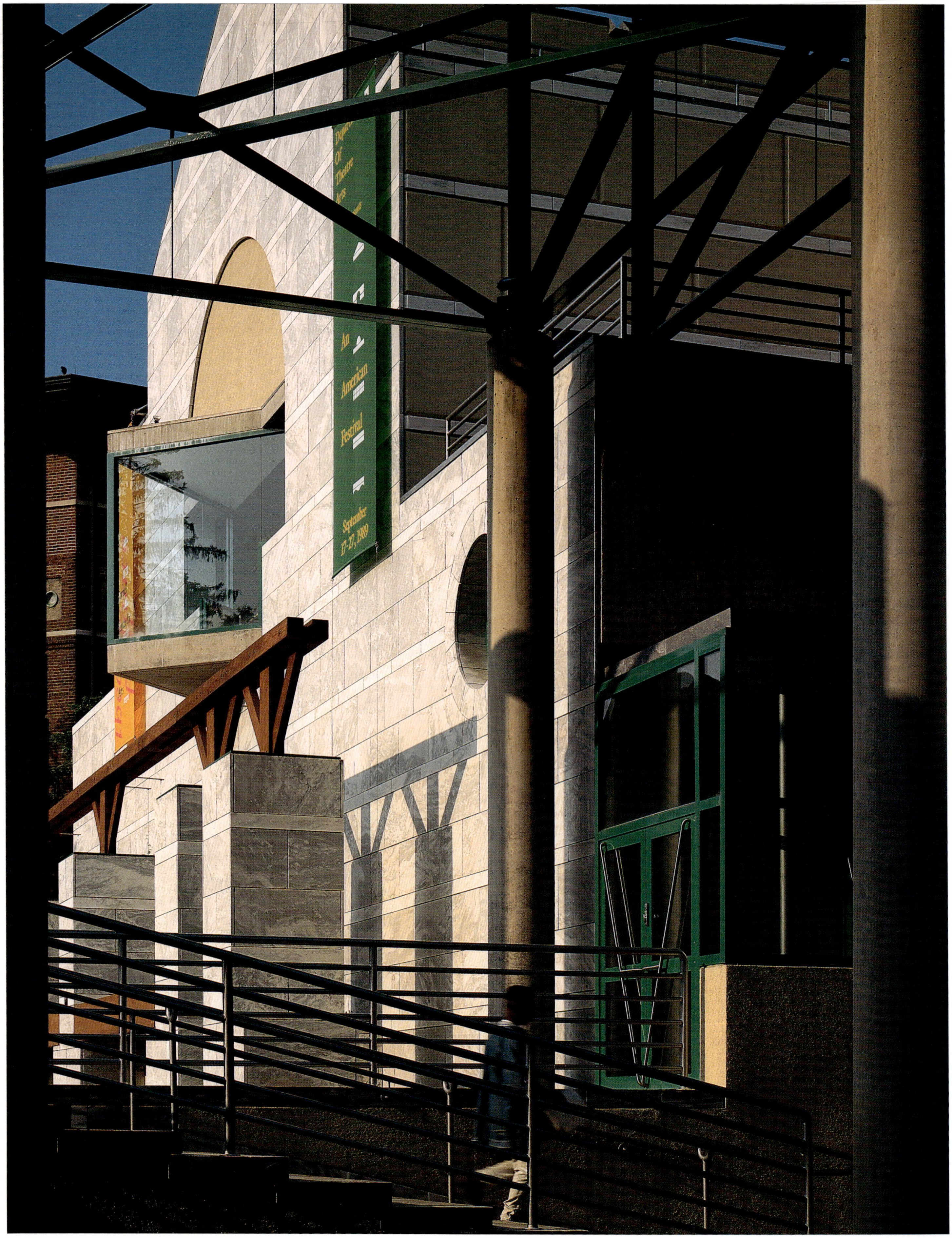

A DECADE OF ARCHITECTURAL DESIGN

Charles Jencks

Ever since Robert Venturi celebrated the notion of contradiction in architecture (1966) the idea of discontinuity has been a conscious tactic of Post-Modernists. Even before this, in the late 1950s, Pop Artists such as Richard Hamilton and Robert Rauschenberg made it a part of their poetics of assemblage and collage. For architects and theorists such as Colin Rowe, collage had the virtues of pluralism, cultural autonomy and all the qualities which might be put in antithesis to minimalism and the Modernist drive towards universalism. An inclusive architecture, it was argued, was better able to deal with social realities than a reduced utopian approach. Modernism and the aesthetics of integration and 'good taste' inevitably led, so the argument went, to the repression of minority cultures. It was crypto-imperialist, or at least smug and middle class, the veiled hegemony of a ruling bureaucratic taste.

Even if this assertion were not entirely true, it had a good deal of statistical evidence behind it: the examples of bureaucratic planning, Park Avenue in New York City and almost any rebuilt downtown area. For artists the position was parallel: the Late-Modern abstraction of Pollock, Rothko and Newman became a kind of aesthetic orthodoxy, upheld by museums and corporate clients, which suppressed the tastes of all but the chosen few. Eero Saarinen's CBS Building in New York, finished in 1965, epitomised both tendencies. Perfectly integrated in its abstract art, simplified architecture and bland furnishings, its good taste was rammed down the throat of every secretary and junior executive. Only the chairman, William Paley, was allowed his personal memorabilia, dark panelled walls and the evidence that he might inhabit Tudor England in suburban Long Island. For the rest it was all colour co-ordination, Knoll International and paintings which might get into MOMA. In case anyone got out of line, or made a mess with a personalised ashtray, battalions of janitors equipped with floor plans and precise aesthetic commands, would march out every night to edit diverse reality and return it to the perfect corporate dream. It was almost aesthetic fascism as everybody knew, including even the editors of *Life* Magazine who ran a story on this corporate control (and soon commissioned a worse version in the same genre). And what finally killed it was not Post-Modern protest, but success and the enormous attendant boredom of this success. Anyone who doubts this is challenged to walk around New York at Sixth Avenue near the Time-Life Building, and keep their pulse above 60.

Anything was better than this *ennui* and one can see why Venturi's *Complexity and Contradiction* was quickly welcomed as a stimulant. Not only was it visually dramatic, it also could handle urban reality in a satisfactory way, accepting the discords and discontinuities of use and taste: for instance the different pressures on the inside and outside of a building, which were invariably suppressed in a Modernist architecture. And yet there was obviously one major problem, which philosophers pointed out: from a contradictory proposition anything can be deduced. When one starts and ends in contradiction there is little at stake and no chance for a coherent architectural language. This problem perhaps explains why Venturi ends his 1966 polemic with the chapter called 'The Obligation Toward the Difficult *Whole*' (my italics): unity must be continually sought amidst the plural languages to give them sense. Otherwise eclecticism degenerates into a trivial and evasive form of collage.

James Stirling, Michael Wilford & Associates, Performing Arts Centre, Cornell University, Ithaca, New York

More recently the French philosopher Jean-François Lyotard has defined 'the Post-Modern condition' (1979) as a kind of perpetual warfare of different language games against each other. Arguing that there are no 'meta-narratives' of religion, politics, social vision or aesthetics that *can* command universal assent today, he pushes the notion of pluralism to an extreme and decides, rather predictably, that this contentious battleground of 'differences' is a good thing and ought to be supported. While one can well agree with his emphasis on tolerance, his 'war on totality' is so obsessive that it leads to a new form of orthodoxy and one which is as oppressive as his enemy the bureaucratic French culture of consensus. Emphasising differences, 'otherness', discontinuity and plural languages, leads finally to a confusing babble; not the competition of language games, but rather their cacophony and mutual cancellation.

It is against such a background that one should see the recent work of James Stirling and Jeremy Dixon – their discontinuous architecture proposed for London – and the paintings of David Salle and Robert Longo, the parallel movement in art. All of this work taken together amounts to a paradigm of discontinuity where one language confronts another, where one theme contradicts another, where cultural pluralism is celebrated as an end in itself. Salle characteristically uses the diptych to set up a dualism of themes that are self-cancelling. Images lifted equally from pulp fiction and high art are juxtaposed, not synthesized, and presented with a studied neutrality. Exotic photographs of the figure are overlaid with graffiti, maps, modern furniture, quotes from Modern art, and all of these contrasts are heightened by the flat, acid colours associated with advertisements. Evidently it's a presentation of the contradictory values purveyed through TV, or any Sunday colour supplement, with no editorial line to supply the meaning, because there isn't any significance in our consumer society. So far so good (or bad, and Salle is on the edge of that tradition valued today as 'Bad Painting'): it's up to the viewer to supply the interpretation and ultimate judgement. Is this a telling indictment of our Faustian predicament, or a cathartic presentation of opposed forces; an allegory about the frustration of consumer nihilism, or an appropriation of its methods? You, the neutral Salle implies, should tell him.

James Stirling has told us, or rather the TV interviewer at the Staatsgalerie in Stuttgart, that he is now interested in the virtues of 'inconsistency', a set of discontinuities generated by contrary urban pressures and internal requirements. His additions, for the Tate Gallery take inconsistency to a new level of poetry. Instead of simply providing a different front, back and sides, as any good urban building celebrated by Venturi might do, Stirling even breaks up these consistent parts into opposed areas. He has called the Clore Gallery extension 'a garden building', hence its symbolic trellis-work and pergola, hence its episodic informality which is almost picturesque. But no garden building, to my knowledge, changes its formal theme seven times and makes those breaks often in the middle or near the side of a façade. Conventionally one changes theme and material in the corner where two planes meet and can be separated by an edge stop. Not Stirling: in nearly every case he has emphasised discontinuity by breaking a theme at an unexpected point. This is true as much in the details as in the larger compositional areas, so one can be sure there is a polemical intention behind the discontinuities. What do they tell us?

First, as Stirling says in descriptions, they relate the relevant parts to adjacent buildings – the cornice and material of the Tate, and the brickwork of the existing lodge and hospital. His 'pergola' relates to the Tate's rusticated base and many building lines, and proportions are also related if not matched. A more literal approach would have produced a more striking incongruity: an unresolvable battle between an Edwardian-Baroque and a brick structure: palace versus house. Instead we find two things which mediate this clash: Stirling's new 'order' of a neutral stone grid and a series of overlapping themes which avoid a clear break, or cataclysmic confrontation.

Both of these tactics are significant contributions to the philosophy of pluralism and the practice of contextualism. They may not be the final word on fitting into a disparate environment, but they begin to formulate a new rule for this most typical of urban problems. Contrast it with the schizophrenic approach of the 19th century – public front/private back, or at St Pancras Station, fantasy hotel/utilitarian shed. Contrast it with Modernist *tabula rasa* or classical integration, which would have papered over the differences between surrounding buildings and denied a valid pluralism. Stirling speaks of 'an architectural conversation' between different parts of the building, and the different buildings, and since at least three sides of his context are speaking different languages, he has plausibly invented a fourth language game – the square stone order – which can speak parts of all three dialects: Baroque classical to the left, brick vernacular to the right and Bauhaus functional in back. The fourth language, like Esperanto, is not yet as conventional as the other three, but it is based on current technologies and plausible, functional analysis. As if to underscore its unconventionality, Stirling has inserted a set of discordant punctuations – particularly the angular bay windows, bright green metal doors and glazing bars. These are even more discontinuous with the surface and adjacent material than the square 'order' is with the adjacent buildings. Finally, in case anyone thinks this discontinuity is accidental, it is underlined by breaking up the 'order' itself into one-to- three bay rhythms on either side of the entrance and by absent stonework just where it is visually expected on the glazed corner. Here brickwork hangs miraculously in tension, emblem of its symbolic, not structural, role. On the inside the square order is repeated again both in its unity and discontinuity, to divide up the wall like a set of pilasters and give proportion and measure to space. The space is a cross between Le Corbusier and Aldo Rossi, the violent triple-height contrast of the one set against the severe serenity of the other. Again colour harmonies at a large scale are penetrated by disharmonies at a small scale, an overall peach and cream is surprised by a pink handrail, or an ultramarine and turquoise archway. Only when we are right inside the Turner galleries do these contrasts and discontinuities calm down, as they should, to a muted contrapunto. The colour and material here is virtually harmonious throughout, with only the doorways and overhead roof lanterns providing accent.

Whether all this juxtaposition and discontinuity make a good gallery remains to be seen, but it does, I believe, make an important contribution to Post-Modern urbanism and is a lesson from which several other designers are learning, if not directly following. Jeremy Dixon's proposal for the Royal Opera House extension is the most eminent successor in this genre. It too changes language three times around four sides of a complex urban site. On the public Covent Garden side where it must complete the square in a desirous way, it adapts the existing Tuscan order and combines it with the typical London grammar of 18th-century stonework. Only

At the corner the square 'order' slides up in a diagonal pattern of brick to meet the brick building to the right. This diagonal avoids a sharp vertical break between the stucco and brick grids. The angular bay windows, somewhat reminiscent of Breuer's usage, break the grid and pergola rhythmn and allow a view out to the Thames.

James Stirling, Michael Wilford and Associates, The Clore Gallery, London, England.

subtle accents are allowed to break this harmony – a row of rectangular voids, based on those of the Uffizi in Florence, which give welcome light to the arcade; a fifth floor loggia which allows the public to survey delights of roof-top London and the square below; and a roof-scape of Post-Modern forms, even the jutting bay window of Stirling (and Breuer). This formula of harmony below the cornice level and *ad hoc* assemblage above is conventional to the Nash terrace as well as extension building in general, but rarely is the duality built from scratch.

In constructing this 'disharmonious harmony' Dixon, like Stirling, is rejecting all models of totalistic planning and imitating the city of memory built over time. In effect he is saying that if we must build 55 million-pound chunks of the environment at one go, then they must look as if many architects constructed them for different, if related, clients. The contrast with the corporate approach, and Foster and Rogers' integrated imagery, could not be greater. Dixon is asserting the image of individualism and autonomy, as in his housing projects, on a reality that is altogether different and in this case as in the others, we can applaud him for the 'lie'.

Of course it's not a complete untruth, there are different functions behind these discontinuous forms and he has sought an appropriate language for each requirement. But just as he favoured urbanistic reality over internal representation at St Marks Road in London, he has made this choice here. Thus many large interior spaces are suppressed on the outside – the shopping mall and side entrance to the grand foyer and staircase – while small-scale shops and offices are represented. These relate to the adjacent fabric in a figurative rather than literal way, just as Stirling related to his context the Tate. On the Russell Street side the language changes abruptly from white stone classicism to a plainer Post-Modern Classicism with a thin layer of cut-out circles, truncated pediments and flat cornice.

There's a virtual knife-cut between these two systems, a discontinuity which is exaggerated by the window rhythms and change of order. And this façade is peeled back at various stages to show its shallow depth and existence as urban representation, precisely to emphasise its symbolic and visual role. The reason for this is not hard to find, for if Dixon had built a regular façade up to the corners and at full height it would have been oppressive in such a small street.

The episodic skin of Russell Street then ends in what is called a 'circular tower', but tower is precisely what it is not: the ribbon windows which spin out of sync exaggerate the horizontal movement, and the overall mass is squat, not vertical. The intention is to relate this curved shape with the turret opposite and had this been done it would have formed a very successful gateway to the square. Here is one case where the strategy of discontinuous urbanism might have been used to more effect, and the choice of a *moderne* treatment seems wilfully off. From here up Bow Street and towards the Opera House the language changes twice more while it also bends to fit into the existing street pattern. Again the basic grammar is a thin skin of Post-Modern Classicism which is eroded and pulled back at various points to reveal a larger mass in back.

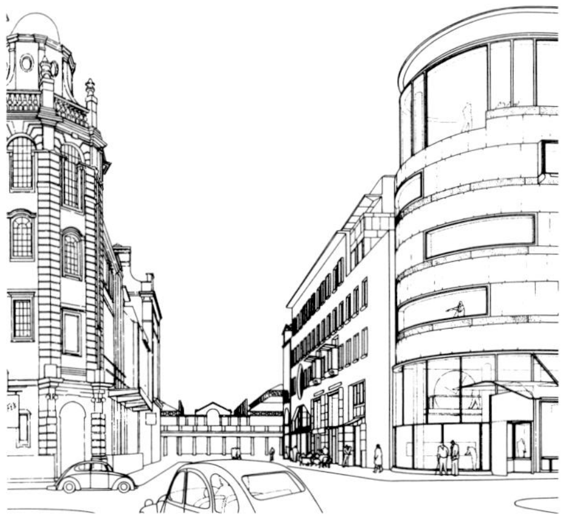

With all these different façades we find a similar conceptual treatment; a formal treatment of classical shapes set below an informal skyline which suggests the corporate mass of the project. In effect Dixon is favouring the illusion of small-scale shops and individual ownership over the reality of a single institutional client. By breaking up his façades into five discontinuous themes he gives them not only an urbane coherence – impossible in an integrated aesthetic at this scale – but a symphonic quality. We can read this score in either direction and still come up with a symphonic ordering, the sonata allegro form, which has a climactic finale at both ends. This musical analogy, which has developed from Stirling's scheme for the Meineke Strasse, Berlin, 1976 – introduction of the theme, exposition, development, recapitulation and coda – has become one of the strongest paradigms of current urbanism. Its virtues are no doubt superior to the totalising model which still prevails in Late-Modernist circles, but like all paradigms it has obvious limits. Discontinuity and fragmentation without an ordering principle and final goal create their own kind of totality, their own style of boredom, every bit as predictable as *La Ville Radieuse*. Evidently all these strategies of collage need a complementary hierarchy and ordering system to be fully effective. And here we can note a lacuna in both Stirling's Tate and Dixon's Opera House scheme: there is no symbolic and ornamental progression to a climax, no clear iconographic programme, no developed centre and sense of climactic arrival. It is true the double-spiral stair and opera auditorium are two centres and climaxes to Dixon's scheme, but they still lack an ornamental and symbolic progression that prepares for them.

This problem characterises, of course, all architecture today and is not an inherent fault of the collage strategy although it may be accentuated by this method. Where one uses many styles and motifs, there is a danger of these languages taking over the plot. 'Intertextuality', the cliché of Post-Modern literature, shows that where there are too many texts there is no author, In architecture of any size the client and architect must work out the plot together, and be quite explicit about this, or the story will degenerate into a collage of professional language games, that implicit war which Jean-François Lyotard asserts is the condition of Post-Modernism. The plausibility of his arguments rests in the idea that no one, and no ideology or religion, has any great authority in our time; a likely truth. And yet the consequences of this need not be an art and architecture of frustration, of mutually incompatible and self-cancelling acts, because there is still a great deal of shared interest and values between different people and taste-cultures. The challenge is to find this area and give it artistic and symbolic expression.

We are thus left with the conclusion that discontinuity is a legitimate, if limited, strategy for art and architecture in a pluralist age, one that expresses our 'contradictions' and 'inconsistencies', as Venturi and Stirling insist. But it is a necessarily incomplete method until it is supplemented by a symbolic programme or some unifying plot.

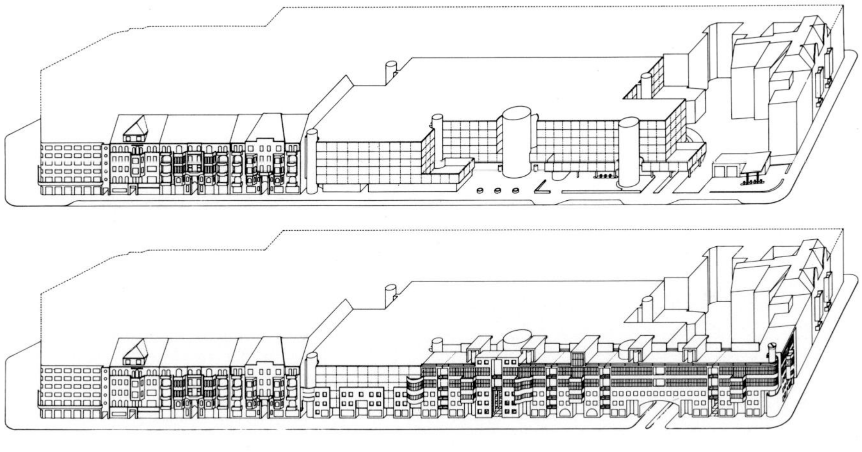

OPPOSITE: The extension changes language at the corner of Russell Street. The arcade is dropped and a thin skin of Post-Modern Classicism is layered over the shop fronts to give an informality similar to that across the street; the office entrance in the curved 'tower' does not provide a sufficient answer to the vertical turret across the street and thus misses the opportunity to create a true gateway to the square beyond. But it does, positively, 'spire' the corner and pick up the horizontal window lines.
LEFT: A thin, changing language of form is wrapped around an existing garage to stitch the environment together. Note the sonata-allegro form and the literal 'hinge' on the corner, a forerunner of current corner turrets.

OPPOSITE: Jeremy Dixon, Royal Opera House Extension, London, England.
LEFT: James Stirling, Meinecke Strasse Project, Berlin, Germany.

A DECADE OF ARCHITECTURAL DESIGN

Japanese Post-Modernism

Kisho Kurokawa and Arata Isozaki, both of whom studied under Kenzo Tange, who was the leader of the preceding generation of Japanese architects, are two of the most visable designers presented here.

Placing maximum emphasis on the urban problems in Modern Architecture, Kurokawa was the most radical of the Metabolists in dealing with systems of growth and change. Recently, revealing a different approach, he has begun using terminology traditional to Japanese culture to interpret his architecture using symbolism to extend it. As he has described this interpretation in *Intercultural Architecture – The Philosophy of Symbiosis*:

'Mood, feeling and atmosphere can each be described as a symbolic order without an established structure. It is through a variety of dynamic, intersecting relationships and juxtapositions – the relationship between one sign and other symbolic elements with which it stands; the way the content of the sign changes when it is quoted; the existence of a medium, an intermediating space introduced between different elements; the relation of the parts to the whole – that mood, feeling and atmosphere are created. In architecture, the meaning produced by the individual elements placed here and there, and by their relationships and disjunctions, is multivalent and ambiguous. When this meaning creates a feeling and an atmosphere, architecture can approach poetic creation.'

Arata Isozaki is also one of the most important architects in Japan today. His Tsucuba Civic Center is one of his most memorable projects, and shows the extent to which he is now borrowing from other sources, which there include Michaelangelo's Campidoglio, Michael Graves, Charles Moore and Robert Venturi, to mention just a few. In more recent projects, such as his Museum of Contemporary Art in Los Angeles, his preoccupation with forms such as the cube and arch continue, and his recent involvement in Computer-Aided-Design is extended.

Kazuo Shinohara, like many architects in Japan today, has been reacting to the urban chaos of Tokyo, which, as he has noted; is the complete antithesis of the Western concept of what a city should be. While he does not promote this chaos; he accepts it, calling it 'progressive anarchy': In his Centennial Hall, in Tokyo; he responds to this anarchy by transcending it entirely, in the creation of what he says are 'the conditions of space that will characterise architecture and cities in the future.'

Hiroshi Hara has responded to this same question of urban anarchy through the creation of man-made landscapes. In these, he has not only addressed the issue of what place such architecture should have in the city, but also the role of metaphor, and especially environmental, or natural metaphor in that architecture. His Yamoto International Building in Tokyo is the most startling of these, creating a metaphor of mountains, sky and sea.

Shin Takamatsu, on the other hand, creates sci-fi, space-age machines that are diametrically opposite to environmental metaphor. In this machine aesthetic, there is also a hint of what Hajimi Yatsuka has identified as 'symbolic Japanese ritualism', once more showing the conflicting influences of past, present and future that characterise this recent work.

The Primary recognition of formalism, which has always been such a substantial part of traditional Japanese architecture, is a connecting thread that runs through the work of all of these designs.

Kisho Kurokawa, Hiroshima City Museum of Contemporary Art, Hiroshima, Japan.

A DECADE OF ARCHITECTURAL DESIGN

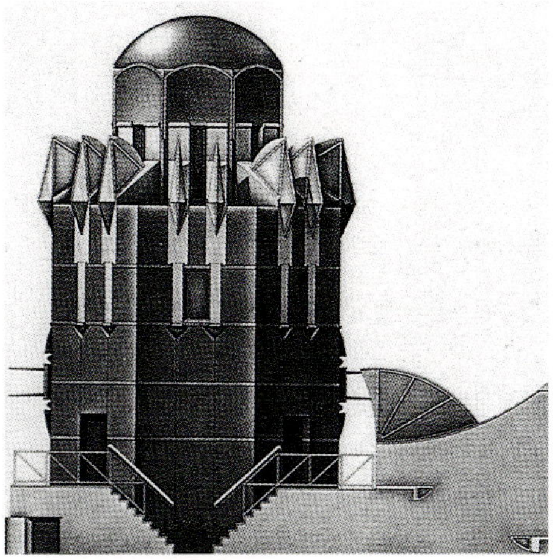

JAPANESE POST-MODERNISM

The appropriate response to be made to the urban growth that has overtaken Japan, just as it has every other industrialised country, can be seen to be different in each of its interpretations.

OPPOSITE: Arata Isozaki, The City Council Chamber Building, Phoenix, Arizona.
LEFT ABOVE: Kazuo Shinohara, TIT Centennial Hall, Tokyo, Japan; CENTRE: Hiroshi Hara, Yamato International Building, Tokyo, Japan; BELOW: Shin Takamatsu, Week Building, Kyoto, Japan.
ABOVE: Shin Takamatsu, Origin III, Kyoto, Japan.

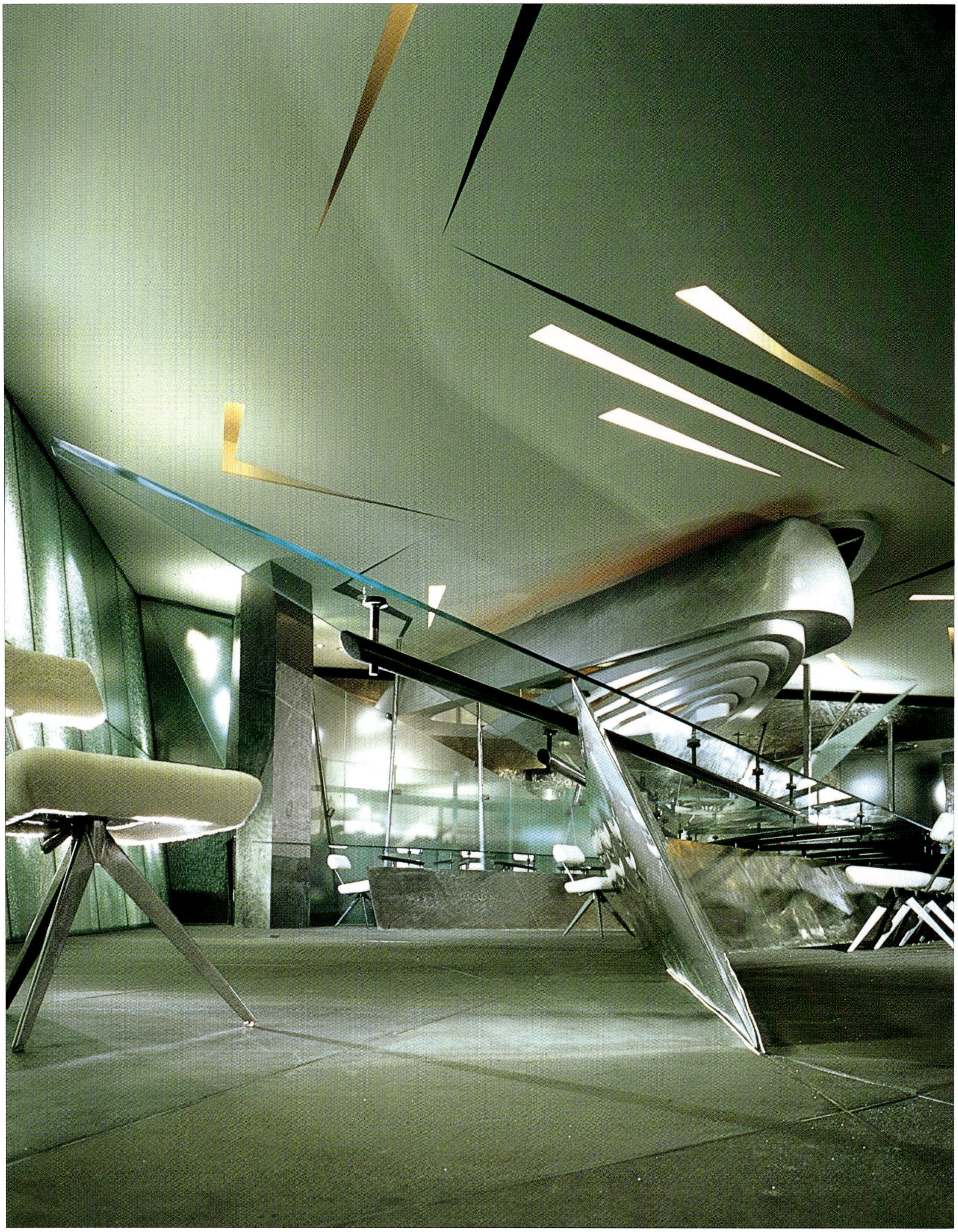

The New Moderns

Andreas Papadakis: Deconstruction and Architecture

Few ideas in architecture have, in a relatively short time, created such a stir as Deconstruction. Even Jacques Derrida, the definer of Deconstruction, was surprised at the alacrity with which Deconstructive thinking, previously the reserve of philosophy and literary criticism, has been applied to a number of different fields. Thanks to the efforts of theoretically-minded architects such as Bernard Tschumi and Peter Eisenman, a connection with architectural theory has been made.

Deconstruction addresses notions in thinking. It operates by suspending correspondence between binary oppositions. According to Eisenman, architecture 'must move away from the rigidity and value structure of the dialectic oppositions. For example the traditional opposition between structure and decoration, abstraction and figuration, figure and background. Architecture could begin an exploration of the "between" within these categories.' Deconstruction creates a disturbance at the signifier's level, employing the strategy of *différance* (a word-play upon the verbs 'to differ' and 'to defer') whereby meaning differs and is deferred from an expected definition. It might appear that Deconstruction defers and even evades a definition of itself. It will not set down strict parameters but constantly questions and examines through a *critique* of dislocated meaning. Architects have thus appropriated the methods of Deconstruction in order to call into question concepts of housing. Bernard Tschumi thinks that Deconstruction is 'not only the analysis of concepts in their most rigorous and internalised manner, but also their analysis from without, to question what these concepts and their history hide, as repression or dissimulation.'

Deconstructivist theories owe a great debt to the early 20th-century Russian Constructivists. 1988, however, was a milestone for the movement in architecture; it began with the Academy Forum at London's Tate Gallery and a coinciding special edition of *Architectural Design*, and was later followed up by the Deconstructivist Architecture exhibition at New York's Museum of Modern Art, which gave rise to controversial debates concerning both the selection of work and the term 'Deconstructivist' itself.

The application of Deconstruction in the visual arts has led to a reassessment of value structures. In Valerio Adami's work, for example, the *critique* lies in a highly conscious juxtaposition of visual and textual elements. Deconstructionist art stimulates the viewer to take part in the analysis of the 'between' and explores – as does the work of Anselm Kiefer – the possibilities of the frame. Additionally, Jacques Derrida has explored the importance of this concept in the *The Truth in Painting*.

Deconstruction, in architecture and the visual arts is in its early stages but the imagery is fresh and appealing. Derrida has pointed out when discussing architecture with Christopher Norris: 'you can't (or you shouldn't) simply dismiss those values of dwelling, functionality, beauty and so on. You have to construct, so to speak, a new space and a new form, to shape a new way of building in which these motifs of values are reinscribed, having meanwhile lost their external hegemony.'

Deconstruction does not simply demarcate a framework. Its critique is continual. Above all, Deconstruction is an activity, an open-ended practice, rather than a method convinced of its own correct reasoning.

Zaha Hadid, Moonsoon Restaurant, Tokyo, Japan.

A DECADE OF ARCHITECTURAL DESIGN

Peter Eisenman

To an incomparable extent Peter Eisenman has been able to objectively construct a quite accurate theoretical model of the Modernist dilemma, in his work. The key to this dilemma as described by Marshall Berman in his currently fashionable book *All That Is Solid Melts Into Air*, is that in the post-industrial age, to be modern is to be equally confronted with unprecedented opportunities and unparalleled destruction. Each of these are part of what Berman calls 'the maelstrom of perpetual disintegration and renewal, of struggle and contradiction, of ambiguity and anguish' that characterises our time. In Eisenman's construct, a clear distinction is made between the need to reflect the nature of what he has referred to as 'the modernist sensibility', and the functionalist doctrine of Modernism itself, which he considers to be a throwback to the humanism of the pre-industrial period. In choosing instead to express a true modern aesthetic in which humanism has been replaced by the objects that have become the central focus of a consumer society, Eisenman has developed a 'decentered' architecture that totally negates function, as well as its direct formal expression. Where his earlier numeralised houses – I through to X – were based on a syntax of structure that was evident by absence as well as presence, he has recently shifted to the use of forms which, unlike Platonic solids, have no easily defined centre, and thus fit well into his 'post-functionalist' posture. Now that the opportunity to design larger, non-residential projects has opened up a new phase in his career it will be interesting to see to what extent that position remains intact. For the moment a passage from Dostoyevsky's *Underground Man*, which is also quoted by Berman as an example of the Modernist dilemma, seems particularly appropriate to Eisenman and the work he has done recently:

'Man loves to create . . . that is beyond dispute. But . . . may it not be that . . . he is instinctively afraid of attaining his goal and completing the edifice he is constructing? How do you know, perhaps he only likes that edifice from a distance and not at close range, perhaps he only likes to build it, and does not want to live in it . . .'

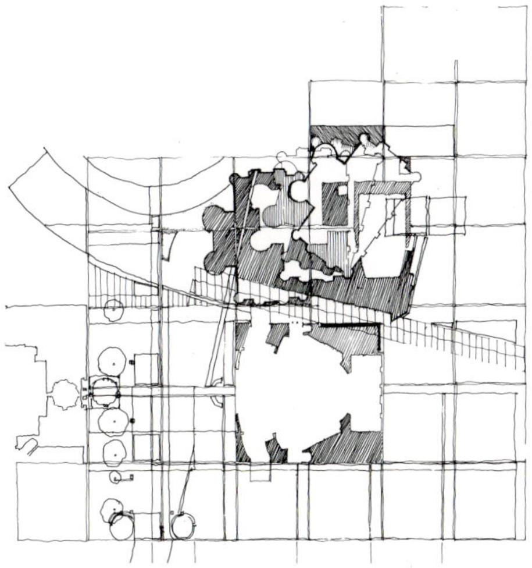

In each of his most recent projects, Peter Eisenman clearly shows the 'in-betweeness' and 'decentering' that now guide his work, as well as his struggle to retain his post-functionalist stance in larger, public commissions.

OPPOSITE, LEFT, ABOVE & OVERLEAF: The Wexner Center for the Visual Arts, Columbus, Ohio.

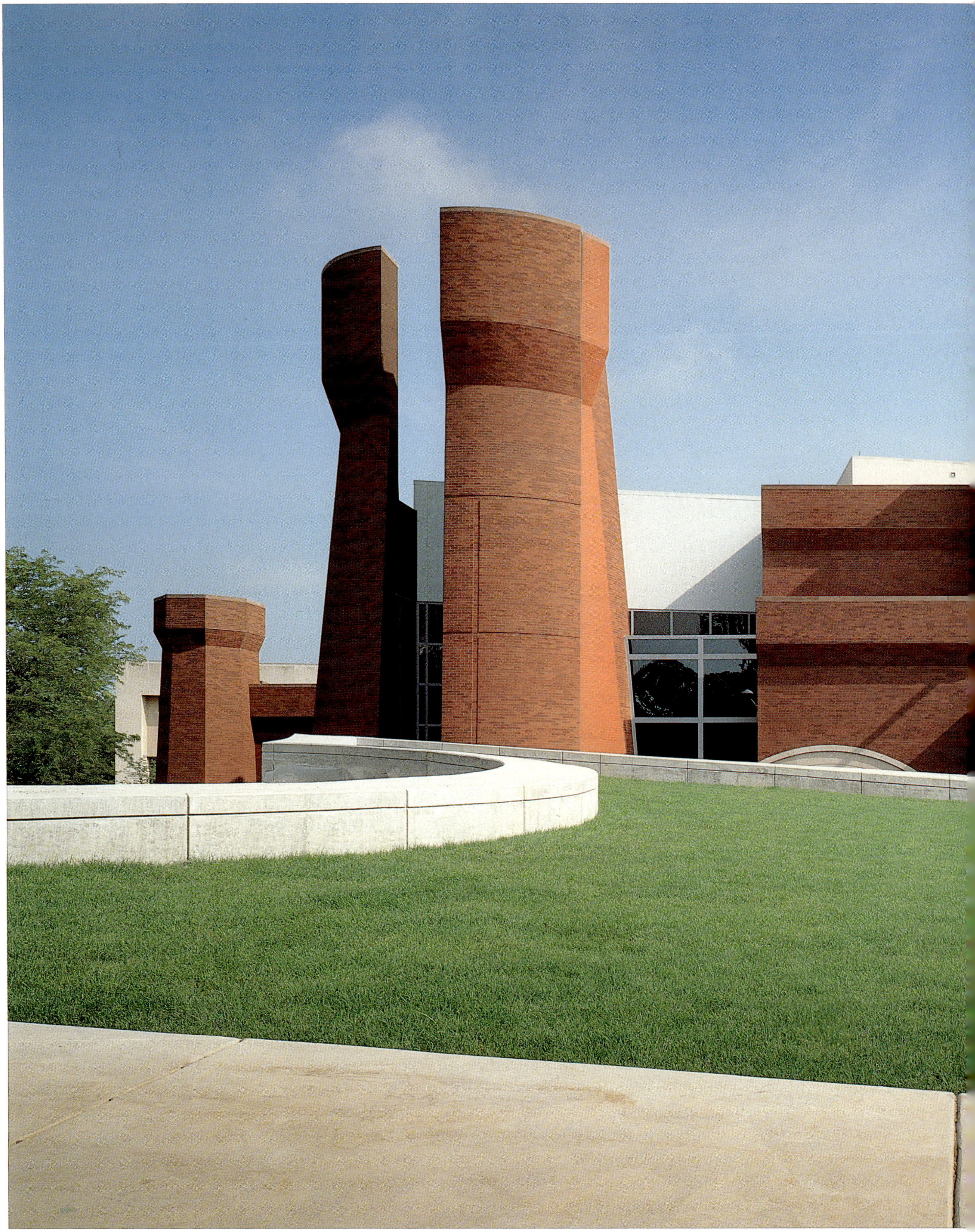

PETER EISENMAN

A DECADE OF ARCHITECTURAL DESIGN

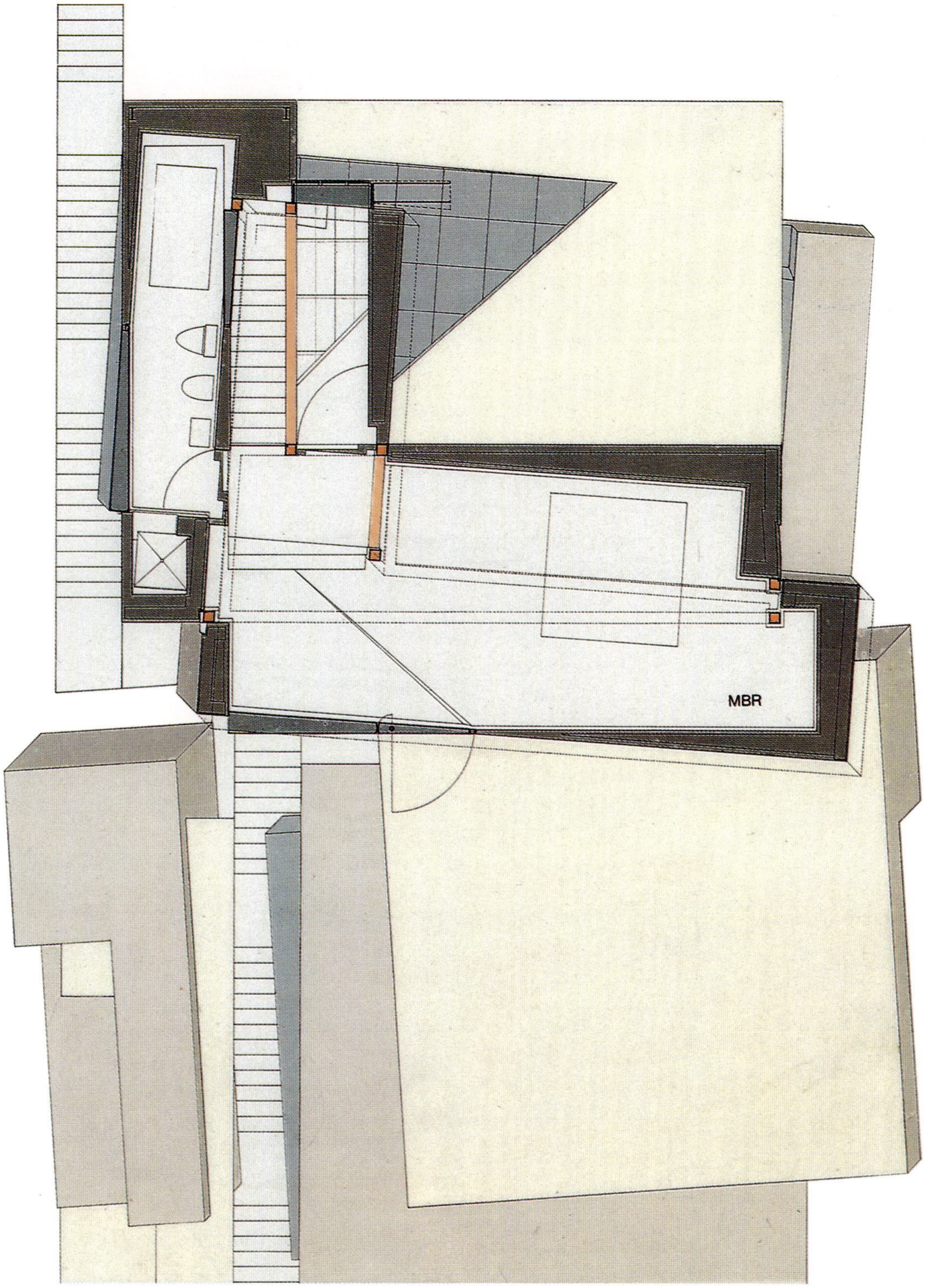

PETER EISENMAN

While others may utilise the grid as a mercator, in order to position their buildings in time and space, it is symbolic here of the displacement that has characterised contemporary life.

OPPOSITE: Social Housing, Kochstrasse, IBA, Berlin.
ABOVE: Guardiola House, Santa Maria del Mar.

173

A DECADE OF ARCHITECTURAL DESIGN

Zaha Hadid

In his brief introduction to the catalogue of an exhibition of Zaha Hadid's work held in the GA Gallery in Tokyo, Arata Izozaki makes mention of his central role in selecting her scheme for the Peak in Hong Kong, which first brought her to world attention in 1983. After providing a fascinating insight into the machinations of a major international design competition, Izozaki says that he personally advocated her approach because of 'the uniqueness of its expression and the strength of its logic.' That strength, in his view, was directly related to what he calls 'a Suprematist composition' indicating his awareness of that tradition, and its impact upon the jury. In closing his introduction, Izozaki provides a concise summary of that style in relation to Hadid's Peak presentation, and in doing so gives an essential clue to her general architectural approach in the five years since it was written. Of Suprematism he says that 'the laws of deployment of the style itself violated and deconstructed the actual architectural programme. In other words, unlike past methods of architectural composition that abstracted certain demands, it involves giving oneself up to the forces inherent in the style itself resulting in the creation of a different type of arrangement that is without parallel.'

The forces that Izozaki refers to were considered by Kazimir Malevich, who developed Suprematism, to involve a metaphysical exploration of an uncharted fourth dimension, hopefully leading to the graphic representation of what was discovered there in what he called 'a semaphore of colour.' That representation often resulted in a series of planes shown as floating, without finite restriction.

For Zaha Hadid, Suprematism has provided the perfect outlet for her use of representation as a design device, allowing her to explore form without the restrictions of gravity, which is the architects' oldest enemy. The results have not only been graphically breathtaking, but also refreshingly free of the functionalist baggage of the past. When finally subjected to the inexorable restraints of gravity itself, those forms are bound to continue to reflect their free beginnings.

Perspectives are chosen that exaggerate the size as well as the feeling of power created by the building.

OPPOSITE; IBA Housing, Berlin, Germany.
LEFT: The Peak Club, Hong Kong.
ABOVE & OVERLEAF: Kurfürstendamm 70, Berlin.

A DECADE OF ARCHITECTURAL DESIGN

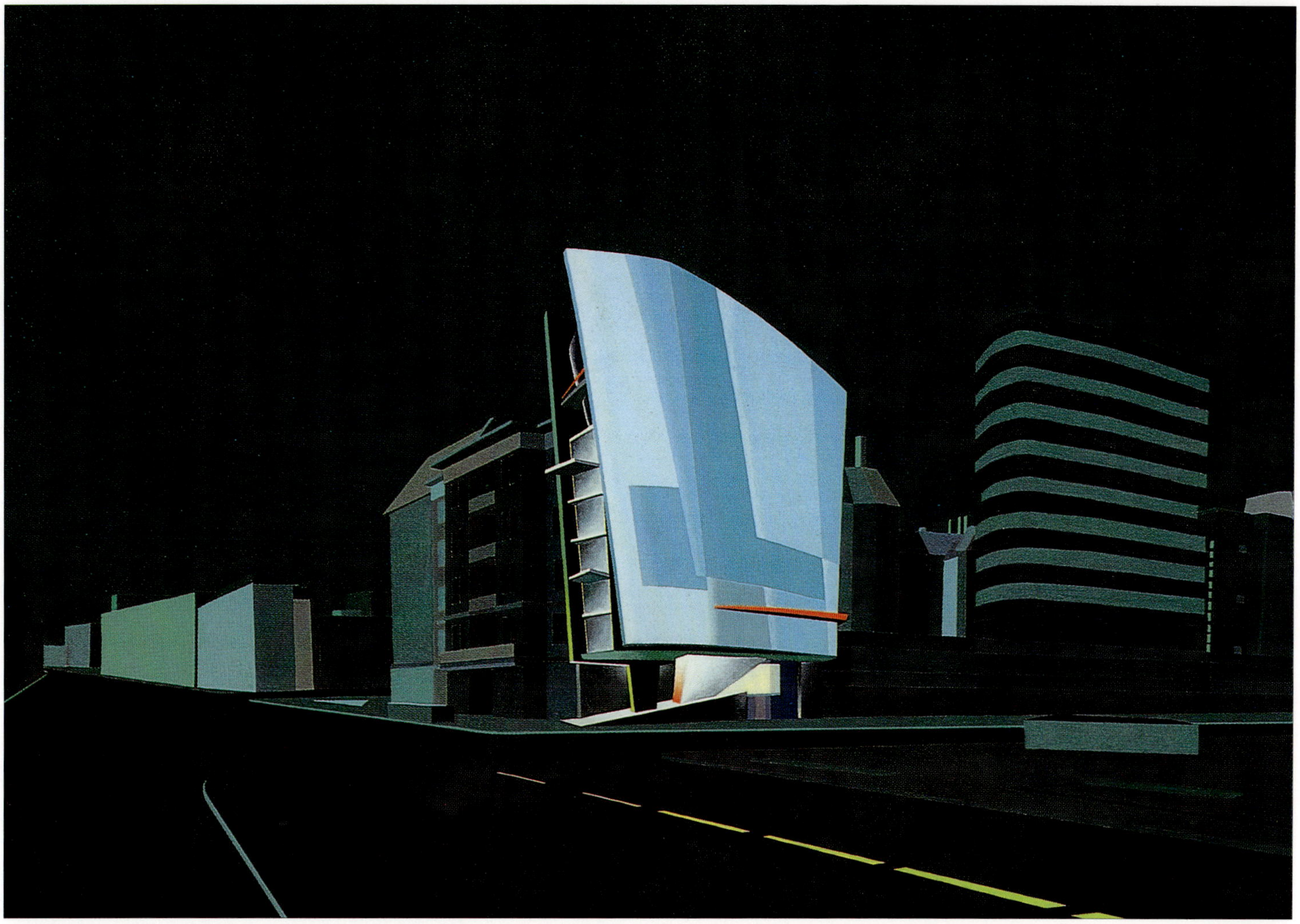

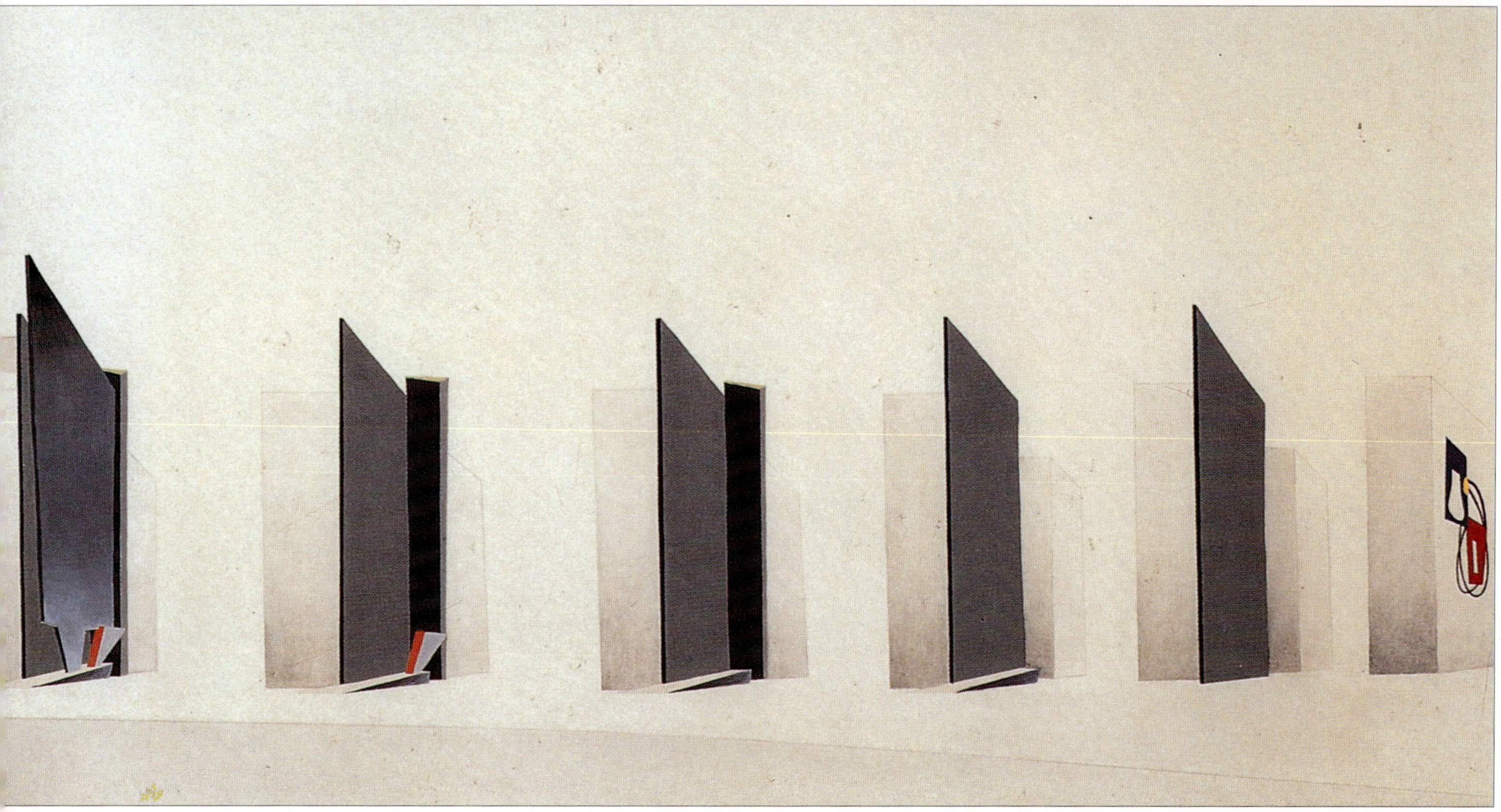

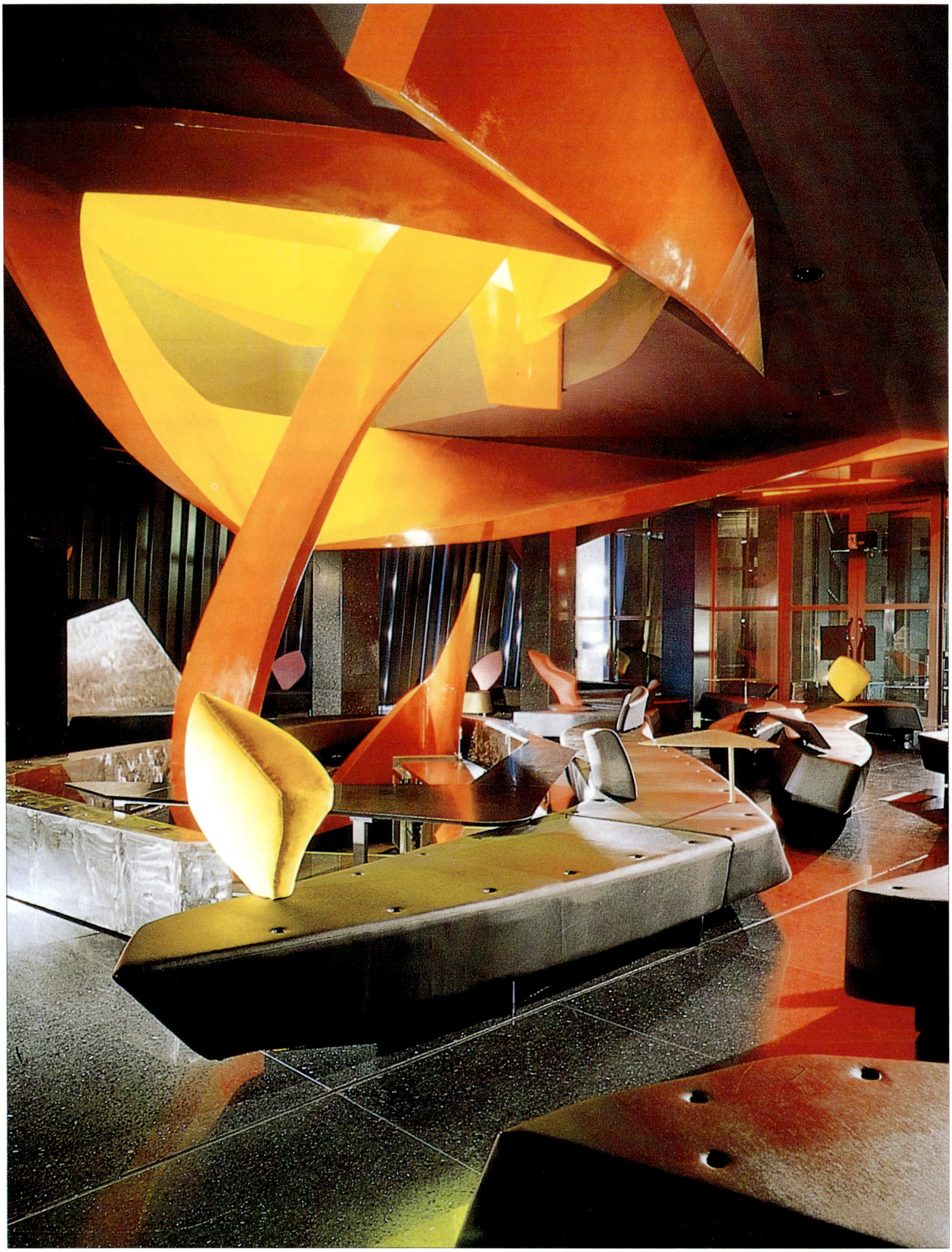

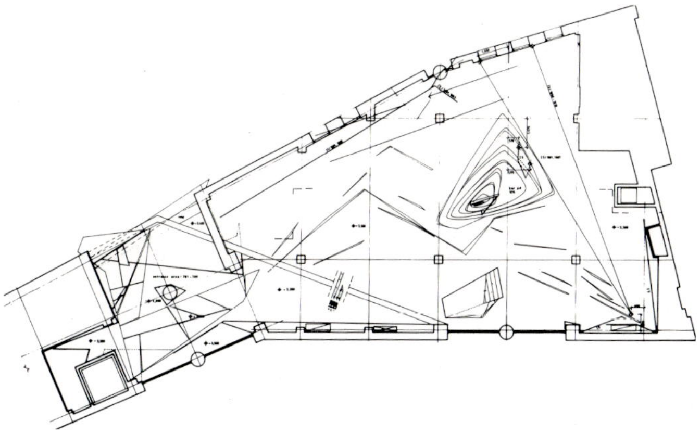

Small scale reproductions, no matter how high in quality, are only a pale shadow of the vivid colour and breathtaking size used in an original painting.

OPPOSITE, LEFT & ABOVE: Moonsoon Restaurant, Tokyo, Japan.

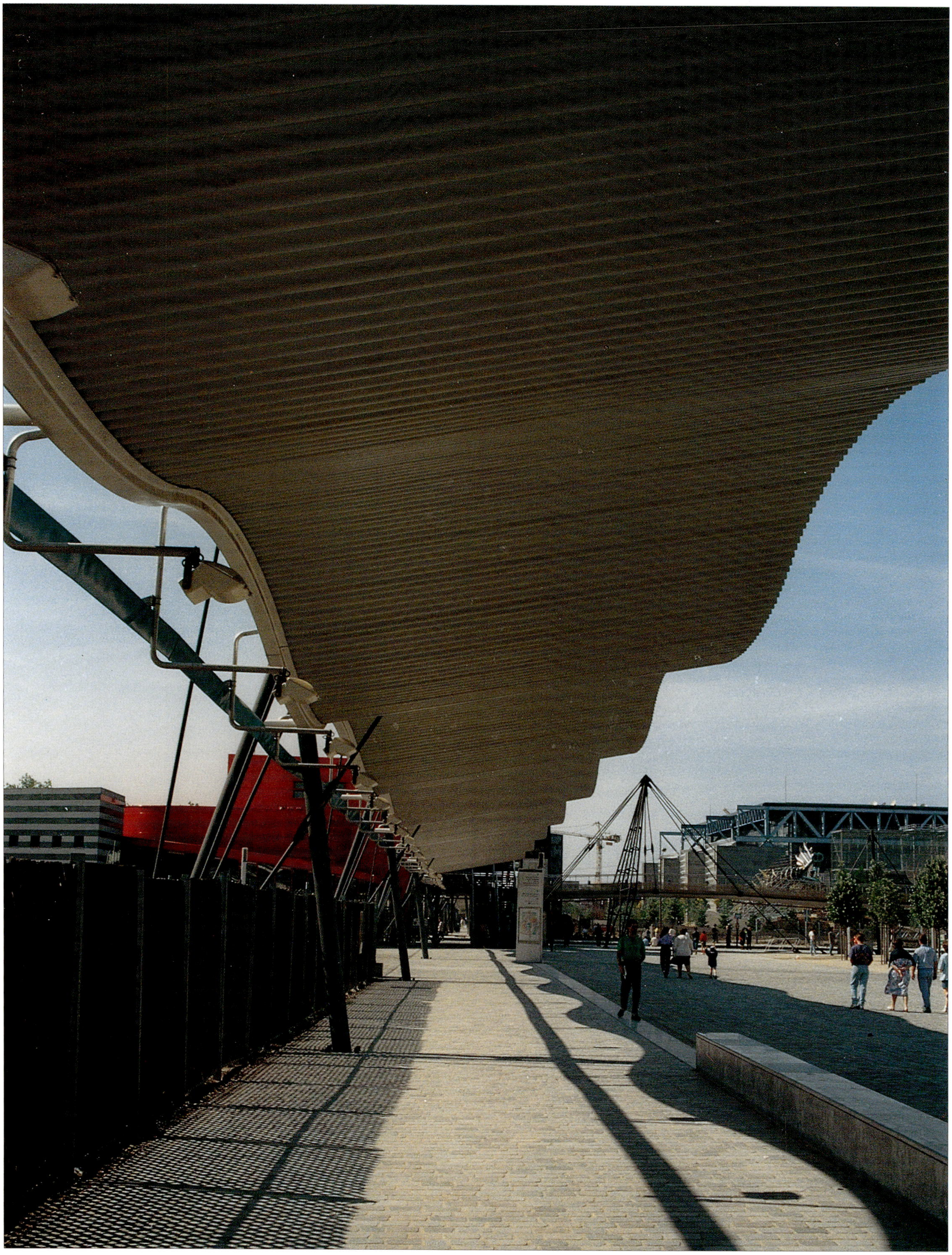

Bernard Tschumi

As one of the first to have explored the use of the disassociative techniques of deconstruction as a bridge between literature and architecture in his *Joyce's Garden* and *Manhattan Transcripts* projects more than ten years ago, and in the actual building of Parc de La Villette, Bernard Tschumi has obviously played a formative role in the establishment of Deconstruction as a distinct theoretical position today. As implemented at La Villette, and in subsequent projects such as his Glass Video Gallery in Groningen, this theory has three distinct parts. These are: the rejection of synthesis in favour of 'disjunction', the replacement of traditional form follows function relationships with the 'superposition' or juxtaposition of each, and the adoption of fragmentation as an analytical device through which to arrive at a new 'architectural system'. The key to his idea of disjunction lies in his perception that a dichotomy now exists between standard practice in the past, and social conditions today. As he has said, this practice has typically depended upon: 'the fusion of form and function, programme and context, structure and meaning. Underlying these is a belief in the unified, centred and self-generative subject, whose own autonomy is reflected in the formal autonomy of the work. Yet, at a certain point, this long-standing practice, which accentuates synthesis, harmony, the composition of elements and the seamless coincidence of potentially disparate parts, becomes estranged from its external culture, from contemporary cultural conditions.' In each of his projects he tries to redress this estrangement through a more realistic appraisal of current conditions. At La Villette, this reconciliation comes through a questioning of the validity of the time-honoured prototypes of park within the modern city today, and that questioning has led to the replacement of landscape, in the traditional sense, with High-Tech trees. In his Glass Video Gallery, architectural stability itself is replaced with the immaterial essence of the electronic image.

Tschumi uses the latest techniques in Computer-Aided Design and Xerox Collage to achieve his 'superpositions' making his architecture a direct extension of today's image-conscious culture.

OPPOSITE & LEFT: La Villette, Paris, France.

A DECADE OF ARCHITECTURAL DESIGN

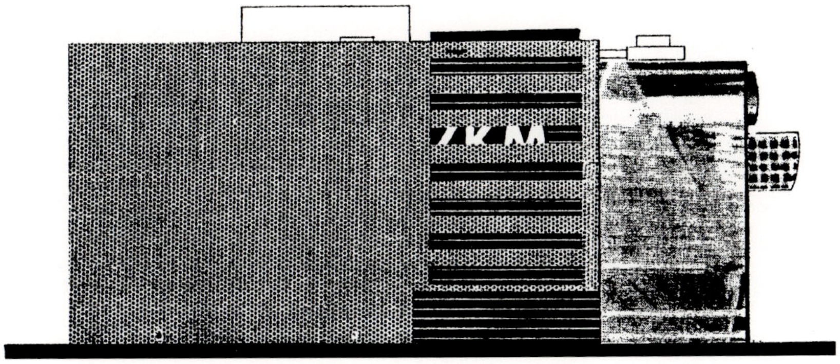

'How', this architect asks, 'can one create a building at a time when the technology of construction has become less relevant than the constriction of technology?'

ABOVE, FAR LEFT & LEFT: Zentrum für Kunst und Medientechnologie, Karlsruhe, Germany.
OVERLEAF: Glass Video Gallery, Groningen, The Netherlands.

A DECADE OF ARCHITECTURAL DESIGN

BERNARD TSCHUMI

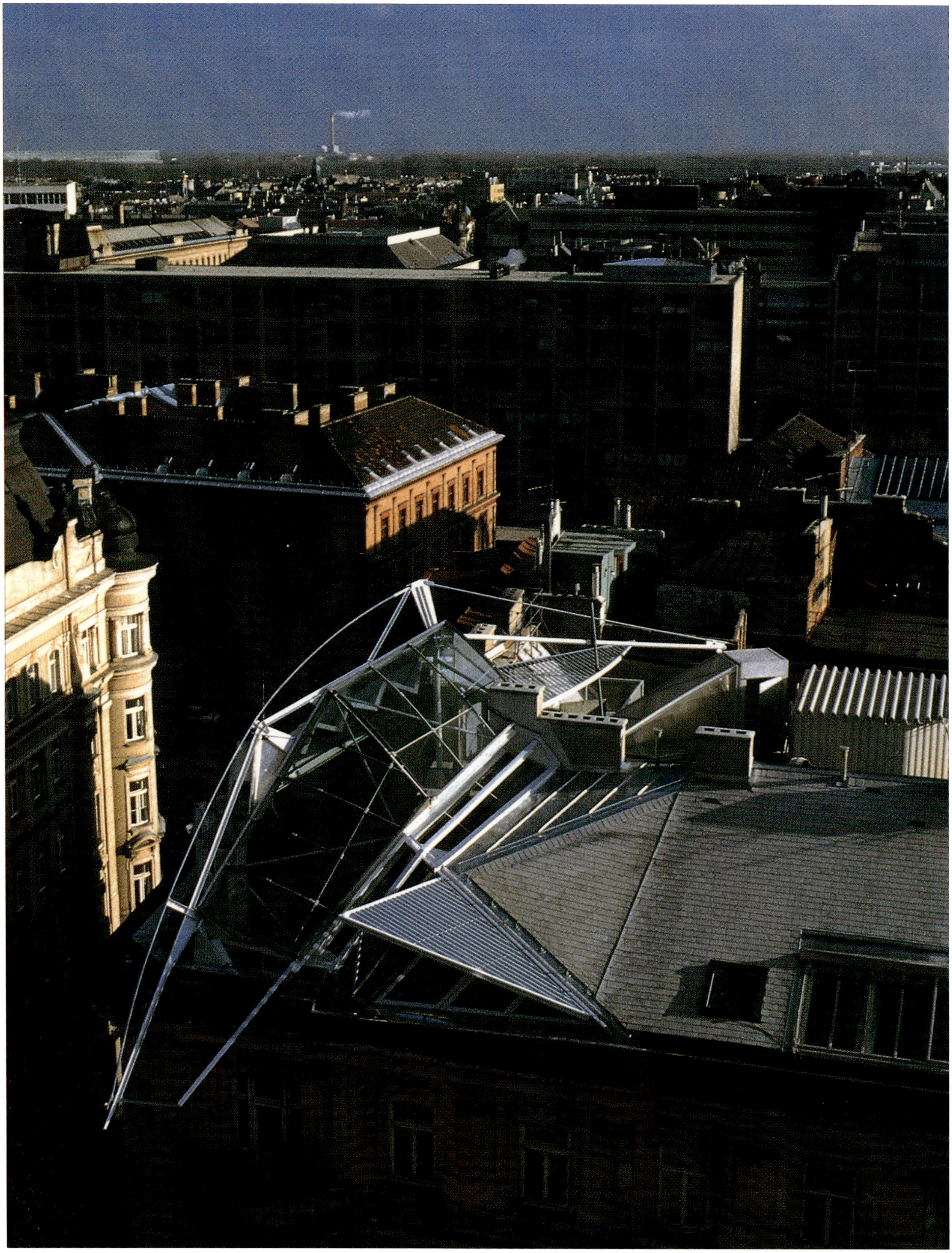

Coop Himmelblau

The Blue Sky Co-operative is a rather ethereal name for a group that seems to be dedicated to the destruction of all existing order, especially in the city. In their belief that 'Tough times demand tough architecture' and that architecture, as we have all come to understand it, 'is over', Wolf Prix and Helmut Swiczinsky have proposed, as an alternative, an aggressive strategy that uses forms like weapons. In explaining their viewpoint they have said that: 'As we . . . are Viennese, we have a close connection to Freud who taught us that suppression requires a tremendous amount of energy. We would like to spend this energy on projects. The safe and sound world of architecture no longer exists. It will never exist again.' Their formal declaration of war on architecture was first issued at the beginning of the last decade by setting fire to a 15-metre high tower that they had built in the middle of Vienna, and had called 'the Blazing Wing'. Their Attic Conversion in that same city, which followed in 1984, has transferred those pyrotechnics into a steel and glass 'taut-bow,' drawn diagonally across the corner of a staid, centuries-old apartment block. This project, while small in scale has since come to symbolise their unique approach to design. Looking like an extruded, crystalline version of an insect from a Franz Kafka short story, this assembly shows the extent to which these architects have condensed what they have called 'the moment of conception' in the design process, using stream-of-consciousness drawing techniques, followed by quickly constructed models to capture the subconscious quality they are after in their work.

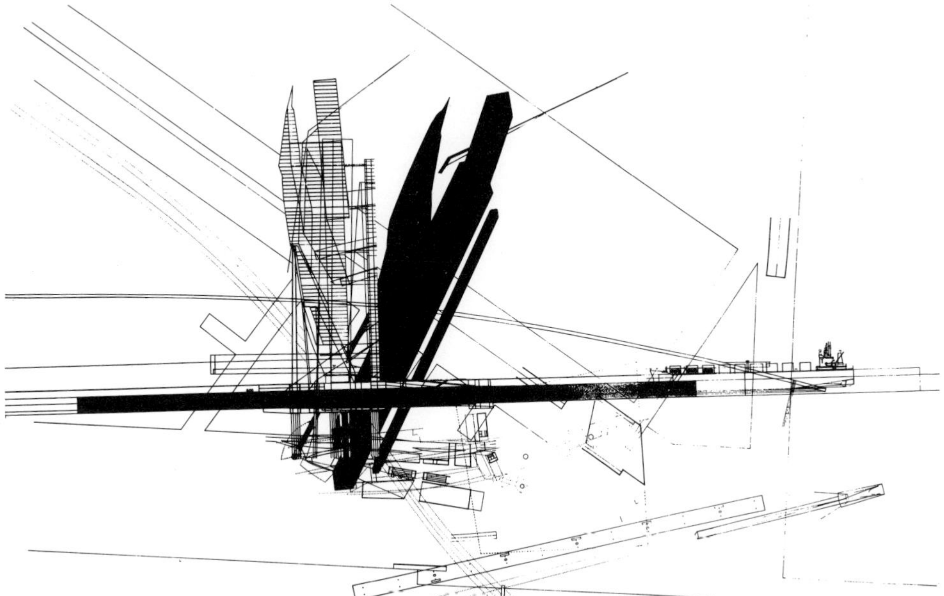

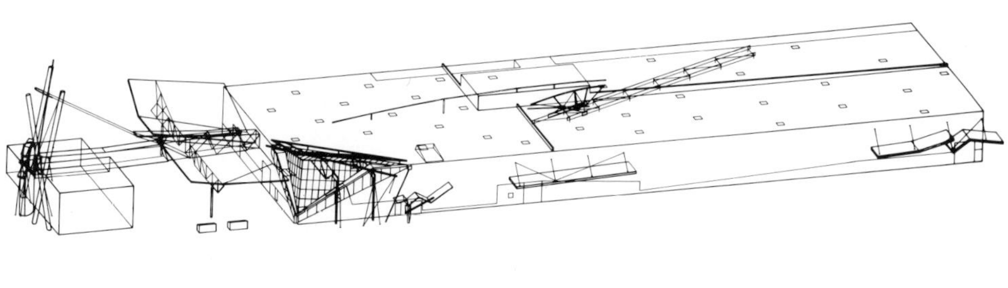

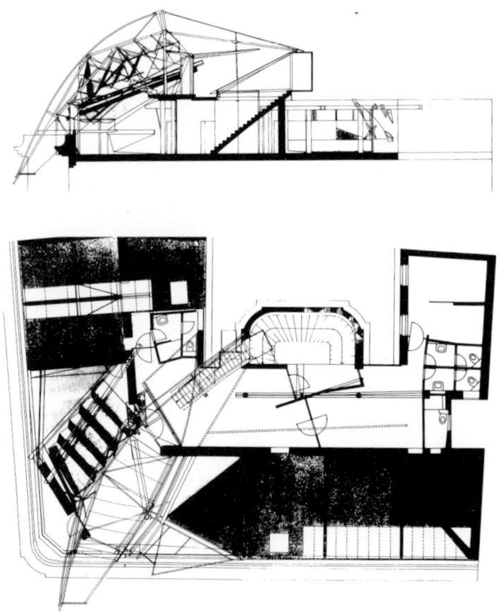

Coop Himmelblau is re-examining all of the conventional aspects of architecture, such as the relationship between form and function, and the way in which structure reflects each.

OPPOSITE & ABOVE: The Rooftop Remodelling, Vienna, Austria.
ABOVE LEFT: Funder Factory 3, St Veit/Glan, Austria.
BELOW LEFT: Skyline Tower, Hamburg, Germany.

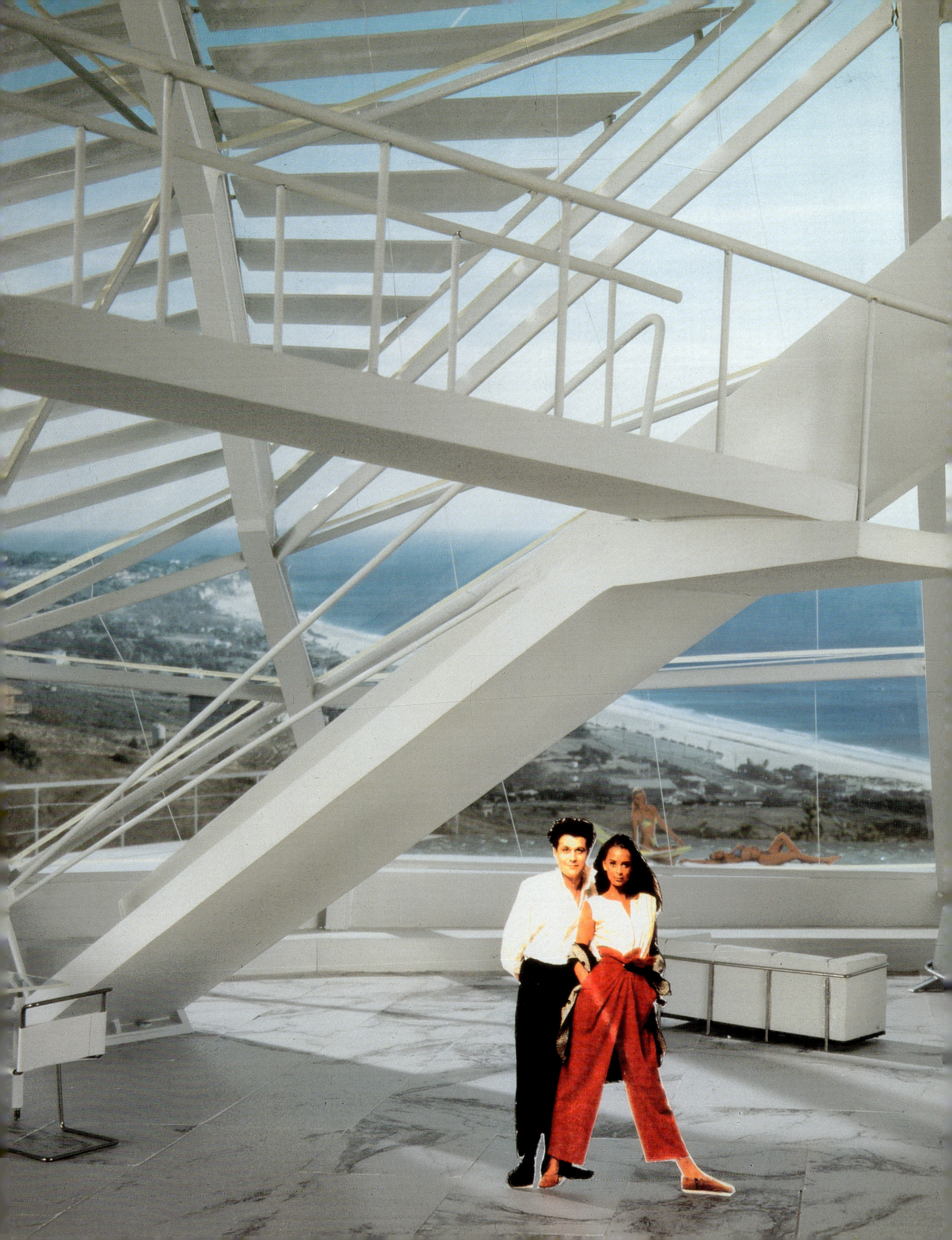

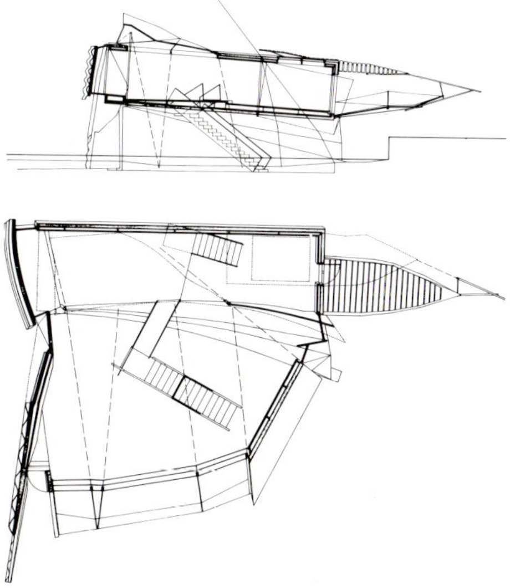

COOP HIMMELBLAU

While glass is ironically a favourite material of these architects, for many of the same reasons that it appealed to the first visionaries of the Modern Movement, the Cooperative is also fascinated by the patterns that light can make in the interior of a space.

LEFT & ABOVE: The Open House, Malibu, California.

A DECADE OF ARCHITECTURAL DESIGN

Frank Gehry

While his name is frequently associated with Deconstructivism, because of the formal disjunctures that have characterised his work, Frank Gehry has not deliberately sought this connection. He has instead been reacting as a sensitive medium to his surroundings, which are temporal, fragmentary and undergoing constant change. As the widely acknowledged father of the 'Los Angeles School' Gehry was the first of that group to reflect the chaos of what has until recently been known as 'the city without a centre', where freeways and automobiles have created a subculture all of their own. This awareness has given his work an intentionally unfinished appearance of being still in progress, making it a very accurate representation of the modern urban condition of not only his own city, but also countless others throughout the world. This look is augmented by his choice of what have typically been considered to be utilitarian materials, such as exposed, unpainted plywood, corrugated metal siding and chain link fence. As such, his work is comparable to a Kurt Schwitters Collage, where found objects that are ordinarily taken for granted are juxtaposed, and presented in a way that brings attention to their intrinsic beauty. Such parallels are intentional, and Gehry has often been known to make direct comparisons between his direction and that of artists such as Robert Rauschenberg, among others. As he once said in an interview with Janet Nairn of *Architectural Record* that later appeared as 'A Search for a No-Rules Architecture':

'My approach to architecture is different. I search out the work of artists, and use art as a means of inspiration. I try to rid myself . . . of the burden of culture and look for new ways to approach the work. I want to be open-ended. There are no rules, no right or wrong. I'm confused as to what's ugly and what's pretty.'

As artist-architect, he has typically seemed to be more concerned with the sculptural and compositional aspects of his work than functional or programmatic requirements, and yet, in spite of his apparent lack of pragmatism, his buildings are remarkably considerate of client needs. This ability to balance between childlike playfulness and professionalism, while consistently making an on-going commentary on modern life, makes Gehry's contribution to contemporary architecture quite extraordinary.

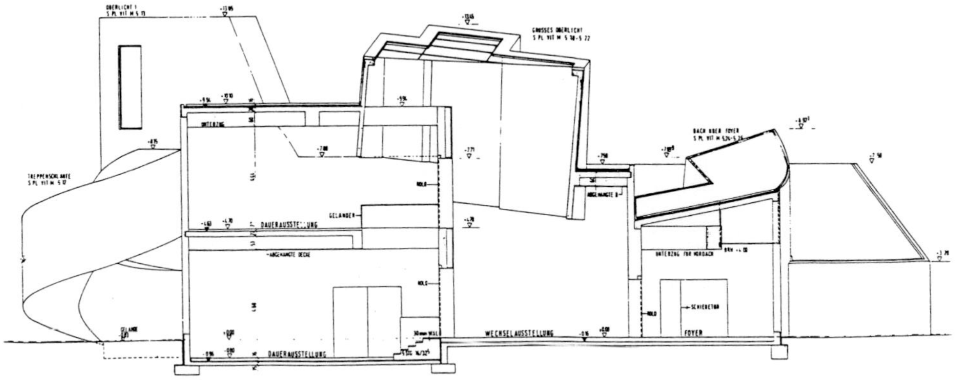

Over time, larger commissions have made more complex formal explorations possible, and have provided an opportunity for the architect to comment on the characteristics of cities other than Los Angeles.

OPPOSITE, LEFT & OVERLEAF: The Vitra Design Museum, Weil am Rhein, West Germany.

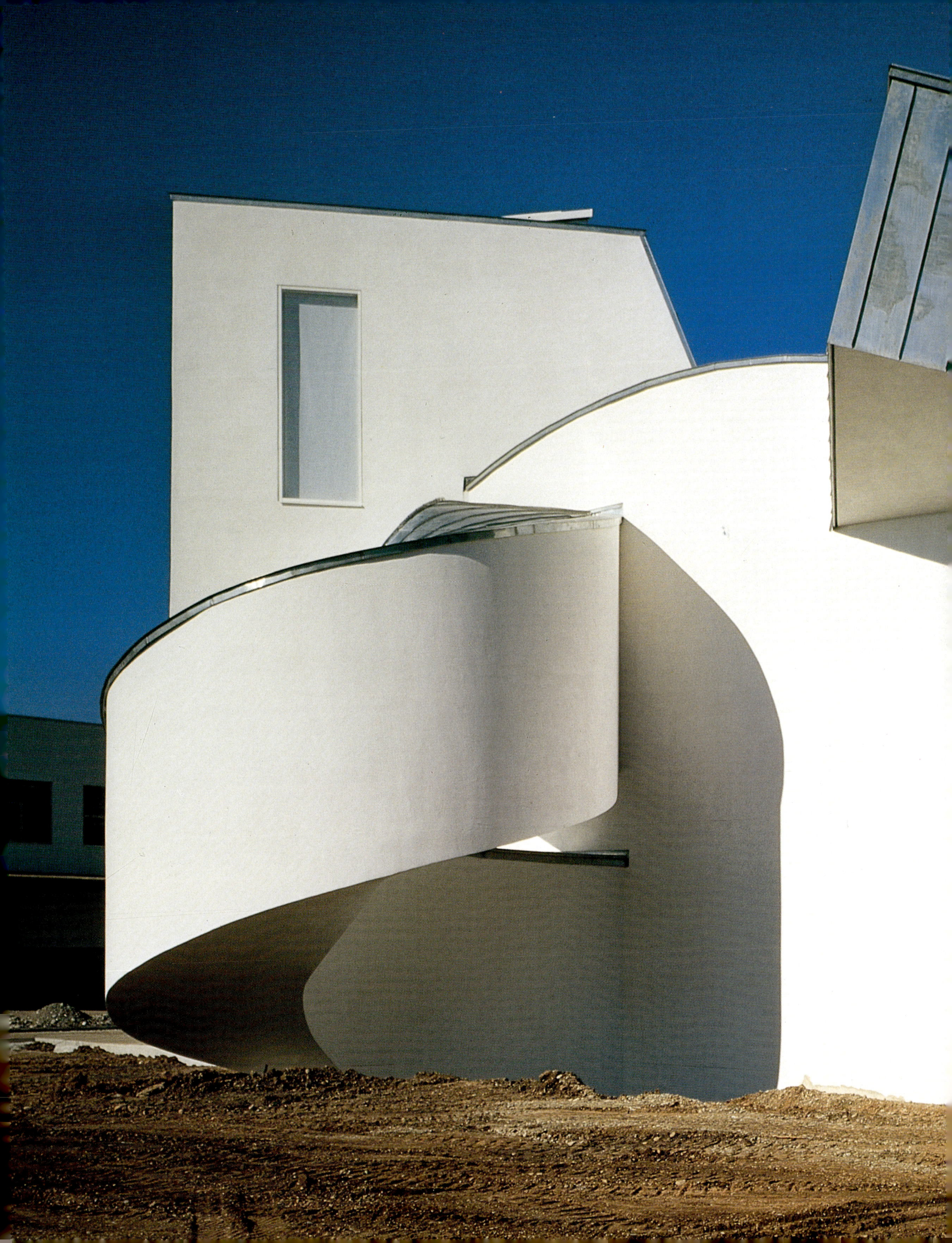

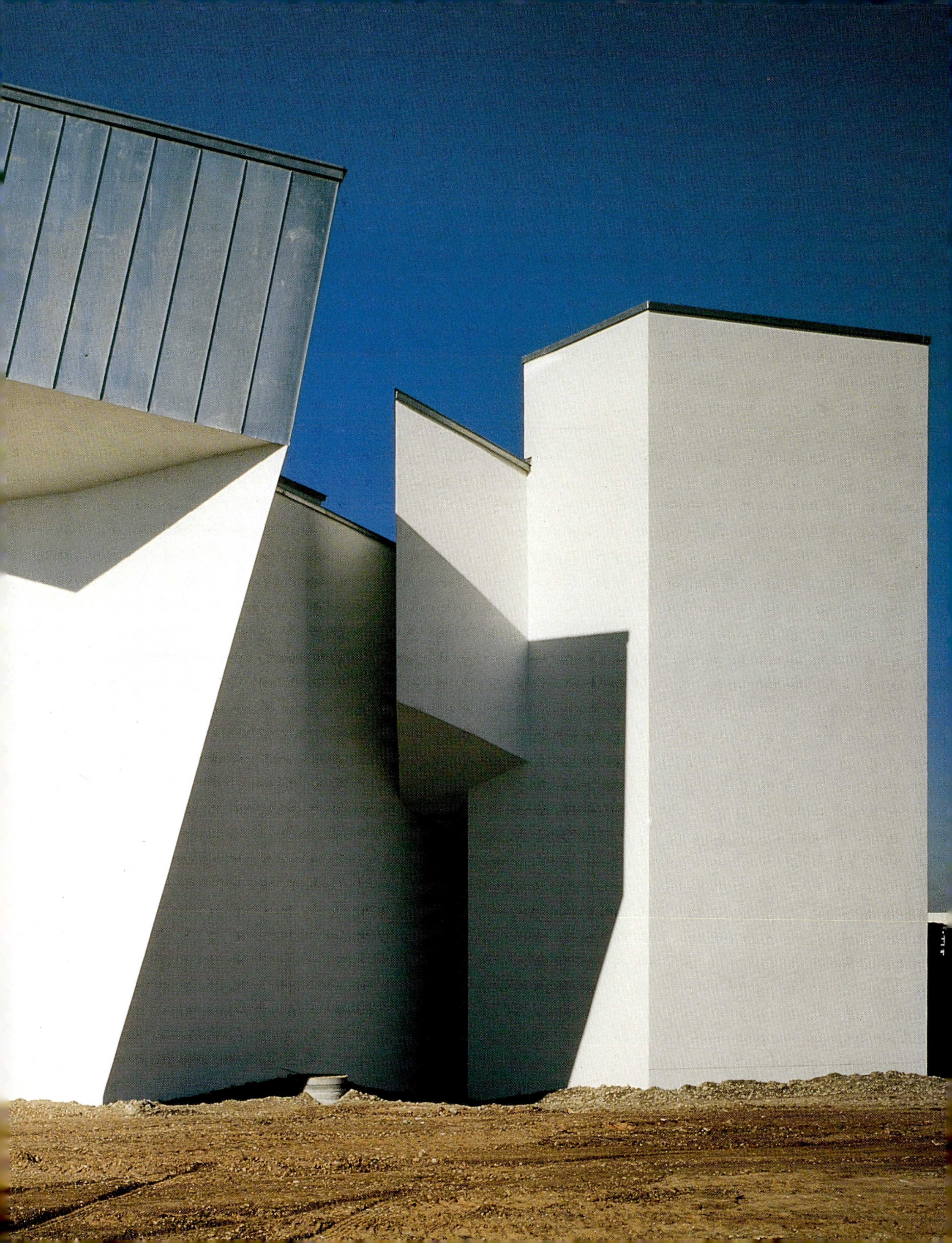

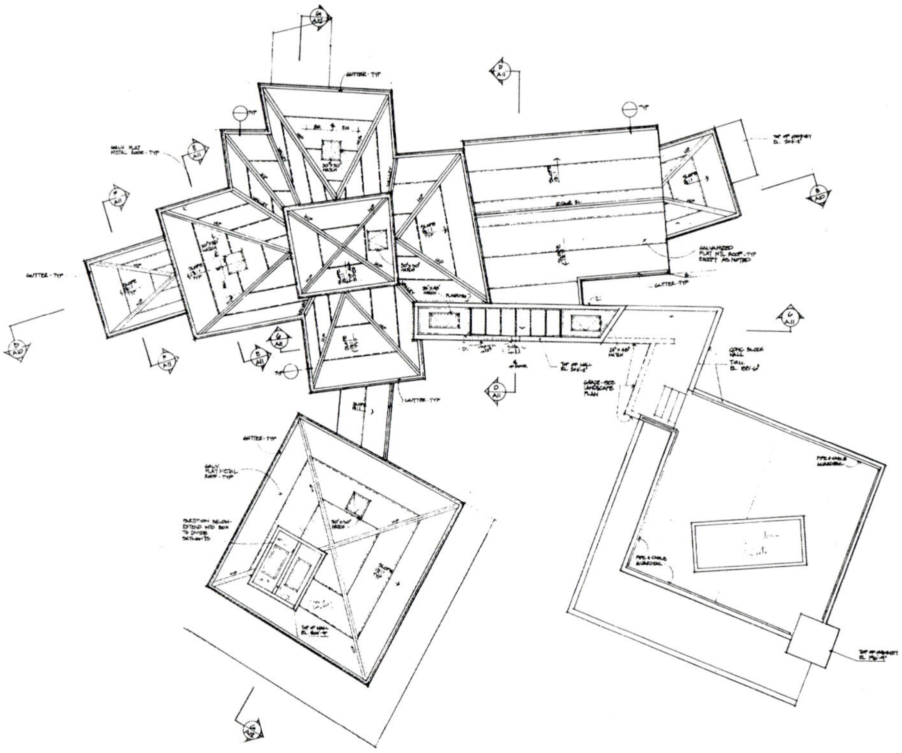

A DECADE OF ARCHITECTURAL DESIGN

Occasionally, Gehry's expression on the basic aggression that is part of contemporary, urban life, is transformed into the creation of an alternative to it, as it was at Loyola, where a protected abstract world is substituted for the harsh reality nearby.

ABOVE: Loyola Law School, Los Angeles, California.
LEFT: Sirmai-Peterson Residence, Thousand Oaks, California.

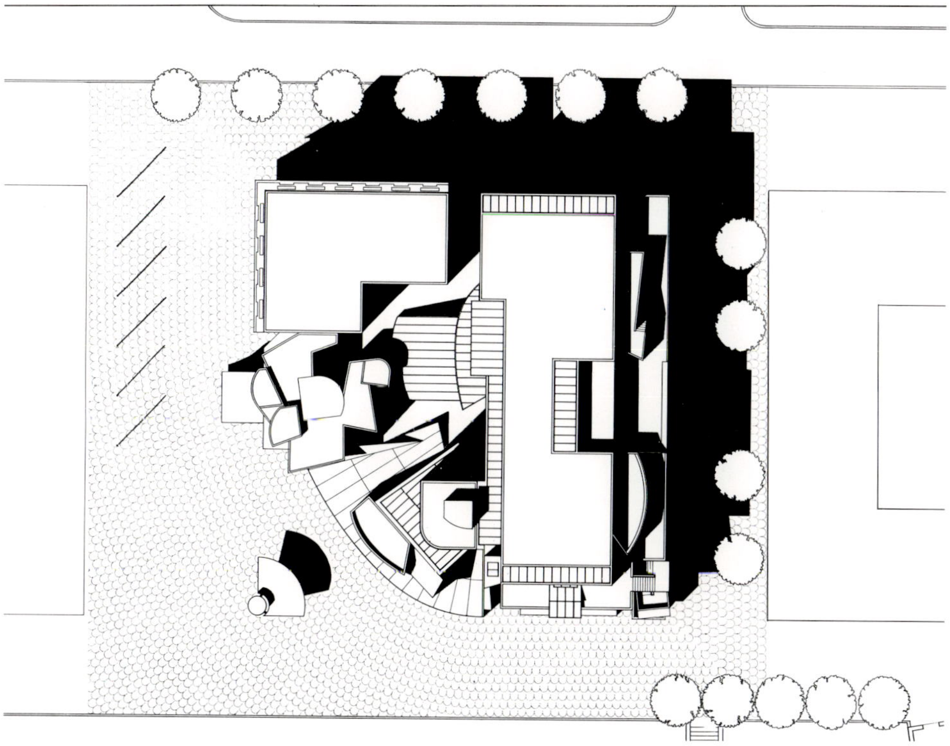

FRANK GEHRY

The fine line that separates art and architecture is often intentionally blurred in Gehry's work, where symbolism and collage are frequently blended into habitable sculpture.

ABOVE: Fish Restaurant, Kobe, Japan.
LEFT; The American Center, Paris, France.

A DECADE OF ARCHITECTURAL DESIGN

Daniel Libeskind

While Umberto Eco may have encouraged some to begin to consider architecture as a palimpsest, Daniel Libeskind stubbornly refuses to accept the fact that erasure means destruction. What he does acknowledge, however, is that the pace of modern life has irrevocably changed the way we must look at that architecture, and that a new language must be formed to allow us to do so. As he has said recently, 'no sooner has one begun a work – touched pen to paper – then the effort lapses, inseminates itself with another one, cancels and overcomes its origins, begets endings that are interminable longer than its own previous history . . . Until today architecture was on the wrong track. Rising up to heaven or grovelling on the ground, it has misunderstood the principles of its existence and has been, not without reason, constantly derided by upright folk. It has not been modest . . . the finest quality that ought to exist within an imperfect being . . . Architectural thought no longer exists – no longer exists as a self-deferential discourse, no more than does any other autobiography [and] architecture becomes past in the sense that today it has entered its coda. A code EX, a code that cannot be decoded; an X, a CODEX which invalidates its origin/ality raises the un/original, founded as it is upon incertitude, upon the void, upon the language of the dead which yet refuses to be a monument to a dead language.'

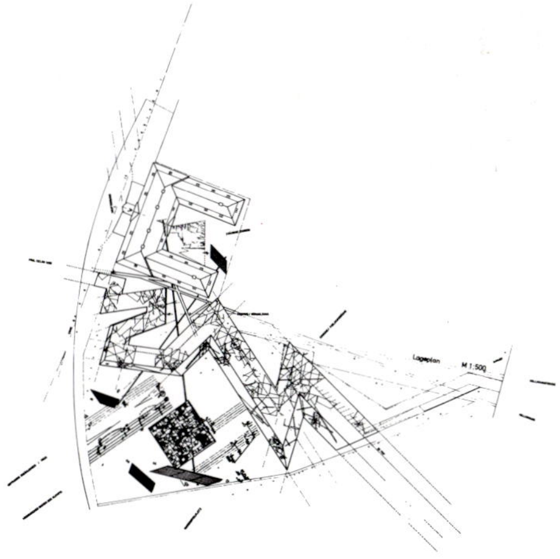

In the CODEX that he seeks to create our ancient language is essential in the formation of a new one, even though the syntax may be completely different.

OPPOSITE: Mies van der Rohe Memorial, 'Never is the Centre'.
LEFT & ABOVE: The Jewish Extension to the Berlin Museum.
OVERLEAF, ABOVE: The Alef Wing Model; BELOW: Berlin, City Edge Competition.
SECOND OVERLEAF: The Jewish Extension to the Berlin Museum.

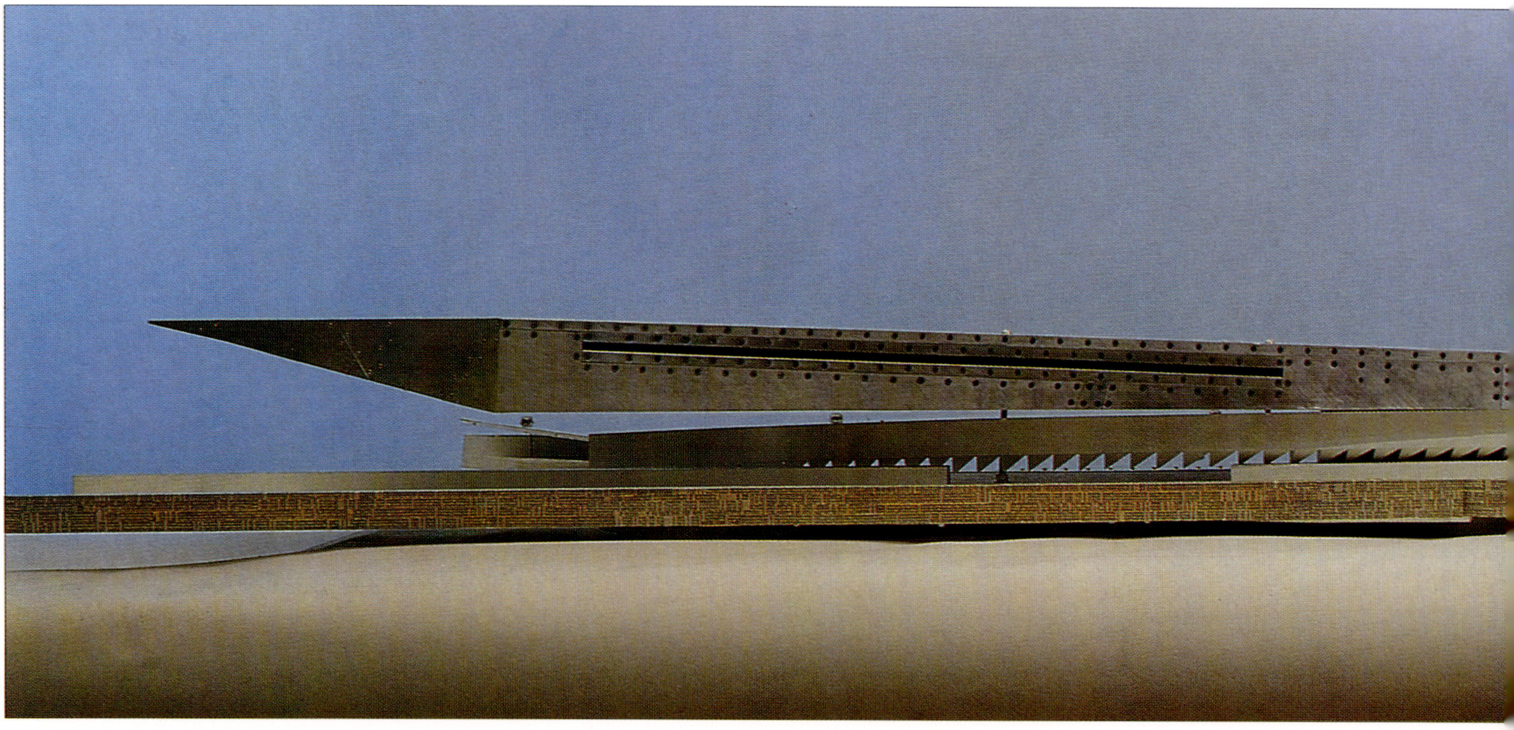

A DECADE OF ARCHITECTURAL DESIGN

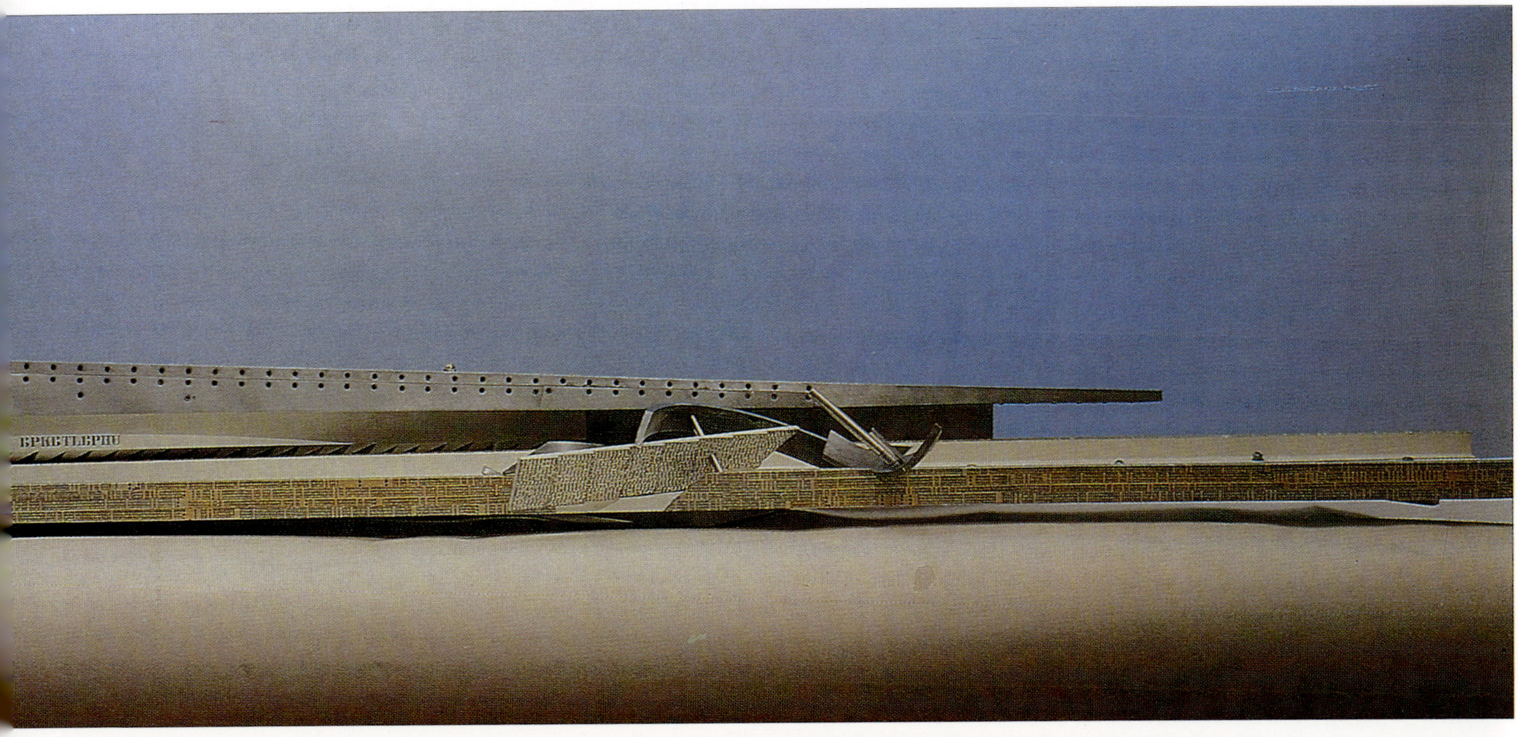

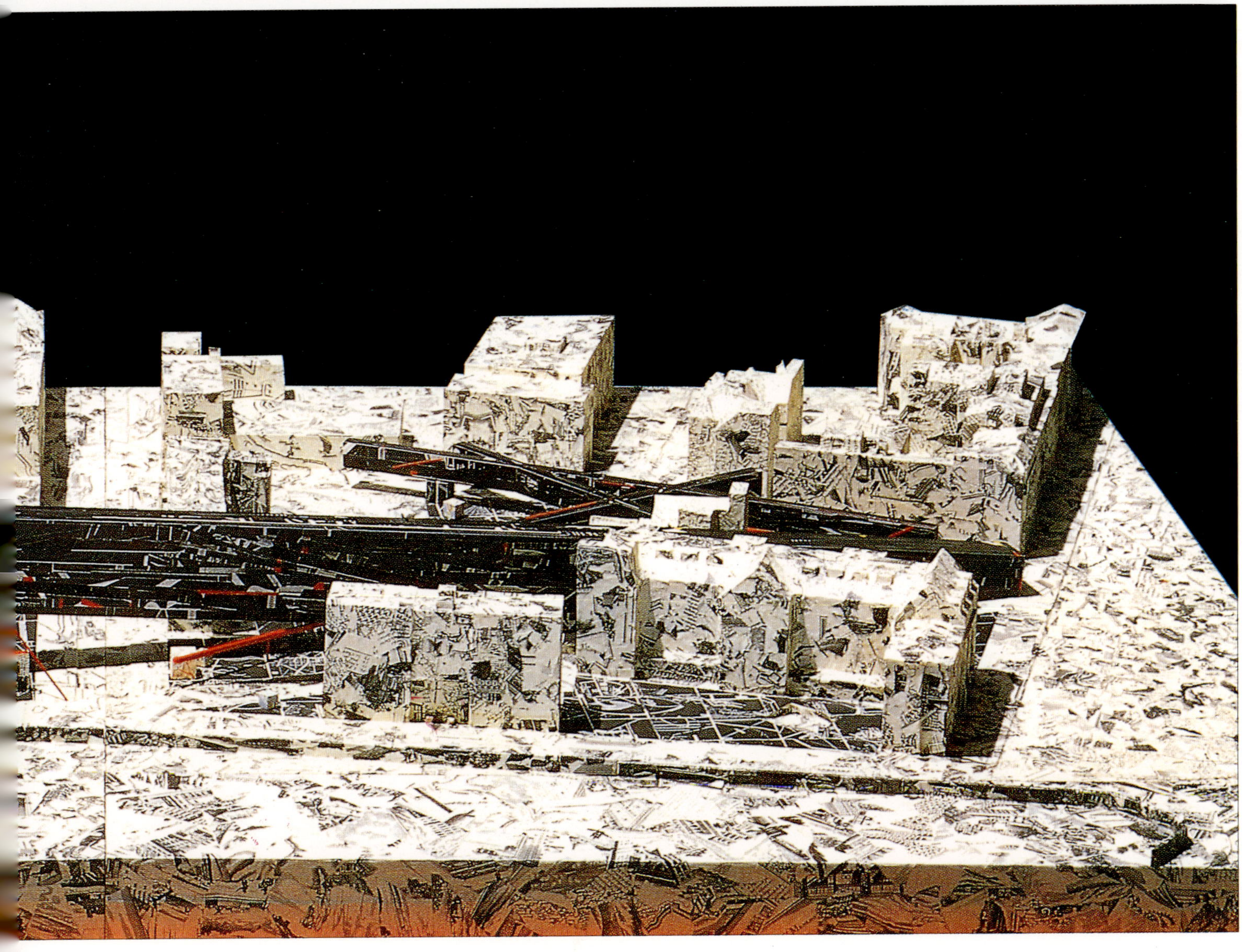

A DECADE OF ARCHITECTURAL DESIGN

200

DANIEL LIBESKIND

A DECADE OF ARCHITECTURAL DESIGN

Günter Behnisch

If the dramatic form of the enormous Olympic Stadia roof that Behnisch and Partners, along with Günther Grzimek, designed for the Munich Games in 1972 remains a dominant image in the collective consciousness, the aesthetic of the firm has most certainly changed noticeably in the years since its completion. While a commitment to lightness of structure, open-ended space and a reluctance to use typological formulae still remains strong, new projects such as the Hysolar Institute, Eichstätt Pavilion and the Postal Museum in Frankfurt all show that Behnisch is beginning to interrogate structure in ways that would have been unthinkable 20 years ago. If categories must be retained, however, that questioning has not served to totally eradicate the sheer love of materials that has made the acrylic tents at Munich so memorable, nor has it destroyed the urge to engage in engineering pyrotechnics just to show that the seemingly impossible can actually be built. All of this relates to what Justus Dahinden has called 'a comprehensive argument with reality' in Behnisch's work, and that argument continues. The reality that Dahinden refers to not only relates to the most obvious natural laws, such as gravity, but also to more mundane questions of institutional power struggles and financial restrictions. In the Hysolar Institute, for example, which is a joint German-Saudi Arabian research project, fast-track building schedules and a tight budget had just as much influence on form as did any prevailing architectural philosophy. Given those restrictions, it is all the more remarkable that such a consistent and powerful expression of the firm's present design direction has emerged at all, showing the extent to which pragmatism has been tempered, conforming to an overall design direction. In this way Behnisch and Partners continue to maintain a precarious balance between slavishly following programmatic requirements and ignoring them completely.

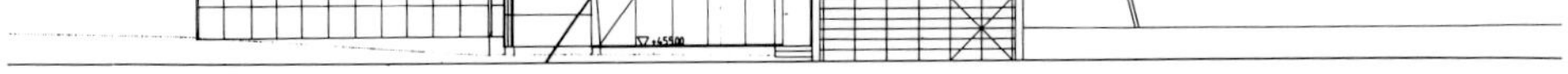

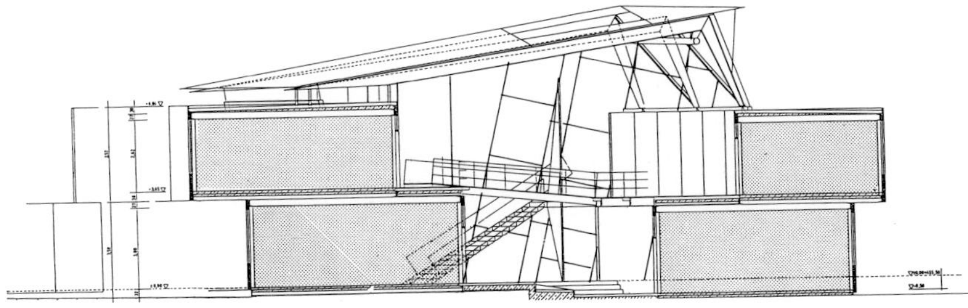

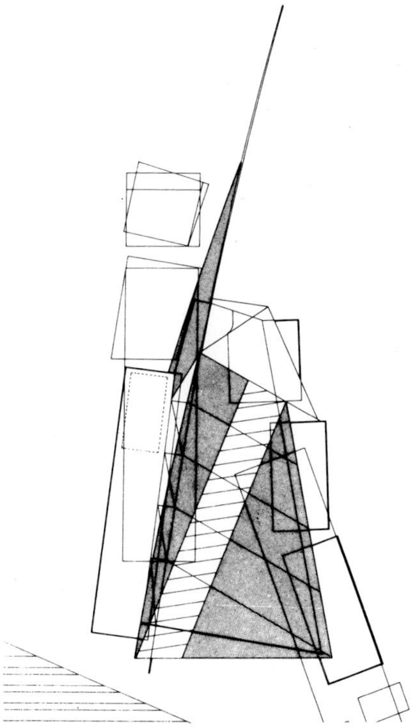

The same love of steel, glass and assembly that have identified this architect's style in the past are still evident in his new work, which now pushes those methods of assembly to the limit.

OPPOSITE, LEFT & ABOVE: Hysolar Institute Building, University of Stuttgart, Germany.

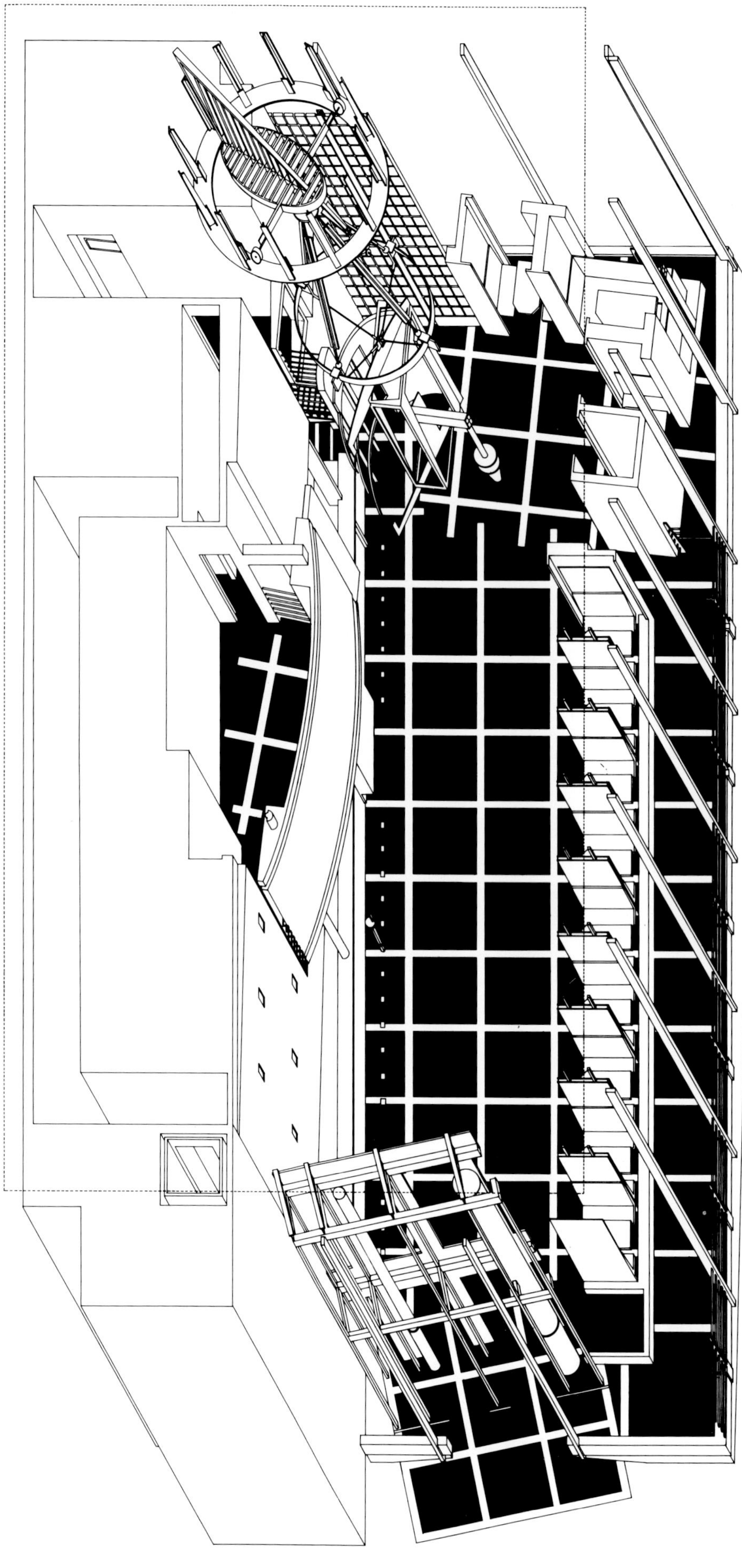

A DECADE OF ARCHITECTURAL DESIGN

Morphosis

In a catalogue for an exhibition of their residential projects, held at the Cheney Cowles Museum in Spokane, Washington in the Spring of 1989, called 'A Decade of Architectural Confrontation', Thom Mayne and Michael Rotondi have provided a brief statement that, while applying only to the houses they have designed, is quite instructive of their attitude towards all of their work. In it, they say, in part, that 'it is the battle or the confrontation which looms as one of the most fundamentally important points of departure from which we begin to understand how our projects develop. In much the same way that one can perceive life as a more or less constant confrontation with the complex and contradictory aspects of modern urban living, so can one perceive the evolution of a building. If the battles of life produce a richness of character, a depth of personality, and result in a final assessment of 'success' in life's experiences, then so do the confrontations dealt within architecture produce a richness of building, a complexity of response, and an ultimately successful solution to the delimitations of site client/program, and architecture. There is a conscious connection in all of our projects dictated by the importation of ideas which draw relationships between the built object and the existing world . . . In sum, our work celebrates the complex.'

While usually categorised as having Deconstructivist tendencies, Morphosis would seem, on closer examination, to have a more finely tuned contextual sense than the majority of metaphysicists who are usually included in that group. The fact that the background in which they work is largely hostile, however, typically prompts a defensive architectural stance that is often misread as being aggressive and destructive, and this tends to obscure their attempts to comment on their surroundings through their work.

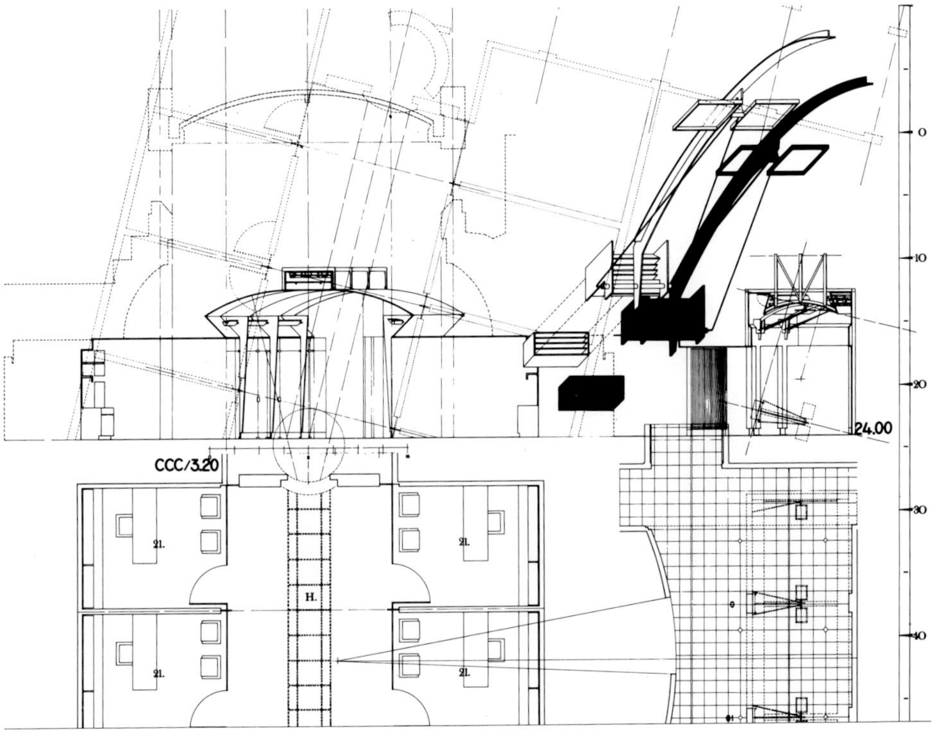

Morphosis presents their work in a way that expands pre-existing concepts of reality, and superimposes various systems of organisation into one complex image.

OPPOSITE: Kate Mantilini Restaurant, Santa Monica, California.
LEFT: The Sixth Street Residence, Los Angeles, California.

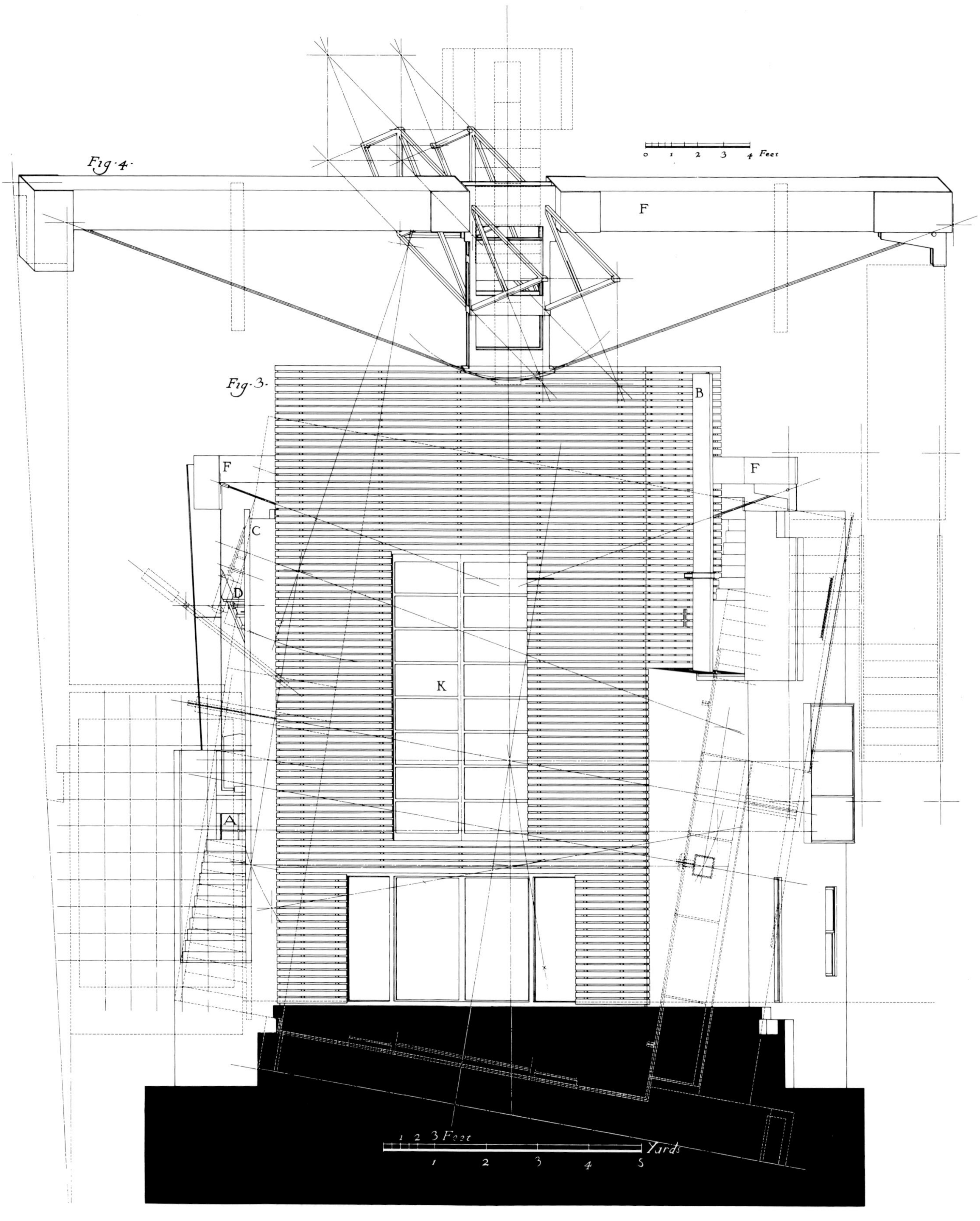

A DECADE OF ARCHITECTURAL DESIGN

206

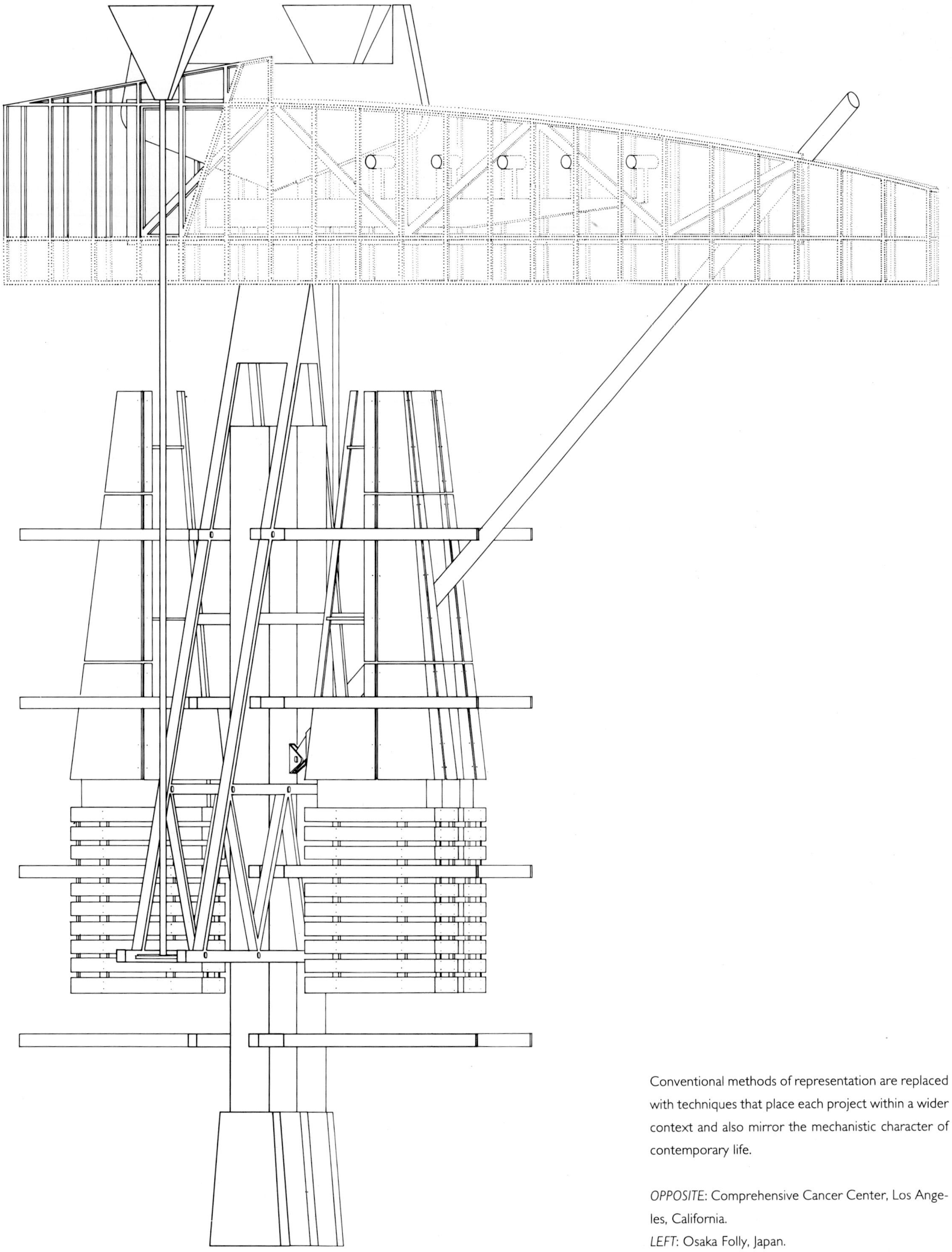

MORPHOSIS

Conventional methods of representation are replaced with techniques that place each project within a wider context and also mirror the mechanistic character of contemporary life.

OPPOSITE: Comprehensive Cancer Center, Los Angeles, California.
LEFT: Osaka Folly, Japan.

207

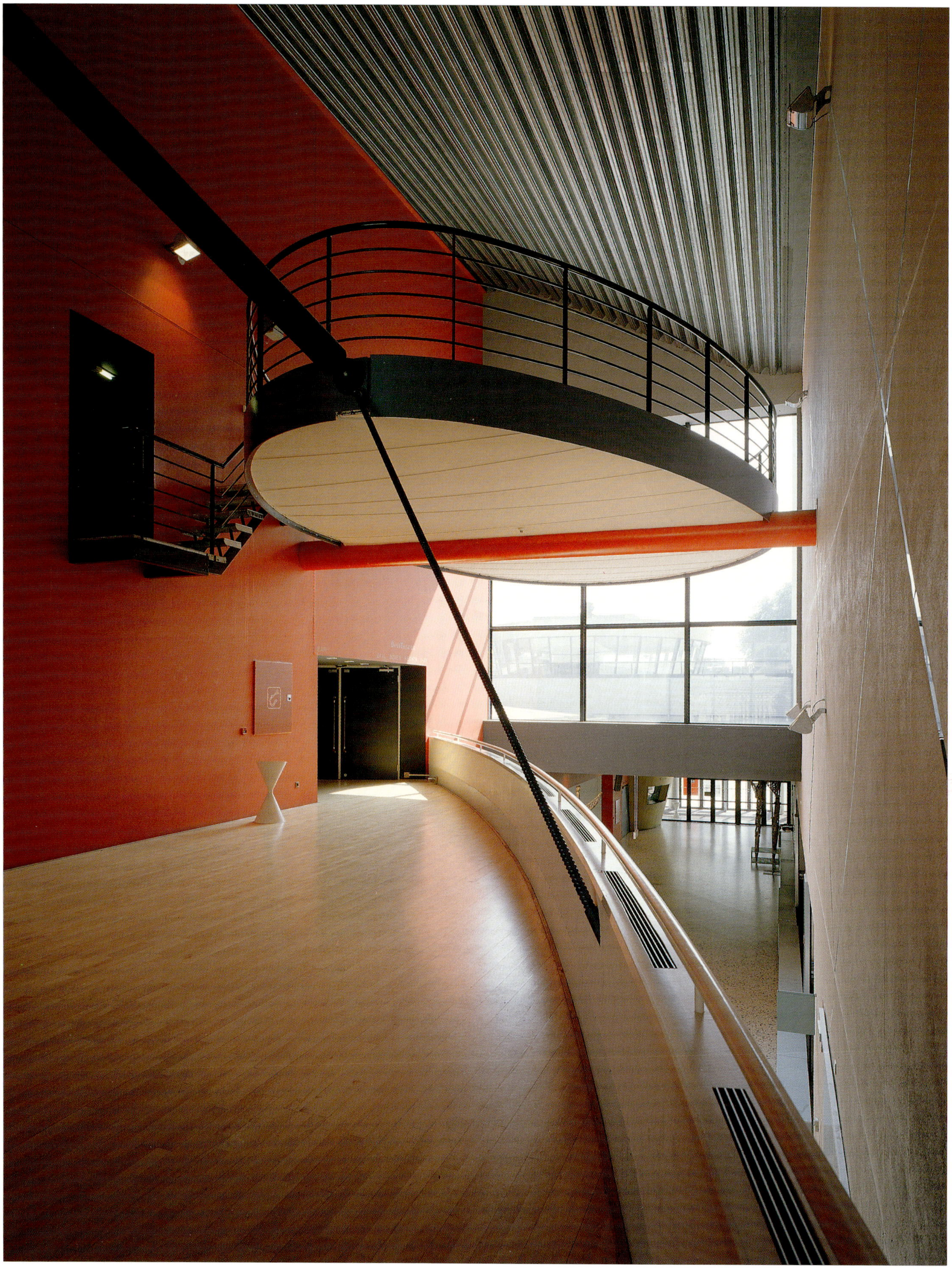

OMA

In 1975, Rem Koolhaas, Elia and Zoe Zenghelis and Madelon Vriesendorp founded the Office for Metropolitan Architecture, which has consistently had as its agenda the realignment of contemporary architecture with modern, and primarily Western cultural values. Koolhaas himself was born in Rotterdam in 1944, coming to London to study at the Architectural Association in 1968. Soon afterwards, in 1970, he published *The Berlin Wall as Architecture* and in collaboration with Elia and Zoe Zenghelis and Madelon Vriesendorp: *Exodus, or the Voluntary Prisoners of Architecture*, in 1972. After winning a Harkness Fellowship for travel and study in the United States in that same year, Koolhaas worked with Peter Eisenman at the Institute for Architecture and Urban Studies, and with OM Ungers at Cornell. Following that, both he and Elia Zenghelis became involved in several projects in New York City that ultimately led to the publication of *Delirious New York*; three years after the founding of OMA. This book, which brought the group such acclaim, shows their fascination with tracking the influence that American urban culture has had upon the architecture of its largest and most cosmopolitan city. After its publication, their focus shifted from America and purely theoretical concerns, towards Europe, and the search for opportunities to build. In 1978, they were able to successfully express their growing interest in the problem of modern intervention into the traditional fabric of the European city by winning a competition for an extension to the Dutch Parliament. Since then, major projects have included the National Dance Theatre at The Hague, completed in 1984, the Museum Park in Rotterdam, planning proposals for Euro Disney and the City Centre for Lille, France, as well as a Housing Project located at the American sector of Checkpoint Charlie, the old border crossing between East and West Germany on Friedrichstrasse.

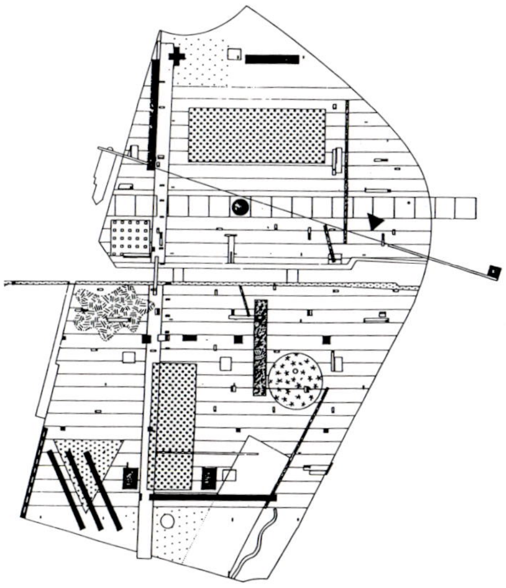

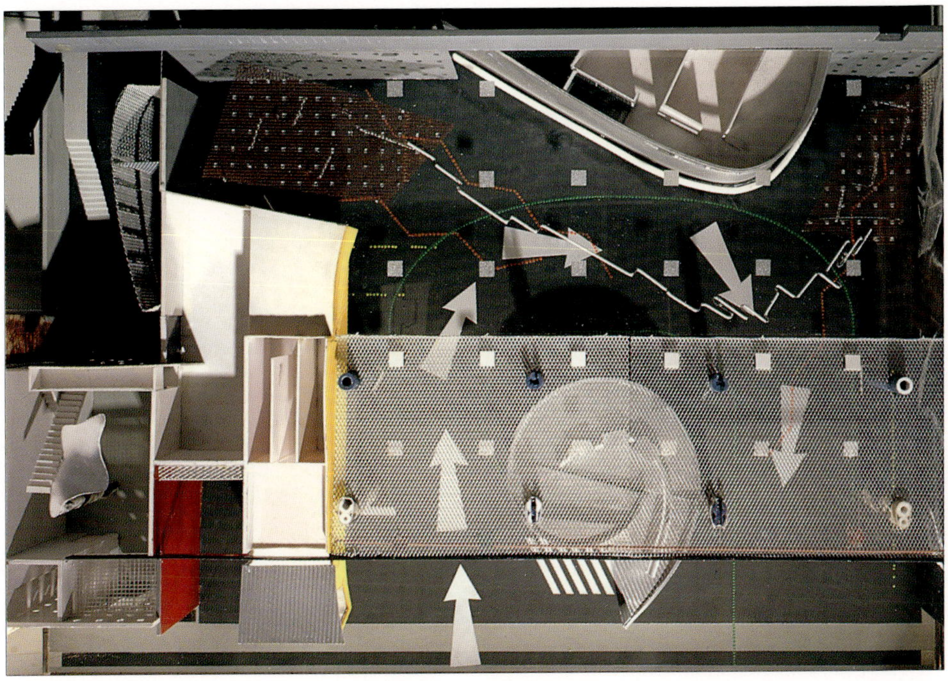

OMA presents an architectural vision that recollects the preoccupation with geometry of the Russian Constructivists as well as a new aesthetic reality.

OPPOSITE: The Netherlands Dance Theatre, The Hague, The Netherlands.
LEFT: Checkpoint Charlie, Berlin, Germany.
ABOVE: La Villette, Paris, France.

A DECADE OF ARCHITECTURAL DESIGN

Emilio Ambasz

In the manner of Luis Barragan, Ambasz has sought to limit his architectural language to the basics in order to achieve maximum effect with minimal means. For his mentor, on whom he has also written an elegaic monograph, those means were limited to the use of surface, landscape, water and colour, all balanced in such a way as to capture the essence of Mexico itself. Barragan understood that however long architecture lasts, it is only an intruder in the natural world and so he sought to limit that intrusion as much as possible through his art. Few architects have understood the physiological and psychological effect that colour in particular may have in architecture, and the influence that Barragan has had through this understanding may now be traced through the work of many architects today.

Ambasz has looked deeper into Barragan's work and has gone beyond colour to the idea of reconciliation with nature that it was used to address, as well as to concepts of beauty and poetry in architecture which many now seem embarrassed to acknowledge. In his lyrical, yet highly realistic solution for the San Antonio Botanical Conservatory in Texas, those concepts are evident. As Ambasz has said:

'By excavating into the earth, the conservatory preserves and harmonises with the gently rolling hills around it, merging the categories of culture and nature. The different roof configurations take their cues from considerations of the wind and orientation of the sun.'

There is a processional aspect to this conservatory that reveals the architect's concept clearly. After entering, there is an extended orangery lined with fruit trees, a misty room of ferns and waterfalls, followed by a desert, tropical rain forest, Alpine meadow, and forest of trees. The conservatory, like all of Emilio Ambasz's work, is a world in microcosm.

Ambasz creates symbolic landscapes that blend with nature rather than intruding upon it, and in San Antonio, he also introduces a building which becomes a world unto itself.

OPPOSITE & *LEFT*: San Antonio Botanical Garden, Texas.

A DECADE OF ARCHITECTURAL DESIGN

Site

With a name that is an acronym for Sculpture in the Environment, the intentions of this firm are not hard to guess. As a multi-disciplinary organisation of architects and artists founded in 1970, Site has taken it upon themselves to explore new conceptual territory; and has done so through what they have called 'De-architecture', which provides a dialogue on the built environment, rather than conventional additions to it. At present, the principals of the Site group are James Wines, Alison Sky, Emilio Sousa and Michelle Stone. Completed projects to date include several showrooms for Best Products Co such as the Peeling Project in Richmond, Virginia, the Notch Project in Sacramento, California, the Indeterminate Facade in Houston, Texas and the Tilt Showroom, in Towson, Maryland, among others. These showrooms have all provided a wry commentary on the increasing need for high visibility in commercial architecture, as well as the impermanence that has become the hallmark of disposable society.

Unlike these earlier, symbolically humorous and intentionally attention-getting projects, the recently completed Four Continents Bridge, in Japan is more subtle, using glass, steel frame and water, as well as landscape elements, to construct a global metaphor. The design focus on a delicate spray waterfall that makes the bridge seem to float, as well as a consistently detailed aquatic cascade that falls in sheets along vertical glass panels serving as a gateway onto the bridge, and the wall of several elevations, effectively place the island nation of Japan within that metaphorical context. In both built and unbuilt work, Site has established a unique position for itself within the current architectural scene, transcending stylistic categories in its commentary.

Ecology is a consistent theme for Site in their 'de-architecture', which provides commentary ranging from the serious and lyrical to the ironic about the place of built additions to the environment.

OPPOSITE: The Four Continents Bridge, Hiroshima, Japan.
LEFT & ABOVE: The World Ecology Pavilion, Seville, Spain.

A DECADE OF ARCHITECTURAL DESIGN

Philippe Starck

Those who believe that Post-Modernism and Deconstruction represent the last gasp of originality in architecture, and that the consumerism of contemporary culture has finally resulted in a bankruptcy of form, must also wish that Philippe Starck does not become very well-known. As if any is needed, his work is additional proof that the cult of individuality is still alive and well today, and that new form, like new music, can be infinitely derived from a fixed number of generators. As has been the case with many others who have sought to experiment with new forms, Starck has found his most receptive audience in Japan, where the originality of designers is highly respected. In Tokyo, which is a city full of individual statements, Starck's are some of the most original of all, standing out as strange, mutational shapes on a skyline full of novelty. As Marco Romanelli has said recently in *Domus* magazine, Philippe Starck's architecture is one of 'signs and signals, of the second generation at least, where things no longer proceed by direct symbolisms . . . but in a more occult way, that is, by concealing the functional and the advertising role at the same time, so that even the enigmatic quality itself becomes the metaphor and the message.'

In this sense 'La Flamme' Building, commissioned by the Asahi Beer Group, and the NaniNani Building for Rikugo are not only playful, sci-fi fantasies, but also a perfectly logical extension of a culture in which a high premium is put on identification with and loyalty to corporations.

A green, pre-oxidised copper skin gives a primitive antediluvian quality to a smooth, computer-generated surface of the NaniNani building.

OPPOSITE: NaniNani Building, Tokyo, Japan.
LEFT: Maisons d'Habitation, Ile Saint-Germain, Issy-Les-Moulineaux, France.

A DECADE OF ARCHITECTURAL DESIGN

PHILIPPE STARCK

Computer-aided design helps in the generation and assembly of the unconventional forms that have become this architect's trademark.

LEFT & ABOVE: NaniNani Building, Tokyo, Japan.

Acknowledgements

The Publishers acknowledge the generous help of architects, authors and artists who have provided work featured in this volume. Every effort has been made to credit each illustration correctly; in the event of an error or ommision we would be glad to modify future editions of this volume. The majority of illustrations reproduced in this volume are extracted from *Architectural Design* Magazine where they have been published over the last ten years. Illustrations provided from other sources are as follows:

PRELIMS
p11 M Pei Extension to the Louvre, photograph by Andreas Papadakis.
p4 Aldo Rossi Il Palazzo, illustration provided by Studio 80, Tokyo.
p8 Nocturne by Rita Wolff.

TRADITION AND CLASSICISM
Demetri Porphyrios, *The Relevance of Classical Architecture* p10-11, is an extract from a paper read at The New Classicism Symposium at the Tate Gallery, London. Painting p10 House in Chelsea Square by Rita Wolff. Leon Krier p12-17, painting p17 Pliny's Villa by Rita Wolff.
Robert Stern p18-23, photographs of Marblehead and Observatory Hill Dining Hall by T Whitney Cox; Mexx International Headquarters by Peter Aaron of Esto.
Andres Duany & Elizabeth Plater-Zyberk p28-29, photograph of Kentlands by Frank Martinez.
Allan Greenberg p30-33, photographs of the Department of State by Richard Cheek; Farmhouse in Connecticut by Peter Mauss of Esto.
Quinlan Terry p36-39, material on the Richmond Riverside Development provided by Mr Thody of Haslemere Estates & Chris Parkinson of Richard Ellis.
Demetri Porphyrios p40-43, photographs of Chepstow Villas by Mark Fiennes.
Aldo Rossi p44-49, all photographs in this section are provided by Professor Graffner.
Robert Adam, *Tin Gods* p50-65; first published in *Architectural Design* Vol 60 9/10 1989, *Reconstruction Deconstruction*. Photograph on p50 by Demetri Porphyrios.

MODERNISM & HIGH-TECH
Ada Louise Huxtable, *On Modern Architecture* p66-67, is taken from 'The Troubled State of Modern Architecture', *Architectural Design* Vol 51 1/2 1981, *From Futurism to Rationalism*.
Richard Meier p68-73, photographs of Madison Square Garden Towers by Esto; Ackerberg House and Museum für Kunsthandwerk by Wolfgang Hoyt.
Henri Ciriani p86-87, photographs provided by M. Gonthier.
IM Pei p88-89, photograph of the Extension to the Louvre by Andreas Papadakis.
Norman Foster p92-99, photographs of Stansted Airport and Renault Distribution Centre by Richard Davies; the Hong Kong Shanghai Bank by Ian Lambot.
Richard Rogers p100-105, photographs of Lloyds Bank by Richard Bryant; Pompidou Centre by Andreas Papadakis; Inmos Factory by Ken Kirkwood.
Cesar Pelli p106-111, photograph of Canary Wharf by Kenneth Champlin; World Financial Center by Charles Jencks; Pacific Design Center by Adrian Velicescu.
Michael Hopkins p112-115, photographs of the Mound Stand, Lords, and Schlumberger by David Bowers.
Jean Nouvel p116-117, photographs provided by M. Gonthier.
Richard Meier p118-119, *The Subject of Architecture* p68-73, is taken from *Architectural Design* Vol 60 7/8 1990, *The New Modern Aesthetic*.

POST-MODERNISM
Robert A M Stern *The Doubles of Post-Modernism* p120-121, is an extract taken from a paper published in *Robert Stern* Academy Editions 1981.
Michael Graves p122-127, photographs of Dolphin and Swan Hotels, Disneyworld and Clos Pegase Winery and Residence by William Taylor & Bill Whitehurst.
O M Ungers p134-135, photograph of Messe Skyscraper by Andreas Papadakis.
James Stirling p136-141, photograph of the Tate Gallery Extension provided by David Lambert, photograph of Staatsgalerie by Charles Jencks.
Ricardo Bofill p146-147, photographs by Charles Jencks.
Terry Farrell p148-151, photographs of Midland Bank by Jo Reid & John Peck and City & Central; Embankment Place by Nigel Young.
Nigel Coates p154-155, photograph of Bohemia Jazz Club and Caffé Bongo by Edward Valentine Hames.
Charles Jencks, *Post-Modernism and Discontinuity* p156-161, is taken from *Architectural Design* Vol 57 1/2 1987, *Post-Modernism and Discontinuity*. Photograph of Performing Arts Center, Cornell University by Richard Bryant of Arcaid.

THE NEW MODERNS
Andreas Papadakis, *Deconstruction and Architecture* p166-167; first published in *Deconstruction Omnibus*, Academy Editions, 1989.
Peter Eisenman p168-173, photographs of the Wexner Center by Jeff Goldberg of Esto & DG Olshavsky of Artog; Kochstrasse Social Housing by Dick Frank.
Coop Himmelblau p186-189, photograph of the Rooftop Remodelling, Vienna, by Gerald Zugmann.
Frank Gehry p190-195, photograph of Vitra Design Museum courtesy of Vitra Ltd; photographs of Loyola Law School and Fish Restaurant, Kobe by Charles Jencks; illustrations of The American Center in Paris were provided by The American Center in Paris.
Günter Behnisch p202-203, photograph of Hysolar Institute by Christian Kandzia.
Morphosis p204-207, photographs of the Comprehensive Cancer Center by Tom Bonner; Kate Mantilini Restaurant by Tom Bonner and Tim Street-Porter.
OMA p208-209, photographs of The Netherlands Dance Theatre and Checkpoint Charlie provided by Mathias Sauerbruch.

Index

A
ADAM, ROBERT *The Tin Gods* 50-65, 35, Dogmersfield Park 34, Crooked Pightle House, 35, Bordon Library 35,
AMBASZ, EMILIO 211, San Antonio Botanical Garden 210-211
ANDO, TADAO 75, Chapel on Mount Rokko 74, Theatre on the Water 75, Koshino House 75-77, Rokko Housing 78-79

B
BEHNISCH, GÜNTER 203, Hysolar Institute 202-203
BOFILL, RICARDO 147, Les Echelles du Baroque 146, Viaduct Housing 147, Palace of Abraxas 147
BOTTA, MARIO 91, House in Viganello 90, House in Origilo 90, Fribourg State Building 90, Rotunda, Stabio 91

C
COATES, NIGEL 155, Bohemia Jazz Club 154, Caffé Bongo 155
CIRANI, HENRI 87, Maison de L'Enfance, Torcy 86-87
COOP HIMMELBLAU 187, Rooftop Remodelling 186-187, Funder Factory 3 187, Skyline Tower 187, Open House 188-189

D
DECQ, ODILE *The Model is the Message* 5
DIXON, Jeremy Royal Opera House Extension 160
DUANY, ANDRES & ELIZABETH PLATER-ZYBERK 29, Seaside, 28, Kentlands 29, Crab Creek 29

E
EISENMAN, PETER 169, Wexner Center 168-171, Social Housing 172, Guardiola House 173

F
FARRELL, TERRY 149, Midland Bank 148-149, Embankment Place 150, 151, Comyn Ching 150, Lee House 151
FOSTER, NORMAN 93, Century Tower 92, Stansted 93, Renault Distribution Centre 94-95, Hong Kong Shanghai Bank 96-97, Milleneum Tower 66, 98-99

G
GEHRY, FRANK 191, Vitra Design Museum 190-193, Loyola Law School 194, Sirmai-Peterson Residence 194, Fish Restaurant 195, The American Center 195
GRAVES, MICHAEL 123, Dolphin Hotel 120, Humana Medical Corporation HQ 122-123, Portland Public Service Building 123, Dolphin & Swan Hotels 124-125, Clos Pegase Winery 126-127, Swan Hotel 127
GREENBERG, ALLAN 31, Department of State Building, Washington DC 30-31, Farmhouse in Connecticut 32-33

H
HADID, ZAHA 175, Moonsoon Restaurant 166, 178-179, IBA Housing 174, Peak Club 175, Kürfurstendamm 70 175-177
HARA, HIROSHI, Yamato Building 165
HASEGAWA, ITSUKO 85, House in Nerima 84, Bizan Hall 85
HOLLEIN, HANS 143, Haas Haus 142-145
HOPKINS, MICHAEL 113, Mound Stand, Lords 112, Basildon Town Square 113, Schlumberger Research Centre 114-115
HUXTABLE, ADA LOUISE *On Modern Architecture* 66-67

I
ISOZAKI, ARATA, Phoenix City Council Building 164

J
JAHN, HELMUT 81, State of Illinois Center 80, Chicago Board of Trade Addition 81, Humana Project 81
JENCKS, CHARLES *Post-Modernism and Discontinuity* 156

K
KRIER, LEON 13, Tegel, 12-13, Turris Burbonnis 14, St Quentin-en-Yvelines 15, Pliny's Villa 16-17
KRIER, ROB 25, Prager Platz 24, Via Triumphalis 25, Plan for City of 25,000 inhabitants 26, Breiitenfurterstrasse 27, Column 27
KURAKAWA, KISHO, Hiroshima City Museum of Contemporary Art 162

L
LIBESKIND, DANIEL 197, Mies Van der Rohe Memorial 196, Alef Wing Model 198-199, City Edge Competition 198-199, Jewish Museum 197, 200-201

M
MAKI, FUMIHIKO 83, Spiral Building, 82-83
MEIER, RICHARD *The Subject of Architecture* 119, 69, Madison Square Garden Towers 68-69, The High Museum of Art 70, Ackerberg House 71, 119 Museum für Kunsthandwerk 72-73
MORPHOSIS 205, Kate Mantilini Restaurant 204, Sixth Street Residence 205, Cancer Center 206, Osaka Folly 207

N
NOUVEL, JEAN 117, Hôtel Saint James, 116, Institut du Monde Arabe, 117

O
OMA 209, Netherlands Dance Theatre 208, Checkpoint Charlie 209, Parc de la Villette 209

P
PAPADAKIS, ANDREAS *Deconstruction and Architecture* 167
PEI, I M 89, The Louvre 1, 88-89
PELLI, CESAR 107, Canary Wharf, 106-107, 109, World Financial Center 108, Pacific Design Center 110-111
PORPHYRIOS, DEMETRI *The Relevance of Classical Architecture* 11, 41, Chepstow Villas 40-1, House in Kensington 42-43

R
ROGERS, RICHARD 100, Lloyds Bank 100, 102-103, Pompidou Centre 101, Inmos Factory 104-105
ROSSI, ALDO 45, Il Palazzo 4, Perugia Administration Centre 44-45, Modena Cemetery 46, Friedrichstadt housing 47, Casa Aurora 48-49

S

SANT'ELIA, ANTONIO drawing, 53
SHINOHARA, KAZUO, TIT Centennial Hall 165
SITE 213, Four Continents Bridge 212, World Ecology Pavilion 213
STARCK PHILIPPE NaniNani Building 215-217, computer aided design 217
STERN, ROBERT *The Doubles of Post Modernism* 121, 19, Observatory Hill Dining Hall 18, 20-21, House at Marblehead 19, Mexx International HQ 22-23
STIRLING, JAMES, MICHAEL WILFORD & ASSOCIATES 137, Science Centre, Berlin 136-137, Tate Gallery 138, Number One Poultry 138, Staatsgalerie 139, Bracken House 139, Tokyo International Forum 140, Bibliothéque de France 141, Performing Arts Center 156

T

TAKAMATSU, SHIN, Week Building 165, Origin III 165
TERRY, QUINLAN 37, Howard Building 36, Dower House 37, Richmond Riverside 38-39
TSCHUMI, BERNARD 181, Parc de la Villette 2-3, 180-181, ZKM 182-183, Glass Video Gallery 184-185

U

UNGERS, O M 135, Messe Skyscraper 134, Fair Hall 135, Galleria 135

V

VANDENHOVE, CHARLES 153, Zuid Singel Project 152, Maison de la Danse 153
VENTURI, ROBERT & DENISE SCOTT-BROWN 129, House on Long Island Sound 128, Trubeck & Wislocki Houses, Nantucket 129, House at Seal Harbour 130, House in Northen Delaware 131, Princeton Urban Design Study 132, extension to the National Gallery 133

W

WOLFF, RITA Nocturne 8, House in Chelsea Square 10, Tegel 12-13, Pliny's Villa 16-17